THE FIGURE OF THE CROWD IN EARLY MODERN LONDON

EARLY MODERN CULTURAL STUDIES

Ivo Kamps, Series Editor

PUBLISHED BY PALGRAVE MACMILLAN

The Figure of the Crowd in Early Modern London

The City and Its Double

Ian Munro

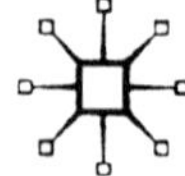

THE FIGURE OF THE CROWD IN EARLY MODERN LONDON
© Ian Munro, 2005.

First published in 2005 by
PALGRAVE MACMILLAN™
175 Fifth Avenue, New York, N.Y. 10010 and
Houndmills, Basingstoke, Hampshire, England RG21 6XS
Companies and representatives throughout the world.

PALGRAVE MACMILLAN is the global academic imprint of the Palgrave Macmillan division of St. Martin's Press, LLC and of Palgrave Macmillan Ltd. Macmillan® is a registered trademark in the United States, United Kingdom and other countries. Palgrave is a registered trademark in the European Union and other countries.

Library of Congress Cataloging-in-Publication Data

Munro, Ian, 1967–
    The figure of the crowd in early modern London : the city and its double / Ian Munro.
        p. cm.—(Early modern cultural studies)
    Includes bibliographical references and index.
    ISBN 1–4039–6642–7
        1. English literature—England—London—History and criticism. 2. English drama—Early Modern and Elizabethan, 1500–1600—History and criticism. 3. Shakespeare, William, 1564–1616—Knowledge—London (England) 4. London (England)—Population—History—17th century. 5. London (England)—Population—History—16th century. 6. English drama—17th century—History and criticism. 7. Crowds—England—London—History—17th century. 8. Crowds—England—London—History—16th century. 9. London (England)—Intellectual life. 10. London (England)—In literature. 11. Crowds in literature. I. Title. II. Series.

PR8476.M86 2005
820.9′32421—dc22   2004053239

A catalogue record for this book is available from the British Library.

Design by Newgen Imaging Systems (P) Ltd., Chennai, India.

First edition: February 2005

10 9 8 7 6 5 4 3 2 1

Printed in the United States of America.

For Becky

CONTENTS

Acknowledgments

The City and Its Double emerged (scarce half made up, it seems in retrospect) from my dissertation, which was directed by Marjorie Garber; without her guidance, inspiration, and constant support it would never have been completed. Jeffrey Masten and Barbara Lewalski deserve special appreciation for their intellectual generosity and exacting advice. Thanks also to Stephen Greenblatt, Marc Shell, and the members of the Harvard Renaissance Colloquium for reading and discussing portions of the work in its early stages. A Mellon Dissertation Year Fellowship funded my initial research, and further research has been generously supported by the University of Alberta. An earlier version of chapter 6 appeared in *English Literary Renaissance* 30.2 (Spring 2000); I am grateful to the publishers for permission to reuse this material.

I am especially indebted to Ivo Kamps, who has remained enthusiastic and interested during the long process of revision. Thanks are also due to Kristi Long and Farideh Koohi-Kamali for their support of the project. The thoughtful and challenging evaluation of the book by the anonymous reader at Palgrave Macmillan was extremely helpful. Principal research for this book was undertaken at the British Library, the Huntington Library, Houghton Library, the Royal Society of Antiquaries of London, and the Bodleian; my thanks to all the staff at these institutions for their assistance. Among the many friends and colleagues who deserve space on this page are Jonathan Hart, Patricia Demers, Robert Appleford, Peter Sinnema, Katherine Binhammer, Sylvia Brown, Garrett Epp, Lynne Magnusson, Elizabeth Hanson, Alexandra Halasz, Paul Yachnin, Rick Bowers, and Ted Bishop. Bryan Reynolds, as always, warrants a special mention. In closing, I want to thank all the members of my family for their continual love and support; nothing would have been possible without it.

This book is for Rebeca Helfer, as it has grown up under the influence of her love, friendship, inspiration, criticism, patience, impatience, encouragement, and support. The debt I owe her for this and for many things will be a long time in the paying; it is an obligation I look forward to with pleasure.

Introduction: Crowded Spaces

Sicinius. *What is the city but the people?*

(Coriolanus *3.1.198*)[1]

This book is a study of the figure of the crowd in early modern London. Its context is London's extraordinary growth in the period: metropolitan London quadrupled in size between 1500 and 1600, and one of the things that this population crisis triggered was a social crisis about the symbolic meaning of the city. Urban crowds became an inescapable presence during the late sixteenth century, and the literature and official proclamations of the time reflect a pervasive unease about the crowdedness and human disorder of the city. Through an examination of the crowd *topos* in a wide variety of literary and social contexts, I argue that the crowd operated as the visible manifestation of an increasingly incomprehensible city, the tangible referent onto which the desires and fears provoked by London's swelling mass were projected. I further argue that in both the streets and the playhouses, the crowd was a powerfully contradictory presence, symbolizing conflicting aspects of the city through metonymy (the city assembled, the public city, the urban community) and metaphor (the city as chaos, random movement, violence, anonymity, and monstrous growth). Metonymy and metaphor are opposing and complementary tropes, figuring the crowd as either an *event*—a physical assembly, either present or invoked—or a *discourse*—the idea of the crowd or of crowdedness, the symbolic associations that attach to it.[2] This interplay between event and discourse produces what I call the *space* of the crowd, a multivalent space that supplements the space of the city, disrupting, reinforcing, or otherwise transforming the social and symbolic dynamics of urban meaning. In the early modern period the urban crowd was always supplemental, always understood as a form of excessiveness and/or superfluousness; it provided the inevitable context for the performance of urban culture and threatened its legibility through its motive force and uncontrollable energy.[3]

I call my subject the *figure* of the crowd in part to establish some distance between this study and the wide and interdisciplinary field known as "crowd theory," which seeks to explain the sociological and psychological dimensions of crowds.[4] Although I am indebted to these analyses, my usage of the term is both looser and directed toward different ends. "Crowd" has always been an omnibus term, referring to almost any collective mass of people, from milling urbanites to theater and street audiences to openly rebellious assemblies; most attempts by historians or social theorists to construct a reified concept of *the* crowd have depended on limiting their analyses to specific and fairly narrow types of collective behavior, especially political demonstrations and popular protest.[5] The focus in this study is more on cultural reception than on political or psychological agency, and I want to suggest that the uncategorizable connotations of the word "crowd" are an important aspect of its cultural character. The crowd is an inherently polymorphous concept, always evading definition; although it is possible to examine the cultural meanings of the crowd, as this study does, a manifested crowd is a kind of blank—meaningless without a context to frame it and a discourse to fill it.

In the work of social historians such as E. P. Thompson, George Rudé, and E. J. Hobsbawm, "the crowd" generally denotes a somewhat cohesive community or social class (in some cases, a nascent proletariat) with coherent sociopolitical beliefs and objectives.[6] Although perceptions of the common populace—what Annabel Patterson calls "the popular voice," Mikhail Bakhtin called simply "the people," and contemporaries tended to call (in a theatrically suggestive image that I will discuss further) "the many-headed multitude"—form an important part of my discussion, my aim is not to use representations and perceptions of the crowd to recover, in a straightforward mimetic fashion, an apparent political reality existing outside the perimeters of the text.[7] Nor is it my intention to establish the crowd as a simple manifestation of legitimate or illegitimate popular discontent. Rather, I see the figure of the crowd as a vehicle by which certain kinds of cultural meanings and conflicts are transmitted and examined. The goal of my analysis is to determine the *function* of the crowd: as a dramatic motif, as a theatrical manifestation, and as a social presence. This is not to de politicize the meaning of representations of the crowd, but to recognize the multiple social and cultural registers in which these representations operate. Figuration always involves a process of displacement, a refracting through a variety of cultural filters, but this is never a hermetic process; as I argue throughout this study, the manifestation of the crowd in theatrical settings renders the perimeters between the dramatic text and the world that surrounds it explicitly permeable. This theatrical permeability lies somewhere near the heart of my project and works in both directions: as dramatic representations of crowds are never just representations, so the cultural significance of the crowd needs to be understood within a framework that recognizes it as a public performance itself, taking place on the streets and in the theaters of London.

The book is thus a study of London and the urban crowd at a particularly significant historical juncture, the fifty years or so at the end of the sixteenth century and the start of the seventeenth century that I consider "England's first population crisis." This is a claim that perhaps requires some justification. On the one hand, as Derek Keene has recently argued, the late sixteenth century was not the first time that London had experienced rapid expansion: "it is at least arguable that the decisive stage in the development of the city as the focus of national power and expenditure was in the late thirteenth century rather than in the sixteenth."[8] It was the Black Death, the "demographic catastrophe of the fourteenth century" as Keene puts it, that reversed this trend, bringing in a long period of relatively stable urban population until the sixteenth century, when subsistence migration, the concentration of mercantile wealth, and a substantial increase of royal residence in and around the capital under Henry VIII once again began to produce the sort of demographic overflow that appeared in the thirteenth century (58–59). On the other hand, London's population growth continued apace through the nineteenth century, thus making it difficult to find a suitable endpoint to the "crisis," and it is undeniable that the political significance of urban crowds generally increased with the city's population. In this regard my study may seem peculiarly *avant le lettre*, not least because it predates the appearance of the word "mob," from *mobilis vulgare*, by almost a century.[9] An argument could be made that it is with the Civil War, immediately after the period I consider, that London crowds first assume a national importance. And, as Tim Harris has demonstrated, it is in the later seventeenth century that public anxieties about the political actions and desires of the crowd, recognized (or misrecognized) as a somewhat cohesive unit, become pronounced.[10]

Nevertheless, as I argue at greater length in chapter 1, there is something special about the late sixteenth and early seventeenth centuries, and not simply that this historical period coincides with what we have come to know as the English Renaissance—though certainly that cultural explosion is related in complex ways to population growth and metropolitan consolidation. London's expansion accelerated during this period, so that between 1580 and 1600 the metropolitan population grew from perhaps 100,000 to 200,000.[11] Complaints about overcrowding in the city became widespread, leading some historians to surmise that the ability of the metropolis to absorb such growth easily (principally through suburban expansion and the subdividing of large properties) was being stretched to its limit.[12] Concern over London's growth was pervasive, to judge by the spate of royal proclamations against new buildings, the increased anxiety in other official and unofficial documents about the gathering of crowds, and the appearance of so many dramatic and nondramatic works that incorporate representations of crowds. These concerns, and the larger social and demographic forces that lay behind them, catalyzed fundamental changes in the understanding and practice of urban significance. Similarly, the years leading up to the Civil War provide a useful terminus, as so much of the urban meaning I examine in this book is connected to royal prerogative and the ancient imagining of London as *camera regis,* the "chamber" of the monarch. Furthermore, as Paul Slack has argued, it seems clear that by the later seventeenth century the terms in which urban expansion and the crowded city were understood had changed.[13]

Perhaps the strongest indication of the unique importance of this urban period is the critical attention it has attracted. My study complements a rapidly growing body of criticism on London, engaging particularly with more recent work that has moved beyond an acknowledgment of the inherent theatricality of early modern London (with its pageantry, theatrical entertainments, and public rituals) to explicitly discuss the space of the early modern city.[14] It also has a corrective function, however, as existing treatments of the urban space and meaning of London have generally not addressed the expansion of the city in terms of *people.* Population growth has typically been treated as something of a critical commonplace, employed as a useful shorthand for the transitional nature of urban life in the period or as a preamble for explorations of the complex sociopolitical relationship between the city and the court. Insufficient attention, in my opinion, has been paid to the phenomenological implications of population growth in the city. The experiential space of early modern London can be fully understood only in a framework that takes into account the visible and tangible presence of more and more *bodies.*

My central concern is thus the *crowded* space of the city. What does it mean for a space to be crowded? What happens, in social and symbolic terms, to a city in a population crisis—especially a city that expressed itself and understood itself so much through the public performance of culture? To answer questions such as these we need a model of the city, and more particularly a model of urban space, that can accommodate the theoretical implications of crowdedness. Though my general approach to this issue is deconstructive, I also rely considerably on the spatial theories of Henri Lefebvre and Michel de Certeau to delineate this model.[15] Put briefly, Lefebvre sees space in material terms, as something produced through a tripartite interaction among physical, social, and psychic factors; it is the *practice* of space—living in it, conceptualizing it, producing it—that defines the meaning of urban space. Similarly, though working in a somewhat different paradigm, de Certeau establishes a strong opposition between the transparent and panoramic space produced by overarching urban strategies—planning, monumental building, organization of labor, place names, and the like—and the opaque and motive space produced by practices—principally, the urban tactics of walking and existing in the city. Though aspects of these analyses are problematic in the historical context of early modern London, as heuristic models they are extremely valuable, demonstrating the importance of bodies in understanding urban space. Central, too, to my approach is the figural opposition I suggest above between metaphoric and metonymic crowds and between the crowd as discourse/subject and the crowd as event/context. These binary oppositions run through all of my discussion and signal the fundamental doubleness of the crowd's function in the creation of urban meaning. It is the corporeal presence of the crowd, whether in the playhouses or in the streets, that turns London into a theater, allowing the unrepresentable complexity of the city to achieve the status and coherence of realized symbol. But within the theatrical economy that dominates early modern urban experience, the crowd is at once audience and subject, at once watching and participating in the performance. This spatial dynamic is particularly significant in the plays I consider, for to place a crowd on the stage is necessarily to create a *mise en abyme* that maps the dramatic space of the urban play onto the urban space of its theatrical performance.

In methodological terms, this approach could be positioned between the older new historicist project and the emerging critical paradigm that Patricia Fumerton has called "a new new historicism."[16] New historicist issues concerning theatricality and the display of power are central to this book, although my main point in engaging with these themes is to demonstrate how the models employed by critics such as Stephen Greenblatt and Leonard Tennenhouse fail to account fully for the complex dynamics of power vested in theatrical (and metatheatrical) entertainments. In contrast to this now traditional attention to hierarchical power structures, Fumerton describes the newer historicist paradigm as focusing "primarily on the common, but the common in both a class and cultural sense" and siting "particular clusters of such myriad commonality within the context of the manifold details of cultural practice and representation—what we might call, evoking Michel de Certeau and Henri Lefebvre, the '*everyday*'" (3–4). Where this study might diverge from this approach is in its treatment of London. As I will explain further, the urban context of this study is not *simply* the everyday but the tension created between the ordinary city and the extraordinary city: the imaginary London whose symbolic space and meaning is principally determined through the interplay of memory, ritual, and theater.

The subtitle of the book, *The City and Its Double,* attempts to capture something of the issues raised by this conjunction of the urban ordinary and extraordinary. My adaptation of the phrase from Antonin Artaud's impassioned examination of the theater is not intended to signal a strong kinship between that manifesto and this study; Artaud's critical deployment of the phrase carries with it connotations of Jungian cultural archetypes and an implied hierarchy of the real and the representation that are uncongenial to my project. However, as I discuss further in chapter 6, the social and semiotic apocalypse Artaud imagines in progress bears a fascinating similarity to the crisis of signification in early modern London: "If confusion is the sign of the times, I see at the root of this confusion a rupture between things and words, between things and ideas and signs that are their representation."[17] As this book extensively illustrates, early modern London was understood and conceived through its doubles; *camera regis,* the theater, civic pageantry, urban literature, the court, the idea of Rome, the plague, and the many manifestations of the crowd itself all catalyzed different sorts of "doubling" of the city. The double in these multiplying cases acts as a Derridean supplement, at once allowing the idea (or ideal) of the city to be enacted *and* undermining the symbolic meaning thus created by threatening to substitute itself for it. In the case of the relationship between the city and the crowd, the question of which is the "sign" and which the "thing" has no straightforward answer.

In the broadest terms, the book could be viewed as an extended meditation on the implicit doubleness in the prefatory quotation from *Coriolanus:* "What is the city but the people?" The tribune Sicinius's rhetorical question is in response to the accusation that he is trying "to unbuild the city, and to lay all flat" (3.1.197) by rousing the plebeians against Coriolanus. The immediate context of the exchange is political; the assembled crowd is seen as threatening the hierarchical nature of Roman rule, and Sicinius's comment is meant to assert the latent power of the populace. But beneath the surface of the exchange lurks a range of social and cultural issues that moves beyond questions of political hierarchy. I want to suggest that we can read Sicinius's rhetorical question as containing real questions: What *is* the city, if not the people? What does the city mean? "Building" the city is more than a matter of bricks and mortar or of political hierarchy; it involves a complex interaction of urban memory, ritual practice, and spatial organization. This complex interaction is particularly visible in the work of John Stow, with whom it seems all discussion of early modern London must start. As well as detailing the customs and composition of the city, Stow's *Survey of London* moves from site to site around the city, listing and explaining the historical importance of each urban locus. This topographical meander lards the city with memory, authority, and cultural significance, producing through elaboration a version of what Kevin Lynch calls urban "legibility," the ease with which the space of the city can be imagined.[18] At the same time, however, Stow repeatedly notes changes in the physical layout and social customs of the city that threaten the legibility of the city and undermine his project. Though central to his narrative, the idea of "London" is far from stable in Stow's account.

The construction of urban meaning in early modern London has received a lot of interest in recent years, producing something of a renaissance in early modern urban studies. Earlier work, such as Steven Mullaney's attempts to model a "rhetoric of urban space" and Gail Kern Paster's exploration of "the idea of London," has been joined by a raft of other analyses by literary scholars and historians—most notably by John Twyning's *London Dispossessed,* Janette Dillon's *Theatre, Court, and City,* and four wonderful collections: *The Theatrical City, Londinopolis, Imagining Early Modern London,* and *Material London, ca. 1600.* Looming especially large on this critical landscape is Lawrence Manley's *Literature and Culture in Early Modern London,* a magisterial reading of London and its cultural production *tout court* over almost two hundred years through the organizing principle of "fictions of settlement," the cultural tactics through which London understood its changing nature.[19] These works have all influenced my analysis, yet my subject is somewhat different and therefore catalyzes significant variances in approach. Manley's work is particularly relevant, although it suffers from the inherent problem of large-scale studies; despite its exceptionally fine analysis of different aspects of early modern London's culture, it works too hard to assimilate everything into the grand narrative being pursued. For Manley, the story of early modern London is a progressive history of cultural settlement and social accommodation: as the city transformed from medieval community to early modern metropolis, fears of social and cultural chaos were inevitably and inexorably brought to rule and order through the invention of new languages and discourses to deal with them. Such a teleology naturally puts considerable pressure on the idea of progress. Thus, for example, despite his innovative attention to figurings of crowded mobility Manley tends to quarantine such descriptions to the early Tudor complaint genre; the crowded disorder of Shakespeare's English and Roman histories, which form a central part of this study, goes unremarked, as do the antitheatrical invocations of a city made monstrous through crowding.[20]

As with most of the other studies cited above, Manley's work owes a great deal to the developments in recent decades in the historiography of early modern London. In the 1970s, historical approaches to London were dominated by what later became known as the "doom and gloom" school, which emphasized the social chaos, economic hardship, and political instability of the early modern city, painting a picture of an urban society reeling out of control.[21] This perspective was challenged by historians such as Valerie Pearl and Steven Rappaport, who argued that reports of pervasive crisis overlooked the fundamental stability of the city during this time; downplaying accounts of rioting and unrest, they instead stressed the strength of urban institutions, particularly within the corporate city.[22] In the early 1990s, Ian Archer's *The Pursuit of Stability* charted a middle course: admitting the potential for catastrophe, and the perception among the elite of such potential, but arguing that the social measures in place served remarkably well to forestall such calamities. With its detailed attention to social customs, urban ceremony, and local cohesiveness, *The Pursuit of Stability* has set the tone for almost all subsequent engagements with early modern London; Archer's work has been instrumental in creating a more nuanced vision of London, shifting the balance of historical research toward understanding the complex web of social interactions and urban rituals that made up daily life in early modern London.

From the perspective of my study, there are a number of limitations to this dominant model, less in its initial form than its subsequent dissemination and reworking by other scholars and Archer himself. The "pursuit of stability," initially clearly an *ideological* pursuit, has incrementally changed into a positivistic way of imagining the city's growth, with order and settlement becoming the end results of an inevitable teleology. Archer was well aware of this danger; describing the evolution of the city' constitution, he wrote:

> There is, of course, something horribly whiggish about the analysis thus far, of a City gradually finding its way to an ordered harmony, reconciling the principles of rule by the better sort and responsibility to the wider community in a set of workable compromises. . . . The underlying tensions in London society, between wholesalers and artisans, freemen and foreigners, servants and householders, all remained. The elite walked on the crust of a volcano, and it was essential to stability that mechanisms be provided to cope with these tensions. (32)

In the historical discourse of the last decade this sort of acknowledgment seems to have become increasingly unimportant; in the process, the *perception* of instability has largely gone missing. Archer deals extensively with this perception in *The Pursuit of Stability;* indeed, it is what provokes the "pursuit" in his title. If more recent studies deal at all with the widespread urban anxiety evident in contemporary accounts, they tend to see it in narrow terms, either as a rhetorical counterpoint to visions of urban utopia or as part of the dialectic of urban growth.[23] If, as Manley argues, representations of urban instability are necessarily part of a larger social process of articulating new forms of stability, the fears that inspired those representations tend to be minimized. Although I have no desire to return to the pessimistic view of the 1970s, I do stress throughout this study that the crowd was seen in terms of social and symbolic instability. What is at issue, perhaps, is a tension between action and reception: if London was indeed much more stable than it appeared in its official and unofficial literature, that appearance is still vitally important—particularly since what is principally under discussion here is the city's understanding of itself through representation and figuration. This book consequently makes reference throughout to the instability of London, to the symbolic chaos produced by the crowd, and to the threatening nature of the crowded city. I should make it clear at the outset that to read this threat only in terms of political upheaval, in the form of rebellions and revolts, would be a great oversimplification. Indeed, the figured crowd, especially in drama, was often extremely loyal and patriotic—excessively so, in fact, in which sometimes lay the threat.

A second limitation to our consensus picture of early modern London, in my view, relates to the dominance of civic institutions and local community in many recent accounts of the city. This is not to say that scholars have generally adopted an economiastic approach to London, or simply valorize its civic patterns and customs. On the contrary, a good deal of effort has been expended on the inadequacy of these structures, the ideological underpinnings of civic works, and the lives of those who remain outside the designation of "citizen"—although it would perhaps be fair to say that such things have typically been treated more as problematic outliers than as fundamental problems. Rather, as I argue in more detail in chapter 1, my point is that the space of the city has largely been constructed as a network of social relations to the general exclusion of other perspectives; London becomes a complex system of local networks of reciprocity, into which population increases were gradually and imperfectly incorporated. This historical perspective has had considerable impact on literary and cultural scholars; seeing London's urban space as a network of social relations underpins such insightful projects as Jean Howard's explication of *Westward Ho* in terms of its urban mapping of foreign and female labor, Garrett Sullivan's reading of Heywood's *Edward IV* in terms of changing labor practices and tensions in guild structure in the city and suburbs, Andrew Gordon's exploration of civic ceremony and urban chorography, and Janette Dillon's investigation of numerous dramatic texts through a focus on "the visible mobility of relations between court and city, as influenced by the development of the market and as represented within the domain of the theater."[24] The effect of this focus on community and social relations, however, is to slip past population as a subject.[25] Dillon, for example, looks at the city and the court, but the city is principally understood through its politics, social relations, rituals, and physical environment. This is potentially a political problem, in that it tends to understand the city primarily in terms of its social hierarchies, but it is also an interpretive problem—by (in effect) emphasizing one term of Lefebvre's tripartite interaction over the others, and constructing urban space principally as the register of social relations, the crowded space of London is rationalized and seems to become transparent.

I particularly resist this move because it threatens to dismantle what an assembled crowd is: an anonymous mass, whose composition is unknown and whose allegiances are unclear. It is important to underscore that what particularly marks the space of the crowd is its *illegibility,* its resistance to being read. As de Certeau says, "Beneath the discourses that ideologize the city, the ruses and combinations of powers that have no readable identity proliferate; without points where one can take hold of them, without rational transparency, they are impossible to administer."[26] At the root, de Certeau imagines the practice of the urban crowd in anti-epistemological terms as "an *opaque and blind* mobility characteristic of the bustling city"; urban dwellers "make use of spaces that cannot be seen; their knowledge of them is as blind as that of lovers in each other's arms. The paths that correspond in this intertwining, unrecognized poems in which each body is an element signed by many others, elude legibility" (93).[27] Returning again to *Coriolanus,* what this elusive dynamic speaks to is the complex, supplemental relation between "the people" and "the city." As with "London" in early modern London, the idea of "Rome" holds crucial significance in *Coriolanus,* and throughout the play we can see impossible efforts to separate the meaning of the city from the people who reside in it. I think that the impossibility of this separation makes Sicinius's question a threat of a different sort; not just a political threat but also a semiotic threat, a threat of the loss of urban significance. In this context, what the crowd threatens to unbuild is not simply the political order but the meaning of the city itself: "What is the city but *the* people?" seems to slip inevitably into "What is the city but *people?*," suggesting a disintegration of urban identity through sheer multiplicity. The example of Stow suggests that this was a crucial question in early modern London as well; the legible city whose passing he fears is presented in the context of the effects of population growth. Early modern London, Stow complains, is "too much pestered with people."[28]

*   *   *

Chapter 1 of this study, "Imaginary Numbers: City, Crowd, Theater," expands upon the Introduction's critical, theoretical, and historical discussion. As the subtitle is intended to indicate, I suggest that what makes population growth in the late sixteenth century so culturally significant is the combination of three factors: transformations in the symbolic and ceremonial meaning of the city; changing perceptions of the multitude, due in part to urban rioting and unrest; and the emergence of the commercial theater as a permanent part of the physical, social, and symbolic landscape of the city. The chapter culminates with an exploration of the theater as both a crowded space and a space for performing crowdedness. I observe that urban crowds were most commonly staged as audiences, a move that doubled the conditions of performance, linking dramatic space to theatrical space and allowing plays to express the contradictions inherent to staging an urban world to a city.

"London's Mirror: Civic Ritual and the Crowd," explores the place of the crowd in the calendrical rituals of civic pageantry. My focus is the annual procession known as the Lord Mayor's show, which presents an allegorical image of the perfect city in order to justify the economic and political power of the mercantile elite—an image whose power depends upon its position in a closed system of allegorical reference. Most modern criticism of civic pageantry in this period has characterized it as a ritual process that expressed the traditional values and deep communal structure of the urban culture. Arguing against this perspective, I contrast the hermetic world of the printed pageant texts to the dangerously open mode of performance that transpired. Chapter 3, " 'Shakespeare's London': The Scene of London in the Second Tetralogy and *Henry VIII*" analyzes royal spectacle in the context of London's traditional role as *camera regis*, the "chamber of the king" and the setting of the monarch's visible power. By transforming London into a symbolic counterpart of the court, the royal entry sought to contain the disruptive energies of the city as figured through the crowd. I explore how this spatial ideology was refracted through Shakespeare's history plays, principally in the second tetralogy. The chapter concludes with an examination of *Henry VIII's* use of a dyadic geography of court and city, focusing particularly on the scenes surrounding Anne's coronation and Elizabeth's christening. I argue that the riotous behavior of the unseen crowd in these scenes parallels the relationship the play establishes with the theater audience. In the christening scene, theater and spectacle are reconfigured in the context of the immediate audience, the proximity of the real city, and the real staging of royal power.

"Distracted Multitude: The Theater and the Many-Headed Monster," explores the early modern discourse of the multitude from its sources in Plato through to the antitheatricalist discourse, the location for some of the most vivid linkings between the figure of the crowd and the space of the theater. I approach Plato's supplemental use of the "many-headed monster" in *The Republic* through the opposition between "arborescent" and "rhizomatic" multiplicities suggested by Gilles Deleuze and Felix Guattari; it is the idea of the rhizomatic—or "distracted," in the full early modern sense of the word—urban crowd, I argue, that animates many of the attacks on the theater, figured as both a place of gathering and a place of dissemination. Detailing how numerous dramatic representations of the multitude employ similar language and themes, I suggest that we can read these negative portrayals in the context of the theater's ambivalent relationship with the urban multitude. Chapter 5, " 'Rome, etc.': *Sejanus, Julius Caesar,* and the Prodigious City" repositions this analysis in the context of staging Rome, particularly in *Julius Caesar* and Jonson's *Sejanus His Fall.* I argue that these plays incorporate the antitheatrical discourse of the multitude, the trope of collective dismemberment, and the idea of the prodigious city as ways of staging (without resolving) the problematic place of the theater in the city. At the heart of both plays is the question of what Rome, the ideal urban location, can signify when presented to early modern London. Jonson connects the dismemberment of Sejanus to the treatment of the play in the playhouse; dismemberment becomes the sign of illegitimate dissemination, and marks the metamorphic movement of the body of *Sejanus* through all modes of urban circulation. Similarly, I argue that the dismemberment of Cinna the Poet in *Julius Caesar* should be interpreted not as a generic representation of unthinking mimicry by the multitude but as a specifically urban symbol. Unlike the imaginary Rome that Brutus and Sejanus understand as an invisible support for their desires, the city of the crowd acts as a supplement to the discourse of power, characterized at once by insignificance and excess.

Chapter 6, " 'A kind of nothing': Plague Time in London," examines the presence of plague in Jacobean London through an analysis of *Coriolanus* and Thomas Dekker's urban literature. For Dekker, plague becomes a master trope of urban description, applicable to all aspects of city life. *Coriolanus* enters the chapter through a discussion of the liminal status of plague in early modern theater. I focus on Coriolanus's use of plague imagery to emphasize his separation from the plebeians, arguing that his rhetoric serves instead to demonstrate his inextricability from the common population. What is ultimately at stake is not only the failure of the one to separate himself from the many, but the very idea of the city: If the city *is* only the people, then what is it but an anonymous location, identifiable only by its ceaseless change and uncontrollable growth?

CHAPTER 1

IMAGINARY NUMBERS: CITY, CROWD, THEATER

The advent of the crowded city, and the significance with which it was invested, is best seen in the initial attempt to eradicate it: Elizabeth's 1580 proclamation against new building or subdividing of houses in London and its environs. This was the first official response to the population crisis of the early modern metropolis, and it begins with an aptly panoramic imagining of "the state of the city":

> The Queen's Majesty, perceiving the state of the city of London (being anciently termed her chamber) and the suburbs and confines thereof to increase daily by excess of people to inhabit in the same in such ample sort as thereby many inconveniences are seen already, but many greater of necessity like to follow. . . . where there are such great multitudes of people brought to inhabit in small rooms (whereof a great part are seen very poor, yea, such as must live of begging or by worse means, and they heaped up together, and in a sort smothered with many families of children and servants in one house or small tenement). . . . Her majesty . . . doth charge and straightly command all manner of persons of what quality soever they be, to desist and forbear from any new building of any house or tenement within three miles from any of the gates of the said city of London, to serve for habitation or lodging for any person where no former house hath been known to have been in the memory of such as are now living, and also to forbear from letting or setting or suffering any more families than one only to be placed or to inhabit from henceforth in any house that heretofore hath been inhabited.[1]

Aimed at stemming the tide of urban immigration, the "excess of people"[2] who "daily" engross the city, the proclamation explains the situation in terms of a particular sort of spatial excess, expressed in the antithesis of "great multitudes of people brought to inhabit in small rooms," and intensified by imagining the people "heaped up together, and in a sort smothered." By any measure, it was a failure, as were its successors; in the years following the proclamation it seems likely that London's rate of growth increased substantially. In 1602 Elizabeth reissued the order, with many complaints that it had been ignored; owing to greedy property owners and negligent and corrupt officials, "the said mischief and inconveniences do daily increase and multiply, to the great contempt of her majesty's royal commandment, the manifest danger of the whole realm, and especially of the said city of London and the confines thereof" (III.246–57). James later issued numerous building proclamations with similarly impotent demands. Although his approach to urban building was largely framed by his desire to beautify and regularize the appearance of the city, the same language of population excess recurs in his proclamation of 1607, which stresses "the filling & pestering of houses with Inmates and severall dwellers (and those of the worst sort) almost in every severall roome."[3] In both cases, the press of population into the city is imagined in extreme terms, impossibly dense and impossibly widespread.

The 1580 proclamation was the first of many attempts to control the growth of the city by regulating its dimensions. The physical contours of London, however, are primarily employed in the document to elaborate a city of symbolic spaces. Initially invoked as a room itself, the "chamber" of the Queen, London multiplies or disintegrates (or both) into a plurality of "small" rooms, each stuffed to the point of overflow with the bodies of the urban populace. What was "anciently" the Queen's chamber, *camera regis*—implying a type of sovereign space both in terms of ownership and habitation—has been appropriated, subdivided for the use of the swelling crowd of the city, an anonymous, polymorphous mass. A room for one has become many rooms for many, a process carrying significant implications for how royal authority manifests itself in the context of the city.

The real and the imaginary mix uncomfortably in the language of the proclamation, offering us both a sketch of "the state of the city of London" and an idea of the political and symbolic significance attached to that state. Despite the hyperbolic intensity of these descriptions of building, subdividing and overcrowding, they evidence an actual state of affairs. The extent of the population crisis can perhaps be most vividly appreciated in a case heard before the Star

Chamber in 1607, during which the Recorder of London mentions four large properties converted into tenements that were alleged to together house eight thousand people.[4] Vanessa Harding suggests that "the expanded early modern population of the inner city found accommodation in divided houses, higher buildings, and the building-over of back plots; in the immediate fringe beyond the walls, development took the form of closes, narrow blind alleys onto which a dozen or more dwellings opened. . . . The texture of the built environment had become much more dense and congested."[5] John Stow's *Survey of London* corroborates this assessment, repeatedly documenting the breaking up of large properties into small tenements and the covering over of common lands with cottages.[6] Indeed, one of the more striking aspects of Stow's perambulatory account of London and its environs is the persistent attention he pays to building and subdividing, referencing more than thirty such extensive physical alterations, in almost half of the city wards and throughout the suburbs. The changes to the built environment of the city were diverse and widespread, both within and without the wall. In Cornhill Ward, "for winning of ground" ancient stone buildings "haue bin taken down and in place of some one of them being low, as but two stories aboue the ground, many houses of foure or fiue stories high are placed"; a mansion in Lime Street Ward "being greatly ruinated of late time, for the most part hath beene letten out to Powlters . . . but now lately new builded into a number of small tenements, letten out to strangers, and other meane people"; in Southwark "on the banke of the Riuer Thames there is now continuall building of tenements about halfe a mile in length" and "also southwest a continuall building, almost to Lambith"; the Bishop of Durham's house, near Charing Cross, was demolished by the Earl of Shrewsbury "and in place thereof builded a great number of smal tenements now letten out for great rents, to people of all sorts," thereby inaugurating the notably insolvent precinct known as Cold Harbour.[7]

As Patrick Collinson has noted, the eastern part of the city receives some of Stow's most severe criticism: Hog Lane in Portsoken Ward "is now within a few years made a continuous building throughout, of Garden houses, and small Cottages" (I.127); on the highway from Portsoken into Aldgate "were some few tenements thinly scattered, here & there, with many voyd spaces between them, vp to the Bars, but now that street is not only fully replenished with buildings outward, & also pestered with diuerse Allyes, on eyther side to the Barres, but to white Chappel and beyond" (I.127); the choir building of St. Katherine's Hospital was "of late yeres inclosed about, or pestered with small tenements, and homely cottages, hauing inhabitants, English and strangers, more in number than in some citie in England" (I.124); Northumberland House, in Aldgate Ward, was first turned into "bowling Alleys" and "Dicing houses," and then further converted "into a number of great rents, small cottages, for strangers and others" (I.149).[8] The area around Aldgate itself is treated with particular disgust:

> without the barres, both the sides of the streete bee pestered with Cottages and Allies . . . into the common field. . . . this common field, I say, being sometime the beauty of this City on that part, is so incroched vpon by building of filthy Cottages, and with other purprestures, inclosures and Lay-stalles (notwithstanding all proclaimations and Acts of Parliament made to the contrary) that in some places it scarce remaineth a sufficient high way for the meeting of Carriages and droues of Cattell, much lesse is there any faire, pleasant or wholsome way for people to walke on foot: which is no small blemish to so famous a city, to haue so vnsavery and vnseemly an entry or passage thereunto. (II.72)[9]

As in many contemporary accounts, London here seems sclerotic and disfigured, its vital arteries clogged from the deposit of humanity, the beauty of its public lands turned into the blemish of private habitation and industry. Nor was it only buildings for the poor that attracted Stow's censure. He remarks of the precincts of Bartholomew Fair, "now notwithstanding all proclamations of the prince, and also the act of parliament, in place of Boothes within this Churchyarde (onely letten out in the Fayre time, and closed vp all the yeare after) bee many large houses builded, and the North Wall toward Long lane taken downe, a number of Tenements are there erected, for such as will giue greate rents" (II.27). The references in these last two quotations to the building proclamations and subsidiary parliamentary acts highlight the inability of those in power to stop London's growth. The intermittent carnival of the fair has turned into a perpetual mocking of authority that seems to emanate less from individual builders than from the growing city itself.

These familiar descriptions offer a vivid glimpse of the experiential impact of London's growth, and speak to the complex relationship between population and urban meaning. The physical, social, and mental spaces of the city are inextricable in Stow's account. To employ the terminology of Henri Lefebvre, new "spatial practices," including socioeconomic forces, change the "representational" or experiential space of the physical city; at the same time the altered representational space of the city produce new spatial practices and new symbolic or ideological "representations of space," including Stow's own work.[10] Put another way, if demographic growth alters the physical fabric of London, this physical alteration itself necessarily changes how the city is lived and, most importantly, what the city means. As in the building proclamations, population crisis is figured here not only as a crisis of physical space, or of social cohesion, but as a crisis of symbolic space.

This chapter seeks to explore the implications of this symbolic crisis by examining some of the discourses, perceptions, events, and institutions catalyzed by the enormous population growth of the late sixteenth century. How was the growing population of London conceived? What languages and discourses were used to describe this growth? What effects did this growth have on the ways that urban meaning was understood, promulgated, and disseminated? I begin with an extended analysis of the 1580 proclamation for several reasons. As the first official response to the growth of the city it inaugurates a new understanding of what London was and what should be done about it. Working in consultation with many levels of government (the Lord Mayor and Aldermen, parish officials, the Star Chamber), the Crown put in place a radical attempt at urban planning of a kind unknown before.[11] At the same time, the proclamation frames this novel project in reactionary and "ancient" terms, showing a traditional understanding of the city, *camera regis*, as threatened by population growth, outlining in this conflict both a historical trajectory and a symbolic opposition of great significance in understanding how the city was conceptualized. The terms of the spatial opposition between the Queen's chamber and the small, packed rooms of the populace engage with my central question in this chapter: what happens to a space that becomes overfull, stuffed, brimming, saturated— a space, that is, that becomes crowded?

The historical trajectory described in the 1580 proclamation is an ideological fiction, of course; there was no golden age of *camera regis*, and the pervasive deployment of this idea in the early modern period could be read as a back-formation, an invented past devised to deal with the challenges of the present. Nor was the late sixteenth century the first time that London had overspilled its boundaries. As Derek Keene has argued, the underlying catalysts for urban growth were already present in the late thirteenth century. In language reminiscent of the 1580 proclamation, he argues that "by 1300 London . . . was a powerful magnet for migrants drawn by opportunities for work and . . . seeking the charitable relief and marginal employment which were always more freely available in the capital than elsewhere."[12] Things were different, however, in the sixteenth century, not only because of the scale of the change to the city but because of the conjunction of various forces and factors related to the construction of urban meaning. It is in early modern London that the ceremonial and symbolic meaning of the city fundamentally altered, as evidenced by the range of new urban ceremonial practices. It is in early modern London as well that the threat of urban disorder caused a substantial change in the way that the multitude was understood. And it is in early modern London that the commercial theater emerged. The issues of crowded urban space become most critical in the context of the commercial theater—dependent on the growth of London for its existence, and already a double of sorts of the highly theatrical space of the city. As its subtitle "city, crowd, theater" indicates, the chapter follows this inventory of concerns. I begin by focusing on metropolitan London, discussing how the space of the city was produced, conceptualized, and controlled. The second part of the chapter moves to a discussion of the crowd itself, working through the classical discourse of the "many-headed multitude" and examining how that trope was applied in the context of London's population. It then turns to a discussion of the theater, first looking at the stigmatization of the playhouses through their associations with crowds and then exploring the conditions under which crowds were staged within the theaters, and the effects and implications of those stagings.

*   *   *

Among its various concerns, the 1580 proclamation particularly focused on two problems of excessive growth that became, in the following decades, ubiquitous and inseparable characterizations of the crowd and thus justifications for population control. First, the document declares that this excessive population could hardly be "well governed by ordinary justice" without an expansion of the power of the state by means of "new jurisdictions and officers for that purpose." The specific subtext of this reference to "new jurisdictions," as indicated by the earlier reference to the poverty of urban immigrants, was the support and policing of the poor. As Michael Berlin notes, "In the late sixteenth century parishes increasingly functioned as units of local government, with greater responsibility for administering the policies of central government and the City corporation, especially with regard to poor relief."[13] The willingness of parishes to accommodate such population increases is a complex historical question.

Ian Archer emphasizes the various social mechanisms available to defuse neighborhood conflicts, the stabilizing effects of local religious and civic ceremonies, and the close, even claustrophobic, nature of parish life: "The parish therefore, subject to some important qualifications, was an important unit of identity, creating mutual ties among its members, rich and poor alike."[14] Berlin, in contrast, emphasizes the social stratification inherent to parish institutions and the degree to which inmates and lodgers were often excluded from parochial government.[15] One incident sounds a familiar rhetorical tone:

> When in 1600, the more substantial inhabitants of the St. Dunstan in the West parish successfully petitioned for a select vestry they claimed that "through the admission of all sorts of parishioners unto their vestries there falleth out great disquietness and hindrance to good proceedings by the discent of the inferior and meaner sort of the multitude of the inhabitants theyre being greater in number and more ready to cross the good proceedings." (53)

If communal participation in local government was thus sometimes (though certainly not always) unavailable for new and impoverished immigrants, the ability of parishes to deal financially with extreme population increases is also in question. On the one hand, Archer notes "the huge surge in philanthropic giving in the sixteenth century" and comments, "It is striking just how many London parishes . . . sought to maximize resources for poor relief by constructing houses to be rented to generate income for the poor."[16] On the other hand, a 1598 Star Chamber case prosecuting two men under the 1580 proclamation makes particular mention of "the ouerburdened and distressed estate of the inhabitants that dwell in sundry the Parishes where the sayd new Buildings and deuided Tenements are, being for the most part but of small ability to beare and sustaine the great charge which is to growe there by meanes of the new erected and diuided Tenements."[17] These cases suggest how the "excess of people" referred to in the 1580 proclamation is clearly a double-edged expression, meaning both an excessive number of people and a portion of the population that was characterized *as* an excess, a surplus population. The 1598 Star Chamber case, echoing the language of the building proclamations, claims that "the City of London, and Suburbs therof, are ouercharged, and burdened with sundry sorts of poore, beggerly, and euill disposed persons, to the great hinderance and oppression of the same" (sig. P1v–P2). Understandably, the growth of the London was

largely perceived in terms of its most visible component, the impoverished economic migrants who flocked to the city in hope of finding work or charity.[18] John Howes's *Familiar and Frendly Discourse
Dialogue Wyse,* first published in 1587, provides a helpful taxonomy
of this sundry surplus:

> [London] draweth unto it all soldiers wantinge warres to imploy them,
> all wounded soldiers comme to London to be cured of their diseases.
> All serving men whose Lord and Maisters are dead resort to London
> to provide them Maisters. All maisterless men whose maisters have cast
> them offe for some offence or other comme to London to seke
> service. . . . There is allso a nomber of other ydel people, as lustie
> rogues and common beggers, whose profession is neyther to be a
> souldier nor a servingman, hearinge of the greate lyberalletie of
> London cometh hither to seke reliefe. These ar the caterpillers of the
> common wealthe, these and the rest, being forreine and not domesti-
> call, ar the people who overchardge London.[19]

Though eminently conventional in its analysis, Howes's inventory is
interesting for the distinctions it attempts to draw between the "forreine" and the "domesticall" population, particularly at a time when
London's population was in such flux. The difference seems less connected with immigration *per se* than with social place; to be foreign is
to have no place in the city, no "profession" and thus no civic role. It
is also striking that the ambiguous word "ouercharged" appears in
both the Star Chamber case and Howes's list; the double image of the
overcharged city conjures up both the idea of financial distress and an
overcharged weapon, set to explode at any moment.[20] The two meanings clearly conjoined in the context of early modern London's surplus population. Vagrants, unemployed youths, and discharged
soldiers and sailors were especially feared, in part because of their
propensity for violence but also in part because of their superfluity to
the normal running of the city and society.[21]

Secondly, the 1580 proclamation positioned population growth as
a particular threat to the health of the city, the country, and the
monarch:

> it must needs follow if any plague or popular sickness should by God's
> permission enter amongst those multitudes that the same would not
> only spread itself and invade the whole city and confines (as great mor-
> tality should ensue to the same, where her majesty's personal presence
> is many times required, beside the great confluence of people from all
> parts of the Realm by reason of the ordinary terms for Justice there

holden) but would be also dispersed through all other parts of the realm to the manifest danger of the whole body thereof, out of which neither her majesty's own person can be but by God's special ordinance exempted. (II.466–67)

I examine the overdetermined relationship between the crowd and the plague in detail in chapter 6, but it is worth pausing on the complex bodily interplay of this description. Here the direction of the earlier images of urban crowding in the proclamation is reversed; the hidden domestic space of the small rooms packed with bodies expands outward, invading the city and the country. The proximate cause identified is the concentrations of population produced by the terms of justice: as the country comes to London, so London's disease will be taken to the country. Yet the source of this disease is clearly the small rooms of the multitudes. Symbolically, the "popular sickness" connotes both infection and population; the excessively plural bodies of the urban multitude threaten the "whole body" of the country, as a superfluous and unbalanced element in the body politic. Such characterizations of London's growth were common. In a speech to the Star Chamber in 1616, James compared London to "the Spleene in the body, which in measure as it overgrowes, the body wastes," going on to complain that this growth did not take place "in the heart of the Citie, but in the suburbes; not giving wealth or profit to the Citie, but bringing miserie and surcharge to both Citie and Court."[22] In other words, London is not only out of proportion with the rest of the country, but has no proportion within itself.[23]

A different sort of symbolic element is introduced in the threat presented by the "multitudes" to the Queen's "owne person." One way of reading the described scene would be symbolically, as an opposition between the grotesque body of the urban crowd and the classical body of the monarch. In contrast to the closed and perfect classical body, Mikhail Bakhtin conceptualized the grotesque body as porous, unbalanced, infectious, and multiple; it "transgresses its own confines, ceases to be itself."[24] In this interpretation the "low" grotesque body transgressively threatens to engulf the "high" classical body of the monarch.[25] But this symbolic frame cannot quite capture the spatial dynamics of the image. Rather than being portrayed symbolically as the head of the body politic, Elizabeth's body is figured as individual and solitary, whose "personal presence" is required by the task of government. From the initial suggestion that London is her chamber, Elizabeth is moved to a peripheral position to the metropolis, made vulnerable by physical proximity to the multiple bodies of the city. The symbolic opposition between high and low is unsustainable; despite the rearguard sacralizing effect of "Gods special ordinance," the threat of the urban "multitudes" (the plural perhaps underlining the dispersed multiplicity of this image) is to make the Queen's body one among many.

In the description of London offered in the 1580 building proclamation we thus see the collision of two imaginary cities.[26] The first is a city of symbolic architecture, *camera regis,* a city represented by the singular body of the monarch, sanctioned by ancient practice and "God's special ordinance." The second is a city of population, a corporeal and migrational city, a city that threatens disease and disorder and defacement, a city whose prime referent is the plural bodies of the multitude. If the first city achieves a symbolic clarity through its imagined status as a single chamber and habitation, the second city threatens this clarity by its spatial superfluity: one room into many, one building into many, one body into many. Elizabeth, "perceiving the state of the city of London" as if from on high, peering into the small rooms and confines of its buildings, seeks to rectify the relationship between symbol and space, to make London legible, to resolve it from something unknown or unknowable into something "anciently" known. Michel de Certeau discusses such a conceptual split between the architectural and the corporeal city in terms of the panorama versus the street: "The panorama-city is a 'theoretical' (that is, visual) simulacrum, in short a picture, whose condition of possibility is an oblivion and a misunderstanding of practices."[27] Against this artificial city, which "makes the complexity of the city readable, and immobilizes its opaque mobility in a transparent text," de Certeau positions the activities of the urban populace, "practices that are foreign to the 'geometrical' or 'geographical' space of visual, panoptic, or theoretical constructions . . . A *migrational,* or metaphorical, city thus slips into the clear text of the planned and readable city" (92, 93).

The opposition that de Certeau sets up is extremely suggestive in the context of the building proclamations, perhaps the earliest English example of panoptic urban planning, but it has certain limitations as a model for exploring the urban space of early modern London. De Certeau imagines a city in which public spatial practice is necessarily peripheral to the official structures of urban meaning; the tactics of living in the city, by their fragmentary nature, become an act of resistance to the strategic and totalizing nature of urban conceptualization.[28] In early modern London, however, the official meaning of the city was based as much on certain ritualized forms of spatial practice as it was on the physical space of the city. As Andrew Gordon points out,

"The city was enacted before it was visualized, it walked before it was drawn, and the early modern viewer or imager pictured a city in terms of the organised spatial practices which were the first statement of the city as concept."[29] Early modern London was in many ways a ceremonial city, as Steven Mullaney has argued, "shaped not by the dictates of urban planning and population control . . . but by the varied rites of initiation, celebration, and exclusion through which a ceremonial social order defined, maintained, and manifested itself."[30] Through the power of ritual London transforms from its quotidian form into an ideal urban space of transparent meaning. As I discuss further in chapter 3, Lefebvre calls such a conjunction an example of "absolute space," in which the mental, physical, and social dimensions of the space of the city work together to produce a moment of transcendent clarity.[31] For Mullaney, this transformed view of London is the root of its urban significance, and takes on a particularly theatrical valence: "In the varied ceremonies and festivities conducted throughout the year in sixteenth-century London, the city's image of itself was at once dramatized and . . . made inseparable from the physical body of the community" (13). To dramatize the city's "image of itself," the city itself is made into a theater.

While chapters 2 and 3 examine some of the implications of seeing public ritual in such an organic and immanent fashion, as well as taking issue with other aspects of Mullaney's urban vision, a few comments are necessary here. In effect, with this figure of inseparability, and the elisions implied in "the physical body of the community," Mullaney's vision of early modern London binds de Certeau's opposition together: the distance between ideological strategies of urban meaning and quotidian practices of urban experience is erased. As Garrett Sullivan has argued, in a Lefebvrian critique of Mullaney's vision of the city, "To read London as a 'monumental record' of ritual, to see even in its everyday spaces only vestiges of civic ceremony, is . . . to neglect the determining (and determined) influence of other, nonritualistic forms of material practice on the landscape of the city."[32] Mullaney's account also minimizes the extent to which the "varied ceremonies and festivities" of the city were not ancient but modern—as Lawrence Manley, Archer, Berlin and others have noted, urban ritual in early modern London was largely innovative; while older rites decayed, new social ceremonies were invented to deal with the changing state and space of the city. Nevertheless, Mullaney's account effectively highlights the *intended* effect of public civic ritual, the ways in which the official theatricalization of urban space sought to produce urban legibility and social clarity. What is typically overlooked in accounts of urban ritual, however, is the degree to which this moment of theatrical transcendence depends on the framing action of the onlookers. The urban crowd, however reviled or marginal in the context of official proclamations, was the inevitable context for official public performances of urban culture. It is the corporeal, observant presence of the crowd that turns London into a theater, allowing the unrepresentable complexity of the city to achieve the status and coherence of realized symbol. But in this moment as well the logic of the supplement applies. The crowd was necessary as a creating (and validating) frame for the performances of urban culture, but it was also a performance itself. Within the theatrical economy that dominates early modern experience, the crowd is at once audience and subject, at once watching and participating in the performance. This doubled structure, which could be called the carnivalization of performance, undermines the controlling intentions of the ceremony of representation.[33]

The performance of ritual is the performance of communal memory. The sacralizing aura that envelops the calendrical public ceremonies of urban meaning in early modern London is produced through a process of repetition that always looks backward, fictively, to a more perfect city. Manley, quoting the City Recorder, comments, "It was important to observe civic rites because, as Fleetwood put it, 'it hath ever been the use in . . . governing men's doing and policies always to follow the ancient precedents and steps of the fore-fathers.' "[34] This necessary connection of past and present is another structure of urban meaning that the crowd transgresses. As a metonym of the urban community, the presence of the crowd validates the ritual's continuity with the past. But metaphorically the crowd is something *new:* an innovation, a disruption of the memorial city, a break from the past. De Certeau suggests a correlation between the metaphoric city and the "migrational" city, and as I will demonstrate in subsequent chapters it is the motion (i.e., the behavior) of the assembled multitude that changes the position of the crowd in public ritual from frame to subject. On a symbolic level as well, the implications of a city *in motion* is fundamentally at odds with the nostalgic city of early modern urban ritual.

The particular nostalgic city of Stow's *Survey* has received considerable historical comment in recent years; in a seminal article on the subject, Archer demonstrates the extent to which Stow skews his portrait of London, ignoring innovations in charity, ceremony, and public works in order to paint a picture of a lost civic world.[35] Collinson, noting the way Stow incorporates William Fitzstephen's twelfth-century account of the city into the *Survey,* comments, "The implication is of a world which had remained more or less static until a vaguely defined moment. . . . The great changes which he alleges, and regrets, had all or mostly happened in his own lifetime, not in the four centuries which distanced him from his rare author."[36] In this regard, I would suggest the *Survey* might be understood less as a reliable (or unreliable) account of early modern London and more as a work of urban theory, a way of trying to think through the changing city by way of reference to an ideal past. Archer notes that Stow's "laments for a loss of a sense of community and for the decay of hospitality have a timeless quality about them," and such reaching backwards to a more perfect civic space is a persistent feature of writing about cities.[37] Urban nostalgia is clearly a motivating factor in Mullaney's description of early modern urban life: "The late medieval and Renaissance city was the fullest expression of a world in which . . . the outline of things were more clearly marked than they are in the world we occupy" (10). Similarly, Lefebvre sees absolute space as a lost social organization, replaced with the abstract space of capitalism.[38] Even de Certeau, arguing against such totalizing constructions of urban meaning, suggests that the concept city arose perhaps "in the sixteenth century," overlooking a conceptual urban discourse that reaches back through Aquinas and Augustine to Plato.[39] In each case, the analysis of urban experience is predicated not only on a sense of loss but on the belief that a time existed when this sense of loss was not inherent to urban experience.

In Stow's *Survey,* this sense of loss is typically conveyed through physical remains. As detailed above, Stow repeatedly describes the long history and past greatness of the large properties of the city, only to conclude his architectural genealogy with a lament for its present disintegration into small tenements. Sometimes an architectural trace will remain of the original building, as in this description of "Barklies Inne," near St. Paul's: "This house is now all in ruine, and letten out in seuerall Tenements, yet the Armes of the Lord Barkley remaine in the stone worke of an Arched gate, as is betweene a Cheueron crosse, 10.three, three, and foure" (II.15). More often, however, there are no ruins from which to reconstruct the past, only names and memory itself.[40] Stow's description of the Tower Royal in the center of London is striking in this regard:

> this Tower and great place was so called, of pertayning to the kinges of this Realme, but by whome the same was first builded, or of what antiquity continued, I haue not read. . . . in the rainge of *Richard* the

> second it was called the Queenes Wardrope, as appeareth by this that
> followeth, king *Richarde* hauing in Smithfield ouercome and dispersed
> his Rebels, hee, his Lordes and all his Company, entered the Citty of
> London, with great ioy, and went to the Lady Princes his mother, who
> was then lodged in the Tower Royall . . . This Tower seemeth to haue
> beene at that time of good defence, for when the Rebels had beset the
> Tower of London, and got possession thereof . . . the princesse being
> forced to flye came to this Tower Royall, where shee was lodged and
> remayned safe as yee haue heard, and it may bee also supposed that the
> king himselfe was at that time lodged there. . . . This for proofe may
> suffice, that kinges of England haue beene lodged in this Tower,
> though the same of later time haue been neglected and turned into
> stabling for the kinges horses, and now letten out to diuers men, and
> diuided into Tenements. (I.243–44)

An entire urban world is packed into this description. Unable to provide a definite origin for the building through his antiquarian research, Stow instead proves its royal pedigree through an anecdote laced with civic significance. In city memory, Richard II's defeat of the rebels of the Peasants' Revolt was principally occasioned through the actions of the mayor, William Walworth, who arrested Wat Tyler; he was immediately knighted for this action, an elevation that became a standard and much celebrated honor awarded to the new Lord Mayor each year. To fix the memory of this building, then, Stow turns to a foundational moment of civic eminence, a moment at which, as later civic memorialists would exhaustively elaborate, London proved her worth as the safeguard of monarchy. On the architectural level, the Tower Royal is thus associated with both the preservation of royalty and the preservation of royal inhabitance—a literal *camera regis*, as the civic tower protected the Queen from the rebels when the royal Tower of London failed. But the story tails off, mid-sentence, as Stow briefly recounts what has befallen this house of fame: the desecration that the rebels were unable to perform has taken place through neglect and base conversion. Once armed against external attack on its precincts and privileges, London has made a shameful conquest of itself, leased out like to a tenement; the monumental architecture of urban significance has been given over to division and "diuerse men."[41]

This sense of lost urban significance informs the building proclamations, too, which are also a type of urban theory, a way of imagining London. The overwhelming desire of the 1580 proclamation is a physical return to the past. To control London, one turns it back to what it once was—or, more precisely, what it is remembered to once have been. In banning new construction, Elizabeth enjoins the Lord Mayor and other officers "to foresee that no person do begin to prepare any foundation for any new house tenement, or building . . . where no former habitation hath been in the memory of such as now do live" (II.467). The physical shape of the city is thus desired to take its form from a memorial city, a city of collective memory cognate with the imaginary city later delineated in Stow's *Survey*. In defiance of a trajectory of urban defacement and displacement of royal habitation like that charted by Stow in his description of the Tower Royal, Elizabeth's proclamation seeks to turn London into an actual memory theater, producing legible urban meaning through the total control of its physical texture. What slips through this conception of urban meaning as a memorial architectural matrix, however, is the population that inhabits it.

*   *   *

It is the *method* of the building proclamations that most reveals how London is imagined. The idea that restricting housing could cure urban overcrowding is manifestly ridiculous; the more restricted the physical space of the city is, the more crowded and congested the city will become. It is not, I think, that Elizabeth and her advisors did not realize this obvious fact, as the portion of the proclamation that deals with the expected result is appropriately nebulous: "such undersitters or inmates may provide themselves other places abroad in the realm, where many houses rest unhabited, to the decay of divers ancient good boroughs and towns" (II.468). The impracticality of this notion is also demonstrated by the actual practice of the authorities. In the Star Chamber case discussed above, the tenants were allowed to stay in the illegal buildings without paying rent, and the buildings were not to be destroyed until they were empty.[42] Rather, I think the method of the proclamation points to a fundamental difficulty in symbolically constructing the crowded city. Urban crowdedness can only be understood as an addition to the space of the city. In all of the images of the urban multitude I have been examining here—the unspecified and imagined "small rooms," the vagrant population without fixed address, the dispersal of disease and infection from the porous body of the city—crowdedness is represented as being *without shape:* a superfluous augmentation to the urban space of London. Though it is the human growth of the city that has changed London and catalyzed this royal decree, on a symbolic level the proclamation cannot grasp this growth; it remains outside the economy of urban meaning.

This is not to say that urban population *tout court* was indescribable. Indeed, the *Apologie of the Cittie of London,* appended to Stow's *Survey* but written some twenty years before, describes London's population in terms that seem specifically meant to rebut the implications of the contemporaneous 1580 proclamation. Speaking of the size of the city, he admits it is "very great, and farre exceedeth proportion of *Hippodamus,* which appoynted 10000, and of others which haue set downe other numbers, as meete stintes in theyr opinions to bee well gouerned," yet, he declares, "whatsoeuer the number bee, it breedeth no feare of sedition"; despite "the miserable and needy sort . . . which although it cannot be chosen, but that in a frequent City as London is, there shall be found many, yet beare they not great sway, seeing the multitude and most part there is of a competent wealth, and earnestly bent to honest labour."[43] He expands upon this portrait in a description of "the multitude (or the whole body) of this populus Citie":

> generally, they bee naturall Subiects, a part of the Commons of this Realme, and are by birth for the most part a mixture of all countries of the same, by bloud Gentlemen, Yeomen and of the basest sort, without distinction, and by profession busie Bees. . . . the estate of London, in the persons of the Citizens, is so friendly enterlaced, and knit in league with the rest of the Realme, not onely at their beginning by birth and bloud as I have shewed, but also verie commonly at their ending by life and conuersation . . . I doe inferre that there is not onely no danger towards the common quiet thereby, but also great occasion and cause of goodly loue and amitie. (II.207–08)

A number of works in the early modern period concerned themselves with a similar cataloguing, analyzing and celebrating of the city in terms of the social and economic relations that "knit" and "enterlaced" the city to itself and to the larger country. In such works, urban population is understood principally through a model of networks and relationships: masters and servants, buyers and sellers, associations well defined and supported by law and custom. The author of *A Breefe Discourse, Declaring and Approuing the Necessarie and Inuiolable Maintenance of the Laudable Customes of London* (1584) uses this socioeconomic model to defend London's privileged position in the country, its unique set of laws and customs, and its size: "Verily, as the citie of London beareth oddes, and prerogatiue ouer other cities in England, being the Metropolis or mother Citie thereof, so are the inhabitantes of it no lesse necessarie than profitable members of the common wealth, in transporting our commodities into other lands, and enriching vs with the benefits and fruits of other countries."[44] This celebratory vision of the city is perceptibly different from the account found in the royal proclamations, though it explicitly subordinates itself to royal authority. Rather, the tone is explicitly bourgeois, emphasizing less hierarchy than *urbanitas,* mutuality, and social ties. These ties, in fact, are taken for the entire city itself; the *Breefe Discourse* declares, "what is a citie but a manifold and ioynt societie consisting of many housholdes, and liuing vnder the same Lawes, freedomes and franchises" (sig. A2v). If Elizabeth sought to *impose* urban legibility through the reinscription of a symbolic and memorial city, these texts seek to show the city's *inherent* legibility by delineating the patterns and channels through which its members move.

In drawing on the language of incorporation and knitting together, the method of the *Apologie's* rebuttal to Elizabeth's proclamation bears a striking parallel to developments in the social history of early modern London over the last generation—with the crucial difference that modern historians reject the straightforwardly econo-miastic tone of early modern urban theorists. As noted in the introduction, social historians have principally rebutted the older "doom and gloom" model of urban disorder by drawing attention to the ways in which London's social communities worked toward integration and stability. Using a phrase I return to, we could call such a vision of the urban space of London the *articulate* city, playing on both meanings of the term; through its interconnections, its friendly interlacing, its manifold and joint societies, the city becomes enunciable and legible.[45] The urban space thus produced is primarily a space of knowledge. As J. F. Merritt writes in her introduction to *Imagining Early Modern London:*

> The early modern city was not fragmented into a mosaic of individually self-sufficient communities, but seems instead more like a complex web of interwoven communities, where, over the course of a lifetime, individuals might vary their involvement. But everyone also had potential access to the "anonymity" of city life, in the shape of other "foreign" parts of the capital, and most of all in the public streets, squares, and gardens. (13)

In this picture of the metropolis, what predominates is the "complex web" that encompasses and defines the city. "The 'anonymity' of city life," that which escapes the articulated web, is recreational and ancillary, located in liminal spaces; "potential access" exists, but is not thrust upon the urban inhabitant and is produced more through a lack of local knowledge than a lack of order. In "other 'foreign' parts of the capital," ordered urban space may be unrecognizable to the observer but it exists nevertheless. Furthermore, by implication, if the imagined individual citizen might be at times be faced by the unintelligibility of the city, the social historian suffers no such impediment—potentially, the entire "complex web of interwoven communities" is legible and mappable.

What this imagining of London elides is the inarticulate city, the realm of the "*blind and opaque* mobility" that de Certeau elaborates (93). This could be understood as a residue or surplus, that which resists incorporation into the "complex web" of the city, as in the "miserable and needy sort" referred to in the *Apologie,* or the activities of foreign immigrants that were typically stigmatized as a threat to the city's customs and privileges.[46] Such an understanding of London has been visible in critical approaches to its suburbs, typically characterized as lacking the social and cultural cohesiveness of the city proper. Following the work of historians such as Valerie Pearl, who opposed the city and the suburbs in terms of order versus disorder, Mullaney's hieratic portrayal of London proper is intended to provide a sharp contrast to its marginal environs, location of quasi-licensed misrule and mimetic theatricality.[47] I would like to suggest, however, that to locate the inarticulate city *only* in through concepts of residue or margin misrecognizes the effects of urban unintelligibility, which is produced less by disorder than by complexity. As Lefebvre comments, speaking of the "dual 'nature' " of social space:

> On the one hand . . . space contains opacities, bodies and objects, centres of efferent actions and effervescent energies, hidden—even impenetrable—places, areas of viscosity, and black holes. On the other, it offers sequences, sets of objects, concatenations of bodies—so much so, in fact that anyone can at any time discover new ones, forever slipping from the non-visible realm into the visible, from opacity into transparency. (182–83)

Lefebvre's phrasing highlights the process of intelligibility, the ways by which we make sense out of the complexities of crowded space through the construction of systems of knowledge—sequences, sets, concatenations—but the reverse is true as well. Urban space, as Lefebvre says, "gathers crowds, products in the markets, acts and symbols. It concentrates all these, and accumulates them," and through this gathering and concentration what is transparent and legible often becomes opaque and unreadable.

An interesting example of this can be found in the fate of Goldsmiths Row in Cheapside in the early seventeenth century. In a fascinating account of the political complexities of urban improvement, Paul Griffiths explains how the renovation of the Row in 1594 catalyzed enormous praise, particularly from observers such as Stow and Thomas Platter: "As such, the Row raised both civic and royal honour, providing a lush background for visual displays of powerful authority."[48] Market forces, and the growth of the West End, however, changed the street's character sharply in the following years, as goldsmiths left the central city in order to be nearer to their wealthy clients:

> Soon, however, this chorus of praise was turned into a commentary complaining of its shocking decay. In 1622 John Chamberlain moaned that "yt is a straunge sight and not knowne in this age till within these two or three years, to see booksellers, stocking men, haberdashers, point makers, and other meane trades crept into the Goldsmithes Rowe, that was wont to be the bewtie and glorie of Cheapeside." (177)

This urban effect is certainly familiar to any modern reader who has seen a downtown shopping area decay, and it produced a similarly familiar combination of hand-wringing, conspiracy theories, and heavy-handed and futile civic intervention; through a policy of forced return, "at least twenty-nine 'mean' traders were told to shut up shop along the Rows, and at least seventy-five 'remote' goldsmiths . . . were ordered to fill their places. . . . Yet, despite some chilling threats . . . by 1640 the complexion of the Rows remained unaltered" (178). What is particularly interesting is the urban rhetoric used to describe the situation:

> The policy of a forced return was set in motion by concern about workers tucked away out of reach in "secret" corners or "creeping" through the city (language like descriptions of theft or the passage of the pox through infected bodies). . . . The [Goldsmiths'] company blasted the "increasing nomber" of strangers who . . . lived in "chambers, garretts and other secret places" where it lacked "access" to search, cutting "deceiptful jewels" and selling stolen plate. A link was made with the Rows: "strangers," it was said, were "partlie the means that the use and exercise of other meane trades are crept into the [Rows]." (179)

In these descriptions we can see the movement from urban legibility to urban illegibility, from transparency to opacity. The Row, "a political space where verbal and visual statements of meanings of order were emphasized" (176), the epitome of the articulate city, was rendered inarticulate, connected to an image of a clandestine London of thieves and furtive immigrants, deceitful and stolen commodities, inaccessible corners, chambers, garrets, and secret places. The economic and social processes involved were transparent, rational, the logical outcome of certain material conditions, clearly rooted in the complex web of interwoven communities that in some senses comprised the city. But the effect these processes produced was fundamentally irrational, unmanageable, disorderly, transforming a civic ornament into a blemish on the face of the city. And the terms chosen to express this irrationality, inevitably, were rooted in corporeal appropriation; as in the multiplying small rooms of the 1580 building proclamation, symbolic architecture is replaced by disorderly buildings and disorderly people.

A similar pattern is visible in the opaque counterpart of the *Breefe Discourse's* "manifold and ioynt" society: the early modern discourse of the multitude. Against a vision of a hierarchical model of urban citizenry stands the idea, expressed in plays, poems, pageants, and pamphlets, of the population as a mindless, misconstruing, rebellious beast, ready at any instance to throw off the constraints of order and reason and rebel against authority. The idea of the common populace as a "many-headed monster" originally derives from Plato, as I discuss at length in chapter 4, although the Horatian tag *Belua multorum es capitum* was probably a more immediate *locus classicus* for the early modern use of the phrase. As several commentators have demonstrated, this classical idea—frequently bolstered with biblical allusions to the recalcitrant Israelites in the wilderness and the mob that called for Jesus' death—had by the end of the sixteenth century become a cultural commonplace whose most frequent application was to incidents of the violence of crowds: rebellions, uprisings, revolts, and tumults.[49] In this application the idea of the many-headed multitude served two purposes, both articulating the fears caused by incidents of collective protest and minimizing the political significance of protest by explaining it as a random eruption of an irrational and inherent violence.

Often the multitude appears in explicit opposition to the city, as in John Marston's *Histriomastix,* which features a scene where the maddened peasants crying "Liberty! Liberty! Liberty!" as they storm toward the city:

> See, see, this common beast the multitude,
> (Transported thus with fury) how it raves;

> Threatning all states with ruine, to englut
> Their bestiall and more brutish appetites. (5.4.29–32)[50]

The desire of these caricatured peasants is to destroy social hierarchy—"faith let's all be Captaines" (4.4.4); private property—"All shall be common" (26); and the architectural fabric of the city that supports such structures—"Let's pluck downe the Church, and set up an Alehouse" (11). Similar motifs pervade the representation of the multitude in the anonymous *The Death of Jack Straw*, Thomas Heywood's *Edward IV*, and Shakespeare's *2 Henry VI*, three plays from the 1590s that respectively chronicle the events of the Peasants' Revolt, the rebellion of the bastard Falconbridge, and Jack Cade's Rebellion. In each case, at least superficially, disorder is something that comes from without London, threatening its peace, stability, and customs. The city stands as something separate and threatened by the multitude, the barbarians at the gate. This symbolic coding reverses the original meaning of the many-headed multitude, which in both Plato and Horace is explicitly informed by its urban location. In these early modern cases, the city appears as something intrinsically well ordered and well governed, a figure of desire for the marauding hordes. This is cognate to the view of the city put forward by the author of the *Apologie*, who imagines the city in general (and London in particular) as a place where the gathering together of people enhances and strengthens the stability of both city and citizens: "men by this means of neareness of conuersation are withdrawn from barbarous feritie and force to a certaine mildnes of manners . . . whereby they are contented . . . to heare and obey their heades and superiors" (II.197). By fortifying both communal bonds and social hierarchy, he argues, the city "approcheth nearest to the shape of that misticall body whereof Christ is the head, and men be the members" (II.199). In this broad discourse the idea of the many-headed multitude is positioned as something extrinsic to the city. The ideological dynamic is of the rude and ungoverned country rising against the peace and order of the city, threatening, as the *Apologie* imagines such a dissolution of *urbanitas*, "to *Metamorphose* the world, and to make wilde beastes of reasonable men" (II.199).

As a portrayal of crowd violence and social unrest, this type of placement was rather at odds with the realities of political disorder in early modern England, especially at the end of the sixteenth century when all these accounts appeared. Although rural uprisings were pervasive, in the period between Kett's Rebellion in 1549 and the Midlands Revolt of 1607 they typically involved very small numbers of people. Furthermore, as a number of historians have documented, enclosure riots (the predominant form of rural unrest) typically involved a deliberate self-containment, employing a strategy of limited and symbolic violence against hedges and property instead of people, with the intention of communicating dissatisfaction without provoking severe reprisals. The most serious rural uprising in the late sixteenth century was the Enslow Hill Rebellion in Oxfordshire in 1596, which, despite the ferocity with which its organizers were tortured and prosecuted, never amounted to more than a few dozen people.[51] The extreme nature of the official response to this uprising can be understood in terms of the potential threat it proposed: the plan of the conspirators was to join forces with the rebellious apprentices in London.

It was in London that large-scale violence was a constant and intractable problem. At numerous points Elizabeth imposed martial law to suppress, as a 1591 proclamation puts it, the "sundry great disorders committed in and about her city of London by unlawful great assemblies of multitudes."[52] It was in London that violent crowds of hundreds or even thousands could assemble, where even small disturbances could grow into large tumults extremely quickly, where harsh disciplinary measures could result in further riots in protest, and where imprisoned rioters were frequently broken out by large mobs. It was in London that rioting could constitute a serious threat to official power, as in the Apprentices Insurrection in June of 1595, where a crowd of perhaps one thousand people besieged the Lord Mayor's home, an action later denounced as "tak[ing] the sword of aucthorytye from the magistrats and governours lawfully auctorized."[53] It was in London, finally, that continuing violence could take place; in 1595, twelve separate insurrections, riots, and unlawful assemblies occurred in the space of three weeks. The rioters could dissolve into the city to reappear the next day or the next week in stronger numbers.

Roger Manning has labeled the late sixteenth century "The Late Elizabethan Epidemic of Disorder," detailing at least thirty-five outbreaks of disorder in the city and environs between 1581 and 1602.[54] More recent historical studies of London have tended to minimize the political and social effects of this disorder, pointing out that stability did prevail; unlike a number of continental cities in the period, London never came close to falling into open rebellion. Archer in particular stresses the unique situation of the 1590s, portraying it as a time when traditional sanctions and responses to urban rioting failed, causing an unusual degree of panic on the part of authorities. He also asserts that urban rioting, like rural attacks on enclosures, was primarily "a negotiating strategy," "part of the process of interaction between rulers and ruled"—a proposition supported by the actions of rioters in many cases, who seemed less interested in overthrowing the elite than in enjoining them to perform their functions correctly by way of violent example.[55] This assertion of a lack of generalized discontent with the elite is further indicated by the targets of many of the riots—strangers, brothels, gentry servingmen—which all "represented groups or activities marginal to city life" (5). While Archer is surely correct about the fundamentally civic motivations of rioters, such a perspective may understate the political risks (and perceptions of risk) involved. Tim Harris comments, "Although London may have been much governed, well regulated, and fundamentally stable, we nevertheless need to recognize the reality of the underlying social tensions in the metropolis, and that the threat of disorder was never far below the surface."[56] In gauging the perception of disorder by authorities it is also important to keep in mind the different responses of the civic authorities, who typically seemed more ready to assuage urban tensions and negotiate with rioters, and the crown, which typically saw such attacks as a clear threat to royal power, to be dealt with through harsh and punitive responses. The dangers of using riot as a negotiating strategy is also suggested by this diversity of authoritative responses. As Harris suggests, "is it really possible to maintain a distinction between riots which did or did not challenge magisterial authority? All riots implicitly challenged magisterial authority because they exposed the civic elite's inability to keep order, which was one of their main jobs" (257). Certainly Elizabeth's perception that civic authorities were ineffective is visible in her imposition of martial law and other repressive measures.

From the perspective of this study, however, the principal problem with seeing urban rioting as comparable to rural uprisings—or of only viewing urban rioting within the narrow context of political stability—is that it tends to elide the *urban* aspect of this rioting. As the examples cited above suggest, urban collective violence presents a different sort of problem, both practically and conceptually, than agrarian violence. The response of the authorities to urban uprisings (beyond prosecution of such leaders as could be located) was repeated proclamations of martial law, bans on assemblies, and attempts to ferret out and expel masterless men from the city. In 1601, repeating an order made many times during the last decades of her reign, Elizabeth placed London vagabonds under martial law, claiming "there is at this time dispersed within our city of London and the Suburbs thereof a great multitude of base and loose people, such as neither have any certain place of abode nor any good or lawful cause of business to attend hereabouts."[57] Here the multitude is not gathered within the city but diffused throughout it, a huge but superfluous and malign population fundamentally out of place in the physical space and economic function of London. The process for dealing with this "dispersed multitude" involved privy searches of dwellings and frequent interrogation of individuals and assembled crowds; as a 1595 proclamation against unlawful assembly explained:

> Her majesty hath . . . for the inquisition and knowledge of all such kind of persons so either unlawfully gathering themselves in companies or wandering about like vagabonds without any known manner of living . . . prescribe[d] certain orders to be published in and about the said city which she will have straightly observed. (III.82–83)

The anxieties articulated by this dynamic of crowds that appear and disappear—a violent multitude that is not attacking the city from outside but emerging from within, a multitude that is dispersed and must be sought out—change the parameters within which the multitude could be understood in an urban context. Rather than an easily identifiable peasant rabble ranged against the order represented by the city, the urban multitude was inherently ungraspable, producing in its evanescence a particular problem of knowledge. If, as Christopher Hill has suggested, London was the greenwood of the late sixteenth century, this was due to the difficulty the state had in penetrating the circulatory anonymity of the city.[58] Crowds are an inescapable part of urban life, and so the banning of assemblies necessarily took place within the context of a process of interrogation to determine their lawful or unlawful status. The process of imposing symbolic order on London could only be imagined through a manifestly impossible panoptic fantasy of total visibility and total knowledge of the city and its inhabitants.

In *A Thousand Plateaus*, Gilles Deleuze and Felix Guattari suggest a useful way of understanding this cognitive opposition. Deleuze and Guattari discuss "multiplicities" in terms of two opposing and complementary conceptual models, "arborescent" and "rhizomatic." Arborescent systems—such as the original Platonic concept of the multitude, the "manifold and ioynt" vision of the population found in the pamphlets, and the panoptic fantasy of urban knowledge displayed by the Queen—are hierarchically organized, "extensive, divisible, and molar; unifiable, totalizable, organizable."[59] Rhizomatic systems, in contrast, operate through principles of connectivity and heterogeneity, where any segment of the multiplicity can connect to any other: "The elements of this second kind of multiplicity are particles; their relations are distances; their movements are Brownian; their quantities are intensities, differences in intensity" (33). In the context of London, and particularly in the context of London's sporadic but persistent unrest, arborescent models of population are superseded by rhizomatic models: the urban crowd is invisible and ungraspable until reaching a certain level of intensity, gathering and scattering and gathering again. The rhizomatic model finds a resonance in the strange image in the 1601 order of the "dispersed multitude," a circulatory image linked with another great fear of Elizabeth's, the spread and circulation of illicit information within the city. In April 1601, in the aftermath of the execution of Essex, the Queen proclaimed that "divers traitorous and slanderous libels have of late been dispersed in divers parts of our city of London and places near thereunto adjoining by some lewd and ungodly persons, tending to . . . the stirring up of rebellion and sedition."[60] Rumor and sedition circulate through the city like people, rhizomatically; a dynamic at play in the image conjured up by Rumor of itself at the start of *2 Henry IV*, "a pipe . . . of so easy and so plain a stop / That the blunt monster with uncounted heads . . . / Can play upon it" (1.Pro.15–20). In this unrealizable image the uncounted heads joined in one body play a single flute, an awkward combination that in its impossibility gestures toward the dynamic of aggregation and dissemination underpinning the rhizomatic idea of the crowd.[61] This idea is also closely connected to the spatial practices of London's vagrant population—the "great multitude of base and loose people" predictably blamed for urban unrest and sedition—which Patricia Fumerton has described in terms of "a spaciousness of itinerancy, fragmentation, disconnection, and multiplicity that produces a very different topographical mapping of societal relations."[62] Finally, as I will discuss extensively in chapter 6, this idea is closely related to the impact of the plague on the urban body.

It is to the rhizomatic city that this study repeatedly returns, highlighting the ways in which it attaches itself, like a parasitical growth, to arborescent structures of urban meaning. The context of urban rioting throws this aspect of the space of the city into sharp relief, but in effect we have been discussing it all along; the opposition between arborescent and rhizomatic parallels the other oppositions I have been using: transparent versus opaque, articulate versus inarticulate, rational versus irrational. This is not construct the city as inherently chaotic, unstable, or in crisis. Rather, it is to argue for the *impenetrability* of much of urban life, the ways in which it escapes the structures we would use to frame and anatomize it. The vision of the city as a "complex web of interwoven communities" operates by imagining metonymic connections between individuals, tracing out genealogies of contact and contiguity, but the multiplicity and heterogeneity of such connections ultimately defeat the possibility of tracing these paths. In the crowded and anonymous city, any urban body may connect with any other; the complexity of the city always exceeds the bounds of rational analysis.

The response of the authorities to urban unrest took the inevitable form of a scapegoating, an attempt to rid the city of an unwanted supplement that it associated with masterless men and vagrants. This was a political action, of course, but one informed by a symbolic desire to make the city pure. Nevertheless, the rhizomatic patterns of urban life that permitted collective violence and seditious rumor to operate as they did were not a contamination of London but a particular application or appropriation of its constituent dynamics, the complex and impenetrable system of the circulation and exchange of goods, people, and information inherent to the existence of the city. The symbolic associations of the many-headed multitude— constant motion, constant change, confusion—were attributes of London itself, a larger framework that both exemplified the multitude and made it difficult to tell which, on a symbolic level, was reflecting which. While it would not be until the mid-seventeenth century that the idea of London as the monstrous city would become a cultural commonplace,[63] in the late sixteenth century the many-headed monster and the city were already inextricable. This inextricability follows a supplemental logic. On the one hand, through the scapegoating of vagrants, the crowd is figured as something that does not belong in the city, a blemish on the perfect body of the city; on the other hand, the rhizomatic multitude mimics London, mirroring it, demonstrating the inextricability of the city and people. Through the competitive relationship between these two images of the city, the crowd becomes something both *extrinsic* and *intrinsic* to London, an eccentric and unbalancing force in the idea of the city. Instead of a city "nearest to the shape of that mystical body," as Stow's apologist put it, where each citizen is content in his place in the articulated networks of urban connection, London appears as a place where "proportion is so broken, harmony confounded, that the whole body must be dismembered."[64]

*　*　*

This last quotation is from Stephen Gosson's *Plays Confuted in 5 Actions;* its context is the urban disorder caused by the lack of recognizable social distinction in London as part of a larger attack on the theater. As many commentators have argued, the commercial theater had a complex and vexed relationship with London. Typically, criticism (especially new historicist criticism) has tended to explain official hostility toward the playhouses in terms of the inherent subversiveness of representation and the marginal symbolic position of the liberties, in which the theaters were located.[65] While these issues are important, it is worth remembering, as Margot Heinemann has pointed out, that the hostility directed toward the theater by civic and royal authorities was directly related to their ability to draw and gather people.[66] In a city where assemblies were often prohibited due to fears of rioting, the playhouses were one of the few locations where large crowds could and did congregate. As such, the political issues raised by the general overcrowding in the city were especially applicable to the problem of the playhouses. In 1594 the Lord Mayor wrote to Lord Burghley claiming that the playhouses were "the ordinary places of meeting for all vagrant persons & maisterles men that hang about the Citie,"[67] and a petition to the Privy Council from the residents of Blackfriars in 1596 made similar claims, arguing against the establishing of the Blackfriars theater for reasons of crowding:

> both by reason of the great resort and gathering togeather of all manner of vagrant and lewde persons that, under cullor of resorting to the playes, will come thither and worke all manner of mischief, and allso to the great pestring and filling up of the same precinct, yf it should please God to send any visitation of sicknesse as heretofore hath been, for that the same precinct is allready growne very populous.[68]

The petition draws, perhaps knowingly, on the same two key political issues that informed the proclamations against new building: ungovernability and the spread of disease. In addition, the behavior of this excessive theater population is characterized in theatrical terms, as playing "under cullor" of attending plays. These issues are expressed in the local context of a district already populous and fearing "filling up," not just as an occasional and temporary phenomenon but as a permanent byproduct of allowing the theater to enter the community. The precinct of playing, it seems, is inevitably the place of the crowd.

Such judgments were ubiquitous in early modern London. In *Vertues Common-Wealth, or the high-way to honour* (1603), Henry Crosse reported of theater audiences:

> Now the common haunters are for the most part, the leaudest persons in the land, apt for pilferie, periurie, forgerie, or any rogorie, the very scum, rascalltie, and baggage of the people, theeues, cut-purses, shifters, cousoners; briefly, an vncleane generation, and spaune of vipers: must not here be good rule, where is such a broode of hell-bred creatures? for a Play is like a sincke in a Towne, wherevnto all the filth doth runne: or a byle in the body, that draweth all the ill humours vnto it.[69]

In Crosse's description we find the same language of the crowd as in Howes's taxonomy of the "forreine" population of London—"the very scum, rascalltie, and baggage of the people," implying an unhealthy and parasitical residue of the commons—coupled with a bestial and biblical language of "hell-bred creatures" and "spaune of vipers." The description of playgoers as "an vncleane generation" implies both biblical sanction and an unclean generative force, a force of multiplication and agglomeration; through inexorable forces this generation is drawn together in the theater, imagined as both a sewer and a boil, where the otherwise dispersed filth of the city is concentrated and made visible. Contemporary accounts of the playhouse scene are filled with observations of the filthy crowding imagined by Crosse. Thomas Platter's visit to the Globe in 1599 caused him to comment on the "great swarms" of prostitutes that "haunt the town in the taverns and playhouses," a metaphor that repeats in Robert Anton's satirical complaint that the theaters draw "Such *swarmes* of *wives* to breake their *nuptiall othes.*"[70] Theater writers contributed their own observations of the crowded space of the theater. In *The Seuen Deadly Sinnes of London,* Thomas Dekker writes of playhouses "smoakt every after noone with Stinkards who were so glewed together in crowdes with the Steames of strong breath, that when they came foorth, their faces lookt as if they had been per boyled,"[71] in *What You Will* John Marston imagines that the theaters "crack with full stufft audience,"[72] and in *The Roaring Girl* a pictured audience is described as almost impossibly dense: "Within one square a thousand heads are laid / So close, that all of heads, the roome seemes made" (1.2.19–20).

For the authorities, this excessive crowding was an inherently dangerous and unstable social phenomenon. Crosse asks, "doth it not daily fall out in common experience, that there is either fighting, whereof ensueth murther? robbing and theeuering, whereof commeth hanging? or spotting the soule with wickednesse, that he becommoneth the very sonne of *Beliall* ?," and indeed it seems such activities were expected adjuncts of theatergoing.[73] In 1612 an order was made suppressing jigs at the end of plays, as "divers cutt-purses and other lewde and ill disposed persons in great multitudes doe resorte thither at the end of everye play, many tymes causing tumultes and outrages."[74] The official attitude toward the theater crowds is also apparent from the decision in 1602 to use the theaters and bowling alleys to press thousands of people for military service—a disastrous policy, as it turned out, since many gentlemen as well as vagrants were inadvertently captured this way.[75] John Davies describes the scene at "the play house dores" as a promiscuous commingling of all social castes of London—"A thousand townesmen, gentlemen and whores, / Porters and serving-men together throng"—and altercations between apprentices and gentlemen often resulted from this close interaction.[76] Among the best known of these is the famous "turn upon the toe" in 1584, in which a gentleman stepped on the belly of a sleeping apprentice. The result was three successive large-scale riots (two of which began just outside the theater) involving between 500 and 1,000 people, many days of riotous disorder, and the inevitable closing of the theaters.[77] The theater served as the flashpoint for rioting at many times in the late sixteenth and early seventeenth century—as Crosse says, "what more fitter occasion to summon all the discontented people together, then Playes?"—and, as Barbara Freedman has argued, city official often used the danger of plague as a pretext for closing the theaters during times of social turmoil.[78]

In such a social context, with open assemblies often prohibited by royal decree, and the theaters already stigmatized as a breeding ground for social unrest and riotous behavior, the *staging* of crowds was an extremely controversial action. A standard political attack of the antitheatricalists was the overwhelming effect that drama had on its audience, who were supposedly ill equipped to maintain a judging distance from the action. Crosse's attack is conventional in this regard; while acknowledging the theoretical possibility of promoting good behavior through drama, he considers the contemporary stage incapable of it:

> in stead of morallitie, fictions, lies, and scurrillous matter is foysted in, and is cunningly conueied into the hearts of the assistants, whereby they are transformed into that they see acted before them: for the

> rusticke & common sort, are as Apes, that will imitate in themselues,
> that which they see done by other. (sig. P4)

Crosse speaks here to the mimetic power of the theater, although significantly reversing its polarity: it is the audience, not the stage, that acts as a mirror, transforming itself into what is presented before it. At the same time, Crosse's description of the theater crowd as "filth" and "an vncleane generation" suggests that the "scurrilous matter" performed on the stage is itself reflecting the composition of its audience. Given the complexities of this theatrical doubling, in which stage and audience each reflect the other, we might ask how a crowd might be staged to a crowd. How might populated London be staged to itself?

The only representation we have of an openly rebellious *London* crowd is in *Sir Thomas More's* dramatization of "Ill May Day" in 1517, when citizens rose against immigrant artisans in response to a series of alleged abuses, beginning a riot that culminated in prison breaks, the looting and destruction of many artificers' shops, and the burning of a number of buildings. The section of the play that deals with the rebellion is very similar in structure to the representation of the Peasants' Revolt in the contemporaneous *Death of Jack Straw*, in that it begins with the local (and justified) grievances of the commons before proceeding to the reaction of the authorities to the insurrection. In both plays as well, rebellion is accompanied by a bumptious quasi-comic clowning that leavens the seriousness of the events. But while *Jack Straw* moves quickly to establish the inherent depravity of its rebels, *Sir Thomas More* works to maintain a guarded loyalty to the leaders of its riots. Lincoln, the originator of the riot, is portrayed as an honest man driven to an action that quickly spirals out of his control; his mistaken execution, taking place just before the King's pardon arrives, is treated in tragic terms, particularly through the reaction of Williamson and his wife Doll. The events of Ill May Day are brought to a close (unhistorically) by the eloquent address of More, who draws parallels between the rioters and the strangers they attack, reminding them of their stake in civil peace and the rule of law, reasoning them around to obedience and surrender. Where *Jack Straw* establishes a clear moral separation between the rural crowd onstage and the urban crowd that watches them in the playhouse, and achieves its civic uplift from the expulsion of that which does not belong in the city, *Sir Thomas More* envelops rioters, strangers, and audience alike in the mantle of civic generosity and urban mutuality; the description of Londoners as strangers themselves would have had strong resonance in a city increasingly composed of immigrants.[79]

As many commentators have noted, this was an explosively topical setting for a play. In the early 1590s anti-alien feeling was running very high, and there had been a number of posted libels threatening violence if the strangers did not depart London.[80] The words of Shrewsbury, as the riot is gathering, must have sounded particularly ominous to authorities:

> I tell ye true, that in these dangerous times
> I do not like this frowning vulgar brow.
> My searching eye did never entertain
> A more distracted countenance of grief
> Than I have late observed
> In the displeasèd commons of the city. (1.3.5–8)

Even more threatening, however, is how this parallel is employed in the play. As in civic ritual and ceremony, past London is explicitly set up as a model for present London. In response to the Clown's suggestion that the strangers' houses be set on fire, Doll exclaims, "Ay, for we may as well make bonfires on May day as at midsummer; we'll alter the day in the calendar, and set it down in flaming letters" (2.1.36–38). In imagining altering the calendar, Doll prophesies a changed ritual year. In place of civic festivities such as bonfires, May Day will become a new local tradition, a new civic ritual of urban purgation to match the quasi-licensed attacks on brothels at Shrovetide. The earlier comments of George suggest a similar mixing of festivity and politics, of carnival and violence: "on May Day next in the morning we'll go forth a-Maying, but make it the worst May Day for the strangers that ever they saw" (1.2.129–31). Doll's reference to "midsummer," however, contains a further charge: the Midsummer Watch, the height of the civic ritual year in Doll's time, had been suppressed in the mid-sixteenth century due to the large and unruly crowds that would gather for the bonfires. As Berlin has explained, "The processions at midsummer gradually became limited to an exclusively military exercise, often combined with so-called 'privy' watches for 'suspect' persons such as masterless men, papists, recusants and idle rogues or special campaigns against petty offenders, sumptuary laws, illegal tavern keepers and 'night walkers.' "[81] The suppressed midsummer festivities were replaced in the civic year by the autumnal Lord Mayor's show, which by the 1590s was already becoming a extravagant celebration of mercantile power and social hierarchy. Doll's carnivalesque proclamation, therefore, could be further understood as an implicit assertion of ancient communal privileges, abrogated by the time of the play's performance in favor of the ceremonies of urban stratification.

Sir Thomas More does work to contain the effects and significance of the riot, which occupies only the first two acts of the play. All the violence takes place offstage, and what we observe is the somewhat frantic movement of groups through the city, pausing and reporting on the damage done or forecasting the damage to come. The scene of public punishment, when the rioters are brought to the scaffold with halters around their neck, is the occasion of a much greater imagined crowding of the city than the riot itself catalyzed; the Sheriff comments that "The street's stopped up with gazing multitudes," and his Officer complains that "there's such a press and multitude at Newgate / They cannot bring the carts unto the stairs / To take the prisoners in" (2.4.18, 31–33). In the next act, as well, the rioting city is replaced by the ridiculous figure of the ruffian Faulkner, who is hyperbolically charged with setting "half the city in an uproar" by fighting in a public street and blocking traffic (3.1.56), and who is comically bested by More through the Samson-like expedient of cutting his hair. Still, the play repeatedly demonstrates its radical ambivalence to the riot through its tone, its appropriation of ritual, and its loyalty to citizen values. In this way, *Sir Thomas More* seeks to straddle genres, balancing itself between a record of treasonous insurrection and a citizen staple, deliberately playing with the tensions inherent to portraying the collective violence of London's citizens on the London stage.

Sir Thomas More was never produced on the stage, due to the command of Edmund Tilney, the Master of the Revels, at the top of the manuscript:

> Leaue out . . . / the insurrection / wholy w[ith] / the Cause ther off & / begin w[ith] Sr Th: / Moore att the mayors sessions / w[ith] a reportt afterwards / off his good servic' / don being' Shriue off London / vppon a mutiny Agaynst the / Lumbards only by A shortt / reportt & nott otherwise / att your own perilles.[82]

Tilney's reasons for this interdiction are doubtless several, but a central one must be that the scene proposed to stage something far too close to the social reality of London at the time. I want to argue that under the possibility of censure—"att your own perilles," as Tilney puts it—theatrical portrayals of crowds typically worked within the limits of a symbolic economy that helped to minimize the threat of the multitude. Rebellious English crowds could be portrayed in the context of London—and were in works like *Jack Straw, 2 Henry VI,* and *Edward IV.* However, as I suggest above, each of these portrayals superficially preserves the social and symbolic integrity of the city by opposing it to the rebellious rabble, thus making the multitude extrinsic to London. Crowds, if properly stigmatized, could also be portrayed in other urban locations, such as the murderous Spaniards sacking Antwerp in *A Larum for London* and the murderous Catholics of Christopher Marlowe's *The Paris Massacre*—or in the mob scenes of Roman plays such as *Sejanus, Julius Caesar,* and *Coriolanus,* all of which I will discuss in detail later in the book.[83] And Thomas Dekker's *Shoemaker's Holiday* perhaps escaped censure due to its explicitly festive and emphatically benign tone, despite the implicit threat in the mid-1590s of armed apprentices calling "clubs for apprentices!" (5.2.32).

The most common way of staging an urban crowd, however, was as an audience. Shakespeare's canon, with which this study is particularly concerned, is especially full of such portrayals; in all of the English history plays, from *Henry VI* to *Henry VIII,* and in the Roman histories *Julius Caesar* and *Coriolanus,* there are crowd scenes in which the staged or imagined urban populace acts as spectators to the affairs of the elite. On one level this could be understood as a form of displacement, a forcing of the dangerous symbolic energies of the crowd into a peripheral and supporting role. On another level, though, the staging of crowds is a natural consequence of the material conditions in which the plays were produced. By staging or invoking spectating crowds, especially through an address to the actual audience, plays linked the bounded space of their drama to the theatrical space of their performance. One space was mapped onto the other, and the contradictions inherent to staging an urban world could be articulated through the relationship between the staged play and its London audience.

An especially vivid and unusual example of this can be found in the closing lines of *Eastward Ho,* written by George Chapman, Ben Jonson, and John Marston:

Quicksilver. I perceive the multitude are gatherd together, to view our comming out at the *Counter.* See, if the streets and the fronts of the Houses, be not stucke with People, and the Windowes fild with Ladies, as on the Solemne day of the *Pageant!*

> O may you find in this our *Pageant,* here
> The same contentment, which you came to seeke;

> And as that *Show* but drawes you once a yeare,
> May this attract you hither, once a week. (Epilogue, 1–8)

This metatheatrical passage links the theater with the city in complex ways. The comic context is that Quicksilver, newly released from prison, has agreed to go through the streets of the city as an example to the "children of Cheapside" (5.5.217); to his surprise, he finds that they are already assembled in front of him.[84] The linkage is expressed not simply through an association of the theater audience with the London populace, but through a transformation of physical space: the variegated space of the playhouse becomes the space of the city, with streets, houses, windows, and all. But the space here produced by the assembled multitude is not the normal space of the city. Rather, the streets, houses, and windows are "stucke with people," creating a crowded and panoptic tableau. The word "stucke" emphasizes both the immobility of the crowd (preserving it as a frame) and the way in which the scene is an atemporal interruption in the play, a break in time. The invocation of the mayoral pageant as a calendrical, repeated ritual underscores the fact that we have moved into a different perception of time; as during the civic rituals themselves, the London that is produced here is not the quotidian city but the iconic, atemporal, transformed city, in which the moral failings and redemptions of the play's characters can be evaluated and validated.

The moment is ironic as well as iconic; throughout its length *Eastward Ho* satirizes the bourgeois pieties and moral fortitude that it here mockingly endorses. The distance that the play establishes between itself and its epilogue may help to explain a perhaps puzzling feature of this book: the relative invisibility of city comedy in a project devoted to representations of urban meaning. Despite the frequency with which critics talk about the "crowds" in city comedy, the plays of this genre typically map a different sort of city than the one evoked through the presence of crowds. London in city comedy is London writ small. In representing London, city comedy avoids the emblem of the crowd, focusing instead on the iterations and reiterations of a deliberately small repertoire of urban characters and situations. Rather than employing an assembled, anonymous crowd to symbolize the city metonymically, city comedy conveys the city through synecdoche, the network of identified and named characters on the stage implying the rest of the city. The interactions of one usurer, one cuckold, one ignoble noble, one harsh master, one potentially unfaithful wife, one lazy or virtuous apprentice, and the like dramatically stand in for the operation of the entire city.

Ben Jonson's deployment of London in *Bartholomew Fair* epitomizes this process, centripetally narrowing and trivializing the dramatic location of London. In the Induction, the metropolis looms around the playhouse; the words of the Scrivener concretize the play's physical location as "the Hope on the Bankside in the county of Surrey" (Ind.59), and the lengthy calculation of the wit of the audience emphasizes the crowded state of the city.[85] The play does begin with the streets and houses of London, but these are quickly replaced by the fair itself, which stands as a microcosm of the metropolis. Tellingly, once the characters enter the precincts of the fair in the second act they never leave it. Within the fair we eventually move, again permanently, to the scene of the puppet theater—which doubles the space of the Hope and thus in effect returns us again to the start of the play in miniature—where we are presented with the drama of Hero and Leander, reduced from Marlowe "to a more familiar strain for our people" as a ballad of a dyer's son and "a wench o' the Bankside" (5.3.103, 109). As the play progresses, the dramatic location and populous complexity of London shrinks, becoming at its parodic nadir the fractious conversation of two hand puppets; what more is the city than such debased interactions, Jonson seems to imply.

The space of *Bartholomew Fair* is fundamentally a space of urban competence and knowledge. Everyone (excepting benighted Overdo and foolish Cokes) knows or comes to know everyone else—if not by straightforward introduction, then by the obviousness of their occupations: the puppet master, the pig woman, the ballad singer, the pickpocket. But where is the anonymous city, the swarm that do not carry the signs of their professions? The urban vision of the city comedics is a long way from the idea of the opaque and unknown crowd, which features most prominently in the histories and historical tragedies of the period. I think the prevalence of the crowd in the history plays is a symptom of the sort of space, urban, or theatrical, that the assembled crowd produces. Despite symbolizing the quotidian city metaphorically, the crowd as a metonymic assembly is an interruption in the daily life of the city, a diachronic break with the normal time and space of urban experience. It is in the history plays that the distance between dramatic time and ordinary time is most carefully examined, and it is in the history plays as well that the drama of the elite is played out before the eyes of the multitude. Most of all, it is in the history plays that the idea of the past as an edifying spectacle—the collective memory of the populace— is both deployed and analyzed, often through a self-reflexive examination of the act of staging. The figure of the crowd—as concept, as validating frame, and as playhouse presence—stands at the center of the issues that shape the theatrical performance of the historical city.

*　*　*

The title of this chapter, "Imaginary Numbers," is a play on one of my favorite Shakespearean stage directions. The appearance of Cade's rebellion in *2 Henry VI* is announced in this way: "Drum. Enter Cade, Dick butcher, Smith the weaver, and a Sawyer, *with infinite numbers, with long staves*" (4.2.31–32). What draws me to this direction—besides its shading from the specific and named to the general and anonymous—is primarily its preposterousness: given the small size of early modern theatrical companies, the infinite numbers of the staged crowd would perhaps number a dozen. Of course, Shakespeare knew how to produce the effect of a cast of thousands, as demonstrated in the Prologue to *Henry V:* through the "imaginary forces" of the audience, which could "Into a thousand parts divide one man" (1.Pro.18, 24). This figure of multiplication and division, carrying with it contradictory implications of unity and dissolution—and expressed in the context of a punning opposition between the "forces" of the massed audience, numbering in the thousands, and the small space of the stage in which the crowd is manifested—is an intriguing imbalance that has been a continual motivation for me in this study.

This book is concerned with "imaginary" numbers in many ways; the imagined multitudes that have populated this chapter recur through the study in various shapes, forms, and concatenations, as do the different ways of imagining numerousness—articulate and inarticulate, arborescent and rhizomatic, rational and irrational—that I have sketched in the preceding pages. Throughout this could be understood as addressing a particular problem of knowledge. Mathematically, an imaginary number is only known through i, its symbolic double; it has no place in the arithmetical progression of the real, but by deploying its sign one can calculate and understand all manner of things otherwise impossible.[86] In a very loose manner, the figure of the crowd shares both this potential for further understanding and this basic unknowability. In the life of the city, the assembled crowd (whether as theater audience, as human frame of urban ritual, or as rioting mob) was evanescent, fleeting, dissolving but certain to return again. This evanescence and persistence, as we shall see, signals its impact on London's understanding of itself.

C H A P T E R   2

London's Mirror: Civic Ritual and the Crowd

> *Thus having (as it were in Lantschip) a farre off shewne you the
> Toppes onely of our* City-Buildings; *and in a little Picture drawn the
> Face of her* Authority . . . *let mee now open a Booke to you . . .*
>
> (*Thomas Dekker, introduction to* Brittannia's Honor)[1]

For James I's ceremonial entry into London in 1604, seven arches were erected at prominent points in the procession through the city.[2] The arches were crowned with various iconographic and allegorical figures: in Cheapside there was a representation of the Garden of Plenty, showing Fortune attended by Peace and Plenty; in Soper-Lane stood *Nova Felix Arabia,* presided over by Fame and the Five Senses; in Temple Bar was the Temple of Janus, which showed Mars groveling at the feet of Peace. The most striking, and now most famous, of the arches was Ben Jonson's creation for Fenchurch Street, called the Londinium Arch. The entire top portion of the arch was given over to a panorama of London. Unlike the other arches, culminating in *desiderata* and pseudomythical constructs, here the focus was a detailed scale model of a real and contemporary fact of life: *the* fact of life, perhaps, for those who lived in the city.

As discussed in chapter 1, Michel de Certeau defines panorama as a conceptual model of urban space, one that makes the city legible through a fiction of totality: "The panorama-city is a 'theoretical' (i.e., visual) simulacrum" that "makes the complexity of the city readable, and immobilizes its opaque mobility in a transparent text."[3] As the context of material simulacra such as the Londinium Arch emphasizes, it should be added that the urban panorama authenticates itself as a true mirror of the city through its ordered complexity and attention to significant detail. In describing the coronation entry, Gilbert Dugdale remarked of the Londinium Arch, "the Cittie of London [is] very rarely and artificially made, where no church, house nor place of note, but your eye might easilye find out, as the Exchange, Coleharber, Powles, Bowe Church, &c."[4] The power of the panorama articulates itself through a process of similitude. Dugdale's imagined city, the image of London he carries in his mind, matches that of the model—or perhaps is made to match, the total order of the model framing and defining the fragmentary mental city.

In the Londinium Arch the legible city suggested by de Certeau is glossed, as it were, by its frame.[5] Directly under the panorama was "Monarchia Britannica"; under her sat Divine Wisdom, and on either side, ranged in a descending arch, were Gladness, Loving Affection, Unanimity, Veneration, Promptitude, and Vigilance—the six daughters of "Genius Urbis," the personification of London, who himself stood more modestly on a lower level.[6] In this representation the joyful submission of the city to the new monarch is not only made explicit but is mapped onto the space of the city: the symbolic clarity of the ranged figures provides the meaning of the urban panorama. At the same time, the realism of the detailed panorama helps to authenticate the social geometry of the iconographic hierarchy. Two visions of the city—one ideal, one apparently real—complement each other, each reinforcing the ideological message they convey. Set in the emblematic frame of the triumphal arch, London moves from mere existence to iconic meaning; the panoramic spread of buildings becomes invested with a significance realizable only as allegory.

This chapter explores the ways in which the idea of the city as a perfect, geometric, and total construct shapes and informs early modern civic pageantry. Its primary context is the annual celebration known as the Lord Mayor's show. Originally a minor ceremony involving a simple procession on horseback, in the late sixteenth century this annual welcoming of the new Lord Mayor to his office rapidly developed into an elaborate production sitting at the head of London's ceremonial year, complete with costumes, morris dancers, minstrels, and complicated tableaux. Noted dramatists wrote and designed the pageants and craftsmen spent many weeks constructing the tableaux. The costs for each production were enormous, often exceeding

£1000.[7] Drawing on both the public theater and the burgeoning emblematic tradition for material and perspective, it acquired a dramatic and thematic complexity unique in civic entertainments. While it took its general form from the religious pageants of the Corpus Christi and Midsummer festivals, the Lord Mayor's show developed a predominantly secular and explicitly urban focus.

In analyzing the Lord Mayor's show I focus my discussion on the context of the performed show, the urban crowd that filled the streets of the city during the mayoral procession. My aim is to examine the place of the crowd, both in the imaginative world of the civic allegory presented by the shows and in the real world of the actual procession, as part of a process of understanding the interaction of the ideal and real Londons juxtaposed by the act of performance. This examination skips across more than forty years of mayoral pageants, and in so doing it generally pays limited attention to the local historical and political contexts in which the shows operated; through this neglect, however, it draws attention to the striking commonality of concerns the shows display over the entire Jacobean and Caroline periods, the persistence of tropes and themes that repeatedly iterate a particular understanding of what the city is and how the shows are important to that understanding. As the chapter title suggests, my continual interest throughout the chapter is in the complex mimetic interplay that the performance of public ritual produces. I argue that the crowd was both the inevitable and necessary frame for the public ritual, the validating presence needed to legitimate the civic values being performed by the show's passage through the space of the city. At the same time, the spatial behavior and symbolic associations of the crowd, in the context of the mirroring function of the shows, served to reveal the contradictions at the base of the allegorical representation of the city.

I frame my analysis with a discussion of the Londinium Arch for several reasons. The early seventeenth-century Lord Mayor's show emulated the 1604 royal entry in both detail and scale, adopting the lavish monumentality of its pageants while mimicking and reworking its iconographic and moral structures into a powerful model of civic rectitude.[8] This was especially true of the Londinium Arch, as representations of the city increasingly filled the mayoral shows. More importantly, the shows employed the spatial ideology used in the Londinium arch, linking panoramic and ideographic visions of the city to present a perfect and readable London. In Thomas Heywood's *Londini speculum: or, Londons Mirror* (1637), Opsis (Sight) suggests that "every forraigne Magistrate" ought to examine London "without, and then within" as a glorious edifice and example of civic virtue.[9] Opsis continues with a panoramic view of the city, "What Architectures, Palaces, what Bowers, / What Citadels, what turrets, and what towers?" (sig. C3v), and then moves "within" the city:

> let them come within to anatomize her.
> Her *Praetor*, scarlet Senate, Liveries,
> The ordering of her brave societies,
> Divine *Astraea* here in equall scale
> Doth ballance *Iustice, Truth* needes not looke pale. (sig. C3v–C4)

Here, as in the Londinium Arch, the perfect geometrical ordering of London's "brave societies" and the hierarchical positioning of her government provide the anatomy, the inner truth, of the city. An explicit model or personification of the city such as this does not always occupy the center of the shows; frequently constructions such as the "House of Fame" or the "Parliament of Honour" are used for the purposes of organizing and elaborating the meaning of the city. But a constant theme is the imaginative reworking of the physical space of London so that it reflects and embodies the structure and ethos of the mercantile elite. In *Himatia-Poleos* (1614), written for the Drapers, Anthony Munday uses the conceit of city walls being the clothing of the city to give the buying and selling of cloth a foundational role in defining the space of London.[10] Similarly, in the preface to *Brittannia's Honor* (1628) with which I introduce this chapter, Thomas Dekker begins with a panoramic description of London, showing "the Face of her Authority," before opening the text of the public ritual to be performed; to read the show is to read the city. The "book" of the city was also the pageant text itself, a commemorative pamphlet distributed to elite members of the mayoral guild as a souvenir of the event.[11]

The elaboration of an ideal image of the city in the Lord Mayor's show served a number of different (and sometimes competing or contradictory) purposes. As many critics have noted, it was partly through the mayoral pageant that the civic authorities renegotiated the symbolic relationship between London and the court and between London and the rest of the country.[12] An image of a unified, peaceful, and powerful London was a potent political tool for defending London's special privileges and celebrating its prosperity. At times the watching crowd was assimilated into this project. This was especially the case when the city was being imaginatively presented to the outside world; a Russian prince and princess in *Brittannia's Honor* are dumbfounded "to see streetes throng'd . . . To see these Braue, Graue, Noble Citizens / So stream'd in multitudes"—a moment also found in Thomas Middleton's *The Triumphs of Truth* (1613) in the figure of a Moorish king, who is "much astonied at the many eies of such a multitude."[13] In Heywood's *London Ius Honorarium* (1631), London asks her "sister Cittyes" of England why they look so amazed:

> Is it to see my numerous Children round
> Incompasse me? So that no place is found
> In all my large streets empty? My yssue spred
> In number more then stones whereon they tread.
> To see my Temples, Houses, even all places,
> With people covered, as if, Tyl'd with faces?[14]

Although taking place within the city, these views of London are implicitly panoramic and exterior; London appears as a figure of desire for those, like the visiting foreigners or the "sister cities," who do not possess her. In Heywood's vision "numerous children" both encompass the personification of London, framing the display of the pageant, and seem to become the city itself. Despite this transformation, the underlying urban form remains coherent; the city is "Tyl'd with faces," the buildings and temples giving shape to the human masses that overlay them in this static, immobile image. The slight suggestion of excess in "more then stones whereon they tread" is effectively contained in the speech that follows, which makes the ideological purposes of the image explicit:

> Will you know whence proceedes this faire increase,
> This joy? . . .
> Behold; my motto shall all this display,
> Reade and observe it well: *Serve and obay.*
> *Obedience* through it humbly doth begin,
> It soone augments unto a Magozin
> Of plenty, in all Cities 'tis the grownd. (sig. B4v)

In this elaboration of the symbolic meaning of the panorama, population growth is represented as the fruit of moral purpose, a purpose conflated with economic endeavor through the mercantile metaphor of the "Magozin" or warehouse. Moral uprightness, proper respect for degree and hierarchy, and economic prosperity are combined, producing both a powerful symbol of London's glory for the rest of the country and a highly flattering self-image for the civic government.

As the moral valence of Heywood's image suggests, the shows also resonated in the more local context of the common inhabitants of London. The power of the guilds was principally a commercial power, one that derived from their ability to organize and control the economic life of the city and the country.[15] The relationship between city official and Londoner was not that of lord and subject, but rather a complex interaction rooted in economic difference. Although in theory the office of mayor was a possibility to any incorporated merchant or artisan in the city, in practice the higher echelons of civic government were in the power of a small number of extremely wealthy merchants and traders.[16] As such, one of the ideological purposes of the shows was to justify and legitimate the power of the mercantile elite.[17] In part this was done through the acts of charity and communal largesse that accompanied the show, and through the symbolic inclusion of a number of "deserving poor" in the procession itself.[18] But the prime means of fostering a positive image of the elite and legitimating their control was the lavish spectacle of the show itself. In the introduction to *Troia-Nova Triumphans* (1612), Dekker explains this edifying purpose:

> As well to dazle and amaze the common *Eye*, as to make it learne that there is some *Excellent*, and *Extraordinary Arme* from heaven thrust downe to exalt a *Superior* man, that thereby the Gazer may be drawne to more obedience and admiration.[19]

Explaining and elaborating this difference between superior and inferior Londoners was the work of the pageant displays and celebratory speeches, which together present an ideal community in which the economic and political power of the mercantile elite is justified by their moral probity and their desire and ability to do good works.

This ideal was validated by the pageant's progress through the city.[20] By tracing a time-honored route through the ceremonial heart of the city, the shows sought to enact an urban space in which the power of the civic authorities was not only calendrically visible but perpetually installed in the physical space of the city. Steven Mullaney uses Charles Pythian-Adams's idea of ceremony as the "living mirror" of a community to infer a complex mimetic reading of the urban significance of this procession.[21] Claiming that London during such ceremonies appeared as "the landscape of the community itself," he suggests:

> When a lord mayor's pageant achieved its plotted course through the city the ceremony itself was at an end, but the concerns of community

thus celebrated and conveyed were not exhausted by their ritual progress. When ceremony ceased, the city remained: a trace, a record, a living memory of the cultural performances it both witnessed and served to embody.[22]

In this reading, the effect of ritual is to reverse the mimetic trajectory of the performance: while the shows are themselves a mirror of the community, the effect of their performance is to make the physical city into a mirror of the ideal ceremonial city of the pageants. By allegorizing the physical city so that it recalls the idea, a hermetic symbolic logic is established: representation and reality become inseparable. The city is already wholly articulate and wholly legible; ceremony becomes almost superfluous, reinforcing a basic symmetry that already exists.

One of Mullaney's purposes in putting forward this model is to discuss its downfall, the loss of the holistic urban world of the medieval and early-renaissance period; a transformation that he associates particularly with the publication of John Stow's *Survey of London* in 1598.[23] His choice of the Lord Mayor's show as a demonstration of this supposed lost world is somewhat surprising, for the glories of civic pageantry belong exactly to this period of breakdown. The Lord Mayor's show rose to civic prominence at the same time that London first began to noticeably suffer from the negative effects and symbolic illegibility caused by its rapid population growth. These changes threatened the civic elite, in part through the vast expansion of population and economic production in the suburbs and in part through the symbolic loss of control that London's growing incomprehensibility connoted.[24] The presentation of the ideal community of the shows was in response to the perceived loss of urban significance and clarity that pervades Stow's account. Indeed, many of the writers used Stow as a prime source for their elaboration of the historical splendor and virtue of the city.[25]

Mullaney's argument is most useful not as a description of the social effect of the mayoral pageants but as an articulation of a certain kind of urban desire, a desire that I would argue informs the ideological underpinnings of the shows' allegorical models. In his study of Baroque tragic drama, Walter Benjamin comments, "Allegory is in the realm of thought what ruins are in the realm of things."[26] What Benjamin means is that allegory takes as its material the forms of the past that have lost their significance. What this loss of significance requires is a constant looking-backward to a supposed time when sign and referent did cohere, significance was stable, and it was therefore not necessary for the legible city to be an allegory. It is this desire for a more perfect time that animates the Lord Mayor's show, and explains in part the importance of public ritual as a means of recuperating such a time.

Yet public ceremony is a slippery mode of performance, continually sliding back and forth between its formal, symbolic structure and its performative, public context. Symbols are performed, and contexts symbolized. The porousness produced by the act of performance, I want to argue, reveals fissures in the celebratory logic of the pageant texts. Like the Londinium Arch, which presents a complete panorama of the city *within* the city itself, producing a sort of spatial dissonance, the allegorical models of an ideal urban community employed by the Lord Mayor's show mesh imperfectly with the surrounding city. Because of the public medium in which civic pageantry necessarily operated, the ideal city was continually threatened by the real city that surrounded it. London served to frame the pageants, to authenticate their rehearsal of power, but it also undermined the ideal they put forward by contextualizing and contemporizing it, bringing to the surface the artificiality of the ritual and the political motivations that guided its expression. The context of contemporary London, as manifested through the bodies of the urban crowd, creates a gap between the city staged and the city *as* stage.

According to the published texts of the inaugural ceremonies, the mayoral pageant was both an exemplum of London's magnificence, wealth, and stability and a time-honored ritual that expressed the traditional values and deep communal structure of the urban culture. The shows often explicitly allied themselves with the triumphal processions of ancient Rome, and few inaugurations went by without asserting the antiquity of both the mayoral office and the ceremony that welcomed him to that post.[27] In *The Trivmphs of Integrity* (1623), Middleton commented, "Of all Solemnities, by which the Happy inauguration of a Subiect is celebrated, I find none that transcends the State and Magnificence of that Pompe prepared to receiue his Maiesties Great Substitute into his Honorable charge, the City of London."[28] Munday's description of the final procession to the Lord Mayor's home in *Metropolis Coronata* (1615) typifies the official view of the proceedings:

> The way being somewhat long, the order of march appeared the more excellent and commendable, euen as if it had been a Royall Maske, prepared for the marriage of an immortall Deitie, as in the like nature we hold the Lord Maior, to be this day solemnely married to Londons supreame Dignitie.[29]

Emphasizing dignity and decorum, this description evokes an image of the show as a stately, solemn ritual. Indeed, "Solemnity" was the pageant texts' favorite label for the shows after "Triumph," emphasizing the quasi-sacred aspect of the ceremony. As with Middleton's reference to the king's "great substitute," Munday's description links the inaugural with the royal pageantry of the Jacobean court, suggesting a rival tradition and rival locus of symbolic and actual power.

Modern interpretation of the shows has often echoed these perspectives. Although usually adopting a less mystical attitude toward the spectacle of civic power than that proposed by Mullaney, more recent criticism continues to rely on a ritual model to explain the social dynamic of the mayoral pageant. Lawrence Manley, in the most comprehensive reading of the shows, is predominantly concerned with the shows as a discursive context in which the mercantile elite could define themselves,[30] but when he necessarily considers how the shows were seen by the common populace, he also resorts to a collective ritual argument to explain the social function of the show: "the inaugural ceremonies were a *calendrical rite,* a periodic collective ceremony . . . which renewed the ongoing life of the community by re-enunciating its most basic principles" (260).[31] Manley's principal theoretical grounding is Victor Turner's conception of ritual as a social drama, in which the performance of the ceremony articulates and refashions the social concerns of the community.[32] The emphasis on the calendrical nature of the ceremony is a useful way of explaining the symbolic logic of the shows; although individual presentations often responded to topical events, the ceremonial syntax of the mayoral pageant was remarkably consistent over the long span of the Jacobean and Caroline periods. Furthermore, the Turnerian model allows Manley to characterize the show as a progressive ceremony, one in which the ideological intentions of the event become the means through which London dealt with a time of great change, through the collective efforts of the whole urban body.

However, the idea of ritual as a social drama is predicated on a number of significant circumstances. Clifford Geertz has complained that Turner's idea of ritual emphasizes "the affinities of theater and religion—drama as communion, the temple as stage" while neglecting the affinities of "theater and rhetoric—drama as persuasion, the platform as stage."[33] In other words, Turner's idea of ritual is *performative,* in J. L. Austin's sense of the word, as well as *performed;* as in religious speech-acts, to say is to do.[34] Another implication in Turner's paradigm is that the communal nature of ritual performance is presupposed by its public presentation; as Turner says, "A congregation is there to affirm the theological or cosmological order, explicit or implicit, which all hold in common."[35] The existence of this congregational participation is axiomatic in Turner's schema. Pierre Bourdieu's comments on the performativity of ritual point to the weak point in this model, arguing that the "symbolic efficacy of the ritual will vary . . . according to the degree to which the people for whom the ritual is performed are more or less prepared . . . to receive it."[36]

The shows repeatedly presented the crowd as the sort of validating and consecrating frame required for the creation of a Turnerian *communitas.* In *Troia-Nova Triumphans,* it is "this Citty, with her Loud, Full Voice" that cheers for the ceremony, and their "twenty thousand eyes" who will prove Fame correct in lauding the new mayor (sigs. B3v, A4). In *Brittannia's Honor,* London greets the mayor by saying, "Ten thousand welcomes Greete you on the shore" (sig. B2v). In *The Trivmphs of Integrity,* Memory says, "'tis a yeare, / To which all Vertues like the people heere / Should throng and cleaue together" (sig. B2–B2v). However, what little we know about the performance of the inaugural ceremony suggests the possibility of different readings of the event. In 1617, Horatio Busino, a member of the Venetian embassy, witnessed the mayoral show from a window above Cheapside and wrote an extensive account of the event.[37] This well-known description has received surprisingly little critical analysis, despite being a rare first-hand account of the scene of the pageant.[38] Accordingly, I quote from it and discuss it in some detail.

After watching the show on the water, which bewildered him with its chaotic and noisy display, Busino and his party go to an upper window in a house in Goldsmith's Row in Cheapside to await the arrival of the main portion of the procession. Looking across the street to the houses opposite his window, Busino notes the "sundry gallants" and "fine ladies" who fill the windows and throw "an incessant shower of squibs and crackers . . . into the mass beneath," the crowd in the street, which he describes in considerable detail:

> On looking into the street we saw a surging mass of people, moving in search of some resting place which a fresh mass of sightseers grouped higgledy piggledy rendered impossible. It was a fine medley: there were old men in their dotage; insolent youths and boys . . . painted wenches and women of the lower classes, all anxious to see the show. (60)

Busino then comments on the extreme "insolence of the mob," who throw mud at the passing carriages and livery men of the wealthy; he goes on to give a particular example of what befell a Spanish nobleman who caught the eye of a "wicked woman," who "urged the crowd to mob him" (61). In short time, "his garments were foully smeared with a sort of soft and very stinking mud, which abounds here at all seasons, so that the place better deserves to be called *Lorda* [filth] than *Londra* [London]" (61). Finally the procession approaches the scene of the melee, as signaled by the arrival of "the City Marshall on horseback" (61), and Busino turns his attention to the progress of the show through the crowd:

> The way was also kept by a number of lusty youths and men armed with long fencing swords, which they manipulated very dextrously, but no sooner had a passage been forced in one place than the crowd closed in at another. There were also men masked as wild giants who by means of fireballs and wheels hurled sparks in the faces of the mob and over their persons, but all proved unavailing to make a free and ample thoroughfare. (61)

While it would be a mistake to view Busino as a completely objective observer (he is certainly relating the story in a manner that he knows will be appreciated in Venice), his narrative receives some corroboration from various performance notes within the pageant texts themselves. In *Camp-bell or the Ironmongers Faire Feild* (1609), Munday regretted that the actors could not be heard "in a crowde of such noyse and uncivill turmoyle,"[39] and in *Metropolis Coronata*, in the same show that produced the solemn description of the civic marriage "to Londons supreame Dignitie" that I quote above, he complained that "neglect in marshalling" had nearly ruined the performance (sig. B2). With a similar irony, Heywood relates in *Londons Peaceable Estate* (1639) that he omitted a speech for one pageant station because of "the trouble of the place, the press of so mighty a confluence."[40] The violence of the marshalls is attested to in a contemporary satire of the pageant: "Whiflers with whight staves and chaines / And marshals men that tooke great paines, / They swore thay'd beatt out poore mens braines, / That were with durt bemyred."[41] In 1617, the year Busino saw the show, the marshalls and whifflers required 288 clubs and 124 spears for their duties.[42]

Busino's description, in conjunction with the notes in the pageant texts, demonstrates the distance between the ideal and real performance of the civic ritual. Rather than the dignified marriage of mayor and city that Munday describes in *Metropolis Coronata*, the image produced by Busino's account is of a near-riot, as armed men try desperately to keep the mob at bay. The crowd is here not the increasingly rich granary of citizens that Heywood imagines in

London Ius Honorarium, but a dense, swarming mass, growing haphazardly and "grouped higgledy piggledy," committing random violence on foreigners and wealthy passersby. Instead of a common audience, we have a clear separation between the wealthy who watch from the windows and the "fine medley" milling in the streets. Instead of the collective participation expected in communal ritual, we have a crowd held back by force. Instead of the "reverence and solemnity" that the pageant texts continually invoke, we have tumult and chaos, such that the speeches cannot be heard and the show itself is thrown into disarray. And against the invocation of the ideal city, expressed in the show witnessed by Busino through a model of Guildhall decked as "the Castle of Fame," we have London as "*Lorda,*" the city of filth and filthy behavior.[43]

My point in making these observations is not to speculate about the actual investment of the crowd in the ritual of the shows, a profoundly intangible and insoluble question. What I am suggesting, however, is that this riotous behavior was a potential source of anxiety. Within the carnivalesque mayhem of the crowd's behavior was the threat of a possible repudiation of the civic allegory with which the mercantile elite clothed its power. In part this can be seen through the occasional concern about the crowd's ability to comprehend the significance of the allegorical message. After complaining in *Camp-bell* about "the weake voyces of so many Children," which "are not any way able to be understood" (sig. B2v), Munday suggests a solution of sorts in *Sidero-Thriambos* (1618): "For better vnderstanding the true morality of this devise, the personages haue all Emblems and Properties in their hands, and so neere them, that the weakest capacity may take knowledge of them."[44] Middleton also speaks of adding "a little more help to the fainter apprehensions" in *The Triumphs of Honor and Vertue* (1622),[45] and John Webster defends the allegedly simple style of *Monuments of Honour* (1624) by saying that "a more curious and Elaborate way" would have "pusled the vnderstanding of the Common People."[46]

These explicit concerns are only intermittent, but they suggest that the possibility that the watching crowd was not participating in the edifying process was of some concern. For the most part the pageant texts are wholly celebratory; as official presentations, carefully vetted by the sponsoring guilds, they could hardly be otherwise. Nevertheless, traces of the anxiety caused by the linking of the ideal and filthy city can be found in a number of shows, especially those that address the intertwining issues of social disorder, ritual performance, and urban legibility.

In both Dekker's *Troia-Nova Triumphans* and Middleton's *The Triumphs of Truth,* crowded urban disorder is given a presence and place unusual in the symbolic logic of the mayoral pageant.[47] The center of Dekker's *Troia-Nova Triumphans* is a moral and spatial confrontation between the figures of Virtue and Envy. The mayor is escorted on his journey by the Throne of Virtue, a geometric representation of an ideal London. Beneath Virtue sit "the Seven liberall Sciences," which Dekker places in a mercantile context as "Mothers to all Trades, Professions, Mysteries and Societies" (sig. B2). The throne is drawn by Desire, Industry, Wisdom, and Time, and proceeded on horseback by "twelve Persons . . . representing the twelve Superior Companyes, every one carrying upon his left arme a faire Sheild . . . and in his right hand a launce" (sig. B2v–B3). Envy, on the other hand, is placed in "a Forlone Castle, built close to the little Conduit in Cheapside" (sig. B4). As the name Envy suggests, her tower is an emulous mimetic creation, mimicking Virtue's procession of iconographic worthies with "Ignorance, Sloth, Oppression, Disdaine, &c." (sig. B4). As Virtue's throne is "the onely glory and upholding of Cities," so Envy's castle represents the chaotic, fallen, violent city. In Dekker's formulation, Envy is less a traditional representation of a deadly sin than a political and social disruption, personifying those in the city that will not celebrate the accession of the new mayor or validate his innate superiority.[48]

To reach Guildhall, Virtue and the mayoral party must force their way past Envy's castle, guarded at the base by "Ryot and Calumny, in the shapes of Gyants, with clubs, who offer to keep back the Chariot of Vertue and to stop her passage" (sig. B4–B4v). As they pass by, Envy cries out, "Stop, stay her, fright her, with your shreekes" (sig. C1). Although initially dazzled by Virtue's raising of her bright shield, Envy and her troops fire arrows at the mayoral party, but to no avail. This spatial dynamic, in which the procession is hemmed in and must force its way past a scene of riot and confusion, full of shrieking voices, vividly recalls the scene of the procession as reported by Busino and the performance notes in the pageant texts. Envy attacks the well-ordered procession with riot, chaos, and disintegration; the monstrous growth of the crowd that Busino described is recalled in Envy's command, "Snakes, from your virulent spawn ingender / Dragons, that may peece-meale rend her" (sig. B4v).

Virtue's ability to triumph over Envy is never placed in doubt, of course, but the method undertaken by Dekker represents a substantial revision of the ritual syntax of the event. Michael Bristol has suggested "In the dialectic of official pageantry, princely splendor and magnanimity . . . defeat discord, because discord has no ontological status."[49] This is true in terms of the moral confrontation presented in *Troia-Nova Triumphans*, but Dekker's decision to *place* Envy in the space of the city does accord it ontological status in performative terms. The show ends, after the return from Guildhall, with the representatives of the twelve companies firing their pistols at the castle, "at which Envy, and the rest, vanish, and are seene no more" (sig. C4v). In the meantime, however, while the Lord Mayor and his party have been viewing the "House of Fame" at Guildhall, Envy's Castle has remained in the middle of Cheapside, a dystopic urban monument set before the crowd of onlookers. This instantiation of the filthy city gives a presence and an iconographic durability to urban discord never before seen in the mayoral pageants.

The Triumphs of Truth, which was performed the next year, employs a similar opposition, replacing "Virtue" with "Truth" and subordinating "Envy" to "Error." However, Middleton develops the morality structure in ways that heighten both the agonistic element of the ritual and make the underlying ideological message more ambiguous. Rather than presenting an opposition between an ideal city and an anchored filthy city that must be bypassed and then destroyed, Middleton uses a single model of the city that is repeatedly transformed by the forces of Error before being rescued by the chariot of Truth. With this symbolic framework, Middleton continually suggests the overlapping and perhaps inherently linked nature of the ideal and filthy cities: not so much opposing forces as different sides of the same coin. Error greets the Mayor right after Truth does, introducing, as it were, another London. In opposition to Truth's "one sacred way," Error describes running through the "back-ways and by-ways," of the city, telling the mayor:

> Ile show thee all my corners yet vntold,
> The very nookes where Beldams hide their gold,
> In hollow wals and chimneies, where the Sun
> Neuer yet shone, nor *Truth* came euer neere.[50]

Error's city, where greed and corruption rule, is hidden, lurking in the interstices of the ideal city. Error offers the mayor secret urban knowledge, suggesting the existence of a London into which the specular power of Truth cannot penetrate.[51] Error's city is also explicitly connected to the surrounding crowd:

>   I can bring
> A thousand of our Parish, besides Queanes,
> That nere knew what *Truth* meant, nor euer meanes.
> Some could I cull out here, e'en in this Throng,

> If I would show my Children, and how strong
> I were in faction. (sig. B3)

While Dekker's show connected Envy to the crowd through symbolic associations of rioting, chaos, and violence, Middleton's show makes a direct theatrical reference, drawing the milling crowd into the pageant as an example of that which the show's protagonists must overcome. The crowd as barrier to the progress of the show also appears in moral terms; Truth's path is that "to which place throngs / All Worlds Afflictions, Calumnies and wrongs" that threaten to dislodge the mayor on his journey (C3v).

With Error and Envy nipping at their heels (though repeatedly forced back by Zeal), the procession soon comes upon the "Mount Triumphant of London," which has been completely obscured with fogs and mists by Error. Truth, who escorts the mayor, exclaims:

> What's here? the Mists of *Error?* dare his Spight
> Staine this *Triumphant Mount?* where our delight
> Hath bene Diuinely fixt so many Ages,
> Dare darknesse now breathe forth her Insolent Rages,
>
> . . .
>
> I see if *Truth* a while but turne her Eies,
> Thicke are the Mists that o're faire Citties rise:
> Wee did expect to recieue welcome here,
> From no deform'd Shapes but Diuine and Cleere,
> In steed of Monsters that this place attends. (sig. C2–C2v)

Like the crowd presented in Busino's account, Error's power is inherently disorderly and mobile; represented by swirling mists, it is shapeless and ungraspable, the opposite of the ordered shape of the urban monument. Error's effect on London is supplemental; London's true, ideal, ordered shape exists underneath, despite Truth's turning of her eyes, but the mist obscures its lines, stains its body, replacing its shape with "deform'd" shape, no legible form. Truth banishes the mists with a wave of her fan, yet Error continues to dog the procession, repeatedly covering over the mount with fogs until Zeal finally shoots a burning arrow at Error's chariot.

Troia-Nova Triumphans and *The Triumphs of Truth* attempt to place the chaotic scene that surrounds them inside the frame of the pageant, to co-opt the actual city into a redemptive narrative of the ideal city. Manley suggests that such representations of order and virtue defeating discord demonstrate "the heroic act of urban settlement," and form part of a meta-discourse of re-civilizing the city (285). While this is certainly congruent within the hermetic logic of the printed shows, in performing such acts of settlement the shows demonstrate how unsettled and disordered the real contemporary city is. In both *Troia-Nova Triumphans* and *The Triumphs of Truth* the moral triumph of the lord mayor is only possible through depicting the real city as a threat to the world of the shows. As the figure of London herself remarks in *The Triumphs of Truth:* "Spots in deformed Faces are scarce Noted, / Faire cheekes are stain'd if ner'e so little blotted" (sig. B1). The imperfections and asymmetries of the contemporary city, as manifested by the filthy and chaotic scene of the pageant, become a threat to the ideal city, showing its fragility.

This destabilizing effect of the contemporary city is observable in other contexts as well. The shows often sought to present contemporary London as the high point of history, that to which history had built itself. Dekker's prologue to *Brittannia's Honor* asks rhetorically, "What Honor can bee greater to a Kingdome, than to have a Citty for beauty, able to match with the Fairest in the World?" (sig. A3). The role of the mercantile elite in erecting and restoring significant buildings in the city was also often stressed. In these moments contemporary London stands at the head of time, a monument to the glory of its leaders. Yet often underlying this affirmation was the contrary suspicion, the well-worn theme of *vanitas* and the inevitable downward spiral of life on earth, chilling the optimistic boosterism of the shows. The invocation of the past deeds of Lord Mayors was intended to construct a chain of civic honor, but it could also highlight how much the city had been degraded by time. In *Metropolis Coronata*, Munday has the resurrected Henry Fitz-Alwine mention, as something of an aside, that the Drapers of his day "did more needy soules maintaine, / Then I feare will be seene again" (sig. B1). In Middleton's *The Trivmphs of Integrity*, the figure of Memory makes the comparison between past and present more emphatic:

> I finde to Godnesse they bent all their powers,
> Which very Name makes blushing Times of ours;
> They heapt vp Vertues, long before they were old,
> This Age sits laughing vpon Heapes of Gold,
> We by great Buildings striue to rayse our Names,
> But they more truely wise built vp their Fames. (sig. B2)

Here Middleton criticizes the very practice of city-building that he praises in other shows. The reference to "Heapes of Gold," like Munday's aside, refers to the lessening of civic charity in the Jacobean period, as well as to the increasing problem of rich merchants refusing office.[52] As such, although it admits the declining character of the civic community, it can be taken as a compliment to the new mayor, who has shouldered a difficult responsibility that many shirk.

Yet "laughing upon heaps of gold" is an odd image to introduce in the context of the gaudy display of a mayoral pageant. In the introduction to *Troia-Nova Triumphans,* Dekker wrestles mightily to reconcile the extravagant excesses of the shows with the sober responsibilities of civic office, a struggle that climaxes with the paradoxical statement, "A *sumptuous Thriftinesse* in these *Civil Ceremonies* managing all."[53] Gold was by far the favorite element of the shows; the Triumphal Mounts and Houses of Fame of the pageants were typically gilded. In *Chruso-thriambos: The Triumphes of Golde* (1611), Munday's central pageant was an actual heap of gold, a "Rocke or Mount of Golde," covered with jewels and precious metals and crowned by the excessive figure of Vesta, "the breeding and teeming mother of al Golde."[54] Even *The Trivumphs of Integrity,* despite Memory's words and despite being an unusually ascetic show in many ways, culminates with a gilded Temple of Integrity: "the Columnes or Pillars of this Cristall Sanctuary, are Gold, the Battlements Siluer" (sig. B3).

The ambiguous symbolic position of the crowded city and the contradictory project of urban definition are addressed in Munday's 1616 pageant, *Chrysanaleia: The Golden Fishing.* The highlight of this show is the resurrection of William Walworth, the mayor who killed Wat Tyler in the Peasants' Revolt of 1382. By the late sixteenth century the heroic act had appropriated an iconic representation; it was widely (albeit erroneously) believed that the red dagger in London's coat of arms represented the bloody dagger with which Walworth slew Tyler.[55] Describing the effects of his deed on "that swarme of rebels," Walworth says, "The rest of that base rout, dismayed thereby, / And all tumultuous troubles calmely ceast."[56] As Manley might suggest, this is an act of civilization, a taming of the wild crowd similar in tone to Munday's 1605 show, *The Trivmphs of Re-Vnited Britania,* in which Brute, the founder of London, tells Britannia "what height of happinesse she hath attained unto by his victorie, being before a vast Wilderness, inhabited by Giantes, and a meere den of Monsters: Goemagot and his barbarous brood, being quite subdued, his ciuill followers."[57] But it takes place in a context that separates the civilizer from the civilized. Walworth's defense of the city, in effect, creates the city, unifying its symbolism by opposing it to an outside force bent on the destruction of social hierarchy and the disintegration of civic values. This model is prevalent in other dramatic representations of the

Peasant's Revolt; in *The Death of Jack Straw* (perhaps written in conjunction with Thomas Nelson's 1590 mayoral pageant, which also featured Walworth),[58] much of the action takes place at the city gates, with the rebels swarming outside the walls demanding to be let in.[59] The rebels emphasize the symbolic power of the walls of the city to define and create a unified urban space—a power also emphasized by Munday, who begins *The Golden Fishing* with a description of how the Goldsmiths and Fishmongers won international renown for rebuilding the walls of Jerusalem after it was captured in the First Crusade.[60]

But as the crowd in front of Walworth's pageant chariot presumably did not suddenly become peaceful at his recitation of this heroic event, Munday's use of Walworth in *The Golden Fishing* had strong contemporary echoes that undermine this act of civilization and urban foundation. By the mid-sixteenth century, the names of Jack Straw and Wat Tyler had become ubiquitous cultural references, used to stigmatize religious dissent, characterize all rebellions, and describe the intentions of unruly or protesting crowds, both within and without the city.[61] Especially during midsummer, a frequent time of social unrest in London's suburbs, the specter of the Peasant's Revolt was often invoked.[62] Indeed, the mid-century failure of the Midsummer Pageant, which the Lord Mayor's show supplanted in the civic ritual year, was at least partly due to the problem of riotous crowds gathering.[63]

A more immediate political background to Munday's pageant is also apparent. Three months before *The Golden Fishing* was performed, James had once again proclaimed martial law in London for the hopeless purpose of clearing it of vagabonds and masterless men. He appointed Provost-marshalls to carry out the cleansing of the city and suburbs, an action despised by the civic elite as an intrusion on their liberties,[64] while expressing blaming "the Maior, Aldermen, and Recorder of Our said Citie of London" for not dealing with the situation themselves as instructed.[65] Munday's use of Walworth as a foundational moment for the city, and a point of honor for the mayoralty, also highlights the still "uncivilized" nature of London, and the failure of the civic elite to control the problem of urban and suburban violence and unrest.

Some of the complexities of urban legibility that are submerged in Munday's pageant come to the surface in Heywood's play *Edward IV, Part One,* written not long after *Jack Straw* and exploring at its outset a similar moment of invasion and civic cohesion, through a dramatization of Falconbridge's assault on London. As in *Jack Straw,* the climax of the invasion occurs at the city gates, where Master Shore makes clear the history, integrity, and impermeability of the city: "look thou upon our Cities arms, / Wherein is a bloody dagger: that is it, / Wherewith a rebel like to Falconbridge / Had his desert" (1.9.109–12).[66] Heywood also presents a further development of the theme of civic foundation by presenting the apprentices as a cohesive army in opposition to the raggedy forces outside the city gates; against the unruly crowd of peasants is placed a coherent, unified urban crowd, bent on preserving the virtues of the city. This act of urban definition, however, is made problematic at its defining moment. The clear demarcation of the scene at the city gate, drawing such strong lines between well-ordered and loyal citizens and the peasant revolters, is undercut by the taunting words of the Second Apprentice to the rebels:

> You are those desperate, idle, swaggering mates,
> That haunt the suburbes in the time of peace,
> And raise up ale-house brawls in the streete. (1.5.37–39)

At this moment the historical frame of the play is brought forward to the contemporary moment; the rebels appear not as peasants but as suburbanites, evidence not of London's integrity as a symbol but of its porousness.[67] In contrast to the time of the play, in the time of its performance not only did the political city extend well beyond the old city walls, but almost half of the metropolitan population lived outside of the city bars.[68] This permeability of London was further emphasized, of course, by the fact that the theater where the play was being performed was in the suburbs, and that the theater's own demarcation from the suburban scene that surrounded it, in both symbolic and physical terms, was ill-defined and ambiguous.

Heywood again confronts the vexing issues of the suburbs and the urban crowd thirty-five years later in *Londons Mirror,* one of the last mayoral shows produced before the civil war. William Hardin has suggested that the crucial political background to this show was the New Corporation;[69] after years of wrangling with London's leaders over political jurisdiction, Charles had finally incorporated the suburbs that surrounded London into a single jurisdiction, with its own economic and political privileges.[70] Perhaps the title of Heywood's show refers obliquely to this doubling; in apparently acquiring the rights of a city, the suburbs doubled London, creating two freedoms, two citizenries, two potential loci of urban power.[71] The explicit playing with questions of urban definition that was permissible in the context of the popular theater is necessarily inappropriate here. Instead,

Heywood resorts to a childbirth metaphor to subordinate the much larger suburban jurisdiction; in his formulation, London has been "brought a bed / Of a New Towne, and late delivered of such a burthen" (sig. C4). This tactic effectively contains the symbolic crisis catalyzed by the suburban incorporation, naturalizing uncontrollable demographic and economic growth into an example of the city's maternal labor.[72] But the symbolic and spatial excesses of the crowded metropolis had already entered the shows in new and significant ways.

Heywood became the prominent pageant poet of the Caroline period, producing seven shows between 1631 and 1639. Although his shows retain many of the common features and symbolic logic of the earlier rituals, as discussed before, Heywood also introduced innovations to the structure and tone of his shows that engage with the inherent contradiction between the ideals and the performance of the public ritual. Most significant among these was the interpolation of antimasques into the pageant progression. In *Londini Artium & Scientiarum Scaturigo* (1632), Heywood introduces this new element by saying, "The third show by Land . . . is more Mimicall than Materiall, and inserted for the Vulgar."[73] His tone becomes more condescending the next year, in *Londini Emporia* (1633):

> The third Show by Land, is a Modell devised for sport to humour the throng . . . And without some such intruded Anti-maske, many who carry their eares in their eyes, will not sticke to say, I will not giue a pinne for the Show. Since therefore it consists onely in motion, agitation and action . . . I therefore passe to the fourth and last [pageant].[74]

The introduction of the antimasque is a supplemental strategy, intended to keep the rest of the show pure by quarantining the vulgar demands of the crowd in one disposable pageant; as Heywood says in *Londini Artium & Scientiarum Scaturigo,* he includes it "as in all Professions wee see Dunces amongst Doctors, Simple amongst Subtle, and Fooles intermixt with Wisemen" (sig. B4). Excluding the antimasques, Heywood's shows are marked by their inward tone, their tendency towards the erudite and esoteric. While earlier writers tended to transform getting and spending into heroic accomplishments,[75] Heywood's shows connect mercantile practice with spiritual enlightenment; as he says in *Londini Emporia:* "Eight offices of Piety are in a Merchant required" (sig. A3). Heywood counterpoints the public display of civic rectitude with private spiritual development; the texts of the shows become a form of emblem book, deliberately difficult to interpret, legible only once one has been initiated to their mysteries.[76]

Yet Heywood's paraleptic strategy also lets the crowd into the text of the show in new ways. As described, the antimasque is indeed "Mimicall," a reflection of its supposed audience; the show for the bustling throng is only "motion, agitation and action," without shape and, as Heywood puts it two years later, "[deserving] no further Charracter."[77] Like the crowds that watched the shows, the antimasque is without shape, without character; an unreadable "intrusion" inserts itself into the legible text of the pageant. Passing over the antimasque again in *Londons Mirror,* Heywood suggests that the problem is related to Busino's "fine medley," the diverse composition of the watching crowd: "in such a confluence, where all Degrees, Ages, and Sexes are assembled, every of them looking to bee presented with some fancy or other, according to their expectations and humours" (sig. C2). Here, it seems, the variegated audience produces a variegated show. In these written descriptions we see two shows, a festive carnival for the masses and a dignified solemnity for the initiated elite, proceeding simultaneously. The symbolic cost, however, is explicitly renouncing the idea of the Lord Mayor's show as a communal regeneration of civic life and reframing it as an entertainment, necessarily responsive to the competing expectations of its nonunified audiences.

This strategy of ceremonial bifurcation works only on the textual level, of course; in the street the chaos of the crowd would be the same. While Heywood may produce a textual progress of quiet contemplation through the private reading of the pageant book after the fact of performance, the performed scene of the show remains inherently mixed and contradictory. Though the shows attempted to create a space within the city that was marked and coded as separate from the city and acted to epitomize it, they could not control the content of the ritual that took place within this space. As the Busino description indicates, the London crowd continually invaded the ritual space, forcing themselves into the picture, refusing to act as mere endorsers. Despite the show's desire to use the crowd to frame and validate its progress through the city, the demarcation between the show and its context—between the performance of the pageant and the performance of the crowd—is faint, constantly obliterated by the movement of the crowd.

This ambiguity is borne out by contemporary literary evocations of the Lord Mayor's show, most of which refer to it as a crowded spectacle produced by the masses of people it attracted. Describing "that solemne day / When as the Pageants through Chepe-side are carried," William Fennor notes "what multitudes of people thither sway, / Thrusting so hard that many haue miscarried" and concludes, "How mighty and tumultuous is that presse."[78] As discussed in the previous chapter, *Eastward Ho* ends with Quicksilver observing "the streets and fronts of the houses" being "stuck with people . . . as on the solemn day of the Pageant!" (Epilogue 1–5). In his epigram "Way in a Crowd," Robert Herrick speaks of "that scum of men" who block the way "on a Lord-Mayors day, in Cheapside,"[79] going on to reprise a popular joke of the time: "A Sturdy Sayler being in cheapside amongst the throng of people, when the Lord Mayor &c. came from Westminster, was thrust and crowded so hard, that with over-labouring to get out into an easier place, hee let out a great Fart."[80] Dekker, though later a pageant writer, uses the Lord Mayor's Show to seriocomic effect in *The Ravens Almanacke,* a mock-prognostication of the year ahead:

> vpon the very next day of Simon and Iude, the warlike drum and fife shall be heard in the very midst of Cheapside, at the noyse whereof people (like mad-men) shall throng together, and run up & downe, striving by all meanes to get into Merces, Silkemens and Gold-smithes houses.[81]

Dekker imagines the procession having to work hard to "breake through the disordered heapes of Tradesmen, and others that will on that feareful day be assembled together" and predicts that "nothing will be heard by noyse, and the faster that fire-workes are throwne amongst these perditious children, the lowder will grow their rage, and more hard to bee appeased" (sig. D3–D3v). Here the public chaos that Dekker was later forced to sublimate into allegorical progress in *Troia-Nova Triumphans* is allowed to run free, creating an image of an urban apocalypse.

These appearances of the Lord Mayor's show are primarily satiric in nature, of course, and to an extent form part of a literary dialectic with the urban pieties of the Lord Mayor's shows. But they nevertheless emphasize the extent to which the inaugural shows could be understood by contemporaries in terms of the violence, density, and impenetrability of the crowd. In contrast to the symbolic strategies of some of the shows, the impression left by these descriptions is not an opposition between the ideal and the crowded city, in which the ideal can triumph over the chaotic forces of the urban crowd. Rather, it is the spectacular excess of the show creating the spatial excess of the scene: *Londra* and *Lorda* produced simultaneously through the performance of the public ritual, crammed together, inextricable.

Reflection, Heywood explains at the beginning of *Londons Mirror,* is only useful if it is accurate: "a glasse . . . is of no estimation or value (though the frame thereof be never so richly deckt with gold & gemmes), unlesse it represent unto us the true figure and obiect" (sig. B2). Despite being itself profusely decked with gold and gems, unsurprisingly, Heywood's show purports to being a good mirror of the city, "a perfect and true Christall, without any falsity or flattery" that "rendreth every obiect its true forme" (sig. B2). The actual pageant of London's mirror, however, describes not one mirror but many, "Perspective, Prospective, Multiplying, &c" (sig. C3), a mimetic excess produced by the impossibility of capturing the city in one frame. Heywood also tells us, "The Pageant it selfe is decored with glasses of all sorts" (sig. C3v). Perhaps by imagining this pageant model progressing through the streets of the city we can get a sense of the unexpected accuracy of Heywood's framing of urban ritual: the Lord Mayor's show covered with a profusion of mirrors, reflecting back a multitude of fractured images of the crowd and the city, indecipherable fragments without order or unity.

C H A P T E R   3

"SHAKESPEARE'S LONDON": THE SCENE OF LONDON IN THE SECOND TETRALOGY AND *HENRY VIII*

Porter. *You'll leave your noise anon, ye rascals; do you take the court for Parish Garden? Ye rude slaves, leave your gaping.*

(Henry *VIII* 5.3.1–3)

CAMERA REGIS

Where do we find "Shakespeare's London"? The old-fashioned possessive phrase could be interpreted in at least two ways, producing two different, though related, answers. If the expression is cognate to "Shakespeare's Rome," meaning his artistic creation of the city, then perhaps Shakespeare's London only ever existed in the past tense. One of the many things that sets Shakespeare apart from other early modern playwrights is that none of his plays is set in his contemporary city; while dialect, custom, and anachronistic detail may reveal Falstaff's London to be Shakespeare's city in disguise, the disguise is significant, reinforcing a sense of temporal dislocation: this is not now, this is then.[1] From such a perspective, the London location of the history plays acts as a boundary, helping to distinguish past from present and play from reality. The boundary can be crossed—through the extra-dramatic efforts of Prologue, Chorus, or Epilogue, for example—but this crossing typically maintains the integrity of the staged world, and thus the theatrical illusion, by making explicit the transposition from one conceptual realm to another. If, on the other hand, we understand "Shakespeare's London" in the usual sense of referring to the world he inhabited rather than created, it would seem (to judge by the critical tradition) that it only exists outside his plays. The apparent insularity of the London of the history plays feeds into a critical tendency to treat what we call theatrical setting in uncomplicated terms, as a neutral fictive world that frames the action of the play.[2] If typical critical practice sees a difference between Shakespeare's urban locations and the Forest of Arden, for example, it is that the former offers us a detailed mimetic world that we can link to Shakespeare's "real" London, the world outside the boundaries of the stage, through the textual strategies of allusion and metaphor.[3]

These settled assumptions have more to do with our own theatrical heritage than with early modern dramaturgy. According to the *OED* the theatrical meaning of "setting" is a recent coinage, dating only from 1885, and derives figuratively from the frame of a jewel.[4] As in the nineteenth-century theatrical tradition that produced it, this terminology implies a clear hierarchy between background and foreground, with a sharp boundary between the setting and that which is set. In contrast, early modern dramatists used the word "scene" to describe a play's location, a term whose multiple contemporary meanings (place, performance, the stage itself) render such hierarchies ambiguous and suggest a more flexible and unstable comprehension of dramatic location. While a London *setting* can be discussed as a background, a conceptual frame, or a network of textual references, the *scene* of London is inevitably a space of performance as well, one that can only be fully understood through its theatrical manifestation. *Henry V* provides an example of how the performance of London blurs the lines between theatrical setting and urban context in non-mimetic ways. Describing King Harry's triumphant return to England, the Chorus exclaims:

> But now behold,
> In the quick forge and working-house of thought,
> How London does pour out her citizens! (5.Pro.22–24)

Read on the page, this passage suggests a wholly imaginary London, one whose creation depends upon the individual effort of an audience member or reader. But in performance during Shakespeare's time these lines must have produced an uncanny moment of self-recognition.

Contemporary audience members would not have had to task their minds to visualize the scene: it was taking place around them. At this moment, "Shakespeare's London" is in the playhouse; the imagined and unseen spectacle of Henry V on the streets of London overlaps with the spectacle of *Henry V* in the Globe theater, into which London has already poured out its citizens.[5]

In *Henry V* Shakespeare's London slips from play to playhouse to city in a complex *mise en abyme* that indicates the radically interpenetrated character of these spaces of performance. How does the space of the urban play relate to the urban space of its performance? How was the space of early modern London imagined, constructed, and contained, especially in the official and commercial drama of the period? How does Shakespeare's construction of London interact with these prevailing spatial ideologies? More simply, what role does London perform—what space does it produce—in the history plays? In this chapter I suggest some partial answers to these questions by examining the intersection of royal and theatrical display in the context of the city. The first half of the chapter focuses principally on the second tetralogy, looking at the ways in which these plays manipulate the trope of *camera regis,* London as the "chamber" of the monarch, in order to control the theatrical space of the city. As I show in the second half of the chapter, the second tetralogy's strategic deployment of *camera regis* is abandoned in *Henry VIII,* a play that reconfigures the relationship between monarch and city, and between efficacy and entertainment, in ways that dismantle simple, zero-sum binaries of power. In proposing this approach, I am not suggesting that Shakespeare's histories should, for the most part, be considered "urban plays"; perhaps only *Richard III, Henry IV,* and *IIenry VIII* would truly deserve such a title. It is also clear, moreover, that the prime focus of the history plays is the nation as a whole, not the city. Yet the urban space of their performance is persistently significant. Since the principal matter of the history plays is the presentation of royalty, on one level they all effect a form of *camera regis:* placing the king in the environment of the city, making the urban space of the theater his chamber. As we will see, the implications of this relationship are most intense when doubled—when, that is, the plays turn to the urban staging of monarchy within their narratives.

It is therefore not surprising that a royal entry causes the historical frame of *Henry V* to become so explicitly permeable. The dramatic presentation of the monarch links the spatial and aesthetic hierarchies of theatrical setting to the political hierarchies of rule; this linkage, as many critics have noted, necessarily pushes the concerns of the play into the present tense.[6] However, the emphasis on location in the above passage, the way that London acts as the conduit between play and present, raises some questions about how scholars have traditionally dealt with the issue of royal theatricality. Shakespeare's history plays, in particular the second tetralogy, form the bedrock of the new historicist concept of theatrical sovereignty, the ruler whose power is based in and expressed through visual display—a concept neatly summarized by Greenblatt's well-known statement, "Royal power is manifested to its subjects as in a theater."[7] This axiom has catalyzed much brilliant criticism, but its unlocalized generality limits its usefulness when discussing the place of the monarch in London. In Greenblatt's usage, "theater" figures not a location but a psychological dependency, produced by paralleling the relationship between viewer and viewed with the hierarchical relationship between subject and ruler.[8] Visual power, however, is always manifested in a particular place, and focusing exclusively on the *mental* dimension of that space overlooks its *physical* and *social* dimensions.[9] As discussed in the introduction, I take the categories of mental, physical, and social space from Henri Lefebvre,[10] who argues that these three aspects of spatial experience are interdependent but irreducible; each acts in concert to produce the other, in a process that Edward Soja has termed a "trialectic" in order to capture the atemporal three-dimensionality of the interaction.[11] To use one branch of this interaction as an example, the mental space that Greenblatt emphasizes is produced in concert by physical and social spaces; the manifestation of royal power in Whitehall received a different audience, in both physical and social terms, than the manifestation of that power in a London street, just as representations of royal power in the Banqueting Hall were presented under a different theatrical *habitus* (in Pierre Bourdieu's use of the term) than that of the Globe playhouse.[12] The example from *Henry V* makes clear that similar shifts in social and mental space can be produced in one locale; the Chorus's words, which urge an imagined London audience as they acknowledge a physical one, initiate a shift from a mental to an environmental setting for Harry's triumph, causing a corresponding shift in the social meaning of the presentation.

In these examples I stress the context of royal power, the *where,* rather than the *what,* of theatrical sovereignty. The two cannot really be separated, however, because the relationship between the monarch and London is never simply a question of actor and audience. Unlike the power of the Lord Mayor, which symbolically expresses itself in terms of primacy among putative equals, the power of the monarch is absolute and magically transformative. In the spatial paradigm expressed in royal entries, court masques, and other celebratory literature, the monarch does not merely act *in* the city; he or she acts *upon* it, changing the symbolic meaning of the urban space.[13] "Troynovant is now no more a city," Thomas Dekker declares in his pamphlet describing James's 1604 coronation entry; the mere presence of the monarch transforms the city into a wide variety of ideal spaces: a "Sommer Arbour," or a "Parke" in which the royal lion plays, or a "Bridall Chamber."[14] Lefebvre calls such magically transformed spaces "absolute space," a consecrated form of space produced by the perfect knitting together of physical, mental, and social spaces.[15] An example of this spatial unity can be found in an account of Elizabeth's coronation entry, which describes London as "a Stage wherein was shewed the wonderful Spectacle of a noble hearted Princess towards her most loving people; and the people's exceeding comfort in beholding so worthy a Sovereign."[16] To call such a moment theatrical alludes to the transcendent clarity of the royal symbol thus publicly displayed; London is described as a stage because the city acts as a backdrop to the monarch, the setting of the royal jewel. But the urban audience of this regal magnificence is not simply an audience. The stage also encloses "the people," reflecting back and enhancing the image of perfect rule with a perfect reciprocal obedience. In this moment, the space of theater becomes the space of ritual, producing the liminal/sacred condition that Victor Turner terms *communitas,* the revelation of the deep truths and values of the community.[17]

From Lefebvre's Marxist viewpoint, absolute space is a historical phenomenon, a holistic social organization perfected by the Romans and lost to Western civilization with the advent of capitalism.[18] In contrast to Lefebvre, Turner's model is liberal and progressive; the liminal space of *communitas* is both the repository of the deep truths of the culture and the form from which new cultural forms can emerge.[19] My own perspective on cultural politics rejects this sort of organic, gradual ideology of social change as much as it rejects Lefebvre's nostalgia for an imagined precapitalist social unity. I want to use the concept of absolute space differently, as what Michel Foucault might call a political dream, through which potentially threatening elements are contained within a symbolic unity.[20]

In the case of the royal entry, as with the Lord Mayor's show but in different ways, the most prominent threatening element is the people on the streets of the city. For regimes dedicated to ceremonies of visual power, the rapid changing nature of London was most visible through the city's manifestation in the urban crowd. As the discussion in the first chapter suggests, John Stow's complaint that London was "pestered with people" echoes an pervasive unease about the London crowd that finds its official voice in the bans against new buildings, the laws forbidding public assembly, the plague orders, and the periodic inhibitions of play-going.[21] David Scott Kastan has suggested that representation itself was subversive in the early modern period, in that the spectacle of rule was imitated by the representation of power in the theaters and thus threatened to make the sovereign a theatrical subject.[22] More precisely, this observation should be limited to the public space of London.[23] Representing royalty (or royalty representing itself) at court or in country-house progresses such as Elizabeth's trips to Kenilworth or Elvetham caused no danger, because it occurred in front of a courtly audience that accepted and condoned the artifice involved.[24] Essex's production of *Richard II,* on the other hand, was a profound threat because it was alleged to have played "40tie times in open streets and houses."[25] Elizabeth's hyperbolic comment indicates how large the urban population bulked in the mind of the monarch; not only could the play be performed forty times, but London was imagined vast enough to provide forty audiences to view it.[26] Whether in the streets or in the playhouses, the crowd was the inescapable context for the public staging of power in early modern London, and controlling the dangerously open theatrical space of the city also meant finding spatial strategies for containing the crowd.

Such strategies are evident in Dekker's account of the 1604 coronation entry. Dekker begins with a description of the crowd that waits to see James enter the city: "The Streets seemde to bee paued with men: Stalles in stead of rich wares were set out with children, open Casements fild vp with women."[27] This public, crowded view of the audience, in which the people seem to become the physical fabric of the city, is quickly replaced with a literalization of London's ancient title of *camera regis.* As we have seen, calling London "the chamber of the monarch" is a pervasive rhetorical trope in the period, signifying at once the city's subordination to the king and his figurative ennoblement of the city.[28] What makes Dekker's use interesting is his spatial application of the title.[29] Dekker continually refers to London as the "Court Royall" of the king, going so far as to identify particular places within the city with the geography of the court. The area around the Italian and Dutch Arches is deemed "not unworthy to beare the name of the great Hall to this our Court Royal" (sig. C1). Cheapside becomes "The Presence Chamber" because of the presence of "so many gallant Gentlemen, so many Ladyes, and beautifull creatures" (sig. E2v). In spatially transforming the city into a court, Dekker transforms the theatrical space of the event, reconfiguring the theatrical *habitus* of the performance. This translation in the audience is shown explicitly in their gaze; the crowd, whose eyes "sparkeled so . . . that had it not bene the day, the light which reflected from them, was sufficient to haue made one" (sig. B3v), is replaced by courtiers, "in whose eyes glaunces (mixt with modest lookes) seemde to dance courtly Measures in their motion" (sig. E2v). If the first audience lights the scene, watching it as spectators, the second joins it, acting as participants whose "modest lookes" demonstrate their involvement in, and subordination to, the royal event.

Dekker's spatial use of *camera regis* reflects Shakespeare's historical practice in the second tetralogy. Dekker's somewhat awkward assertions of urban courtliness can be understood as elaborations on a relationship that has lost its symbolic purchase: if Troynovant is now no more a city, magically transformed by the arrival of the monarch, then how can its emphatically urban presence be subordinated to the regal performance? These same issues underpin the space of London in the second tetralogy, which plays in complex ways with the spatial implications of seeing the city as the chamber of the monarch. The second tetralogy has often been understood as charting a restorative path, whereby Hal redeems royal authority from its wreckage in *Richard II*. A similarly redemptive path can be seen in the plays' engagement with the space of London. The ceremonial public display of the monarch occurs only twice in the plays of the second tetralogy: in Bullingbrook's politically ambiguous triumph in *Richard II* and in the imagined scene from *Henry V* that I discuss above. The former play uses Richard's public disgrace to effect a movement away from the unrestricted space of the city to a private space of royal theatricality; the latter returns to the public sphere of London, but only within certain careful parameters. Between these two moments the second tetralogy recuperates urban space as an unthreatening location for royal power, a recuperation that operates in a similar manner to Dekker's transformation of London into an analog of the royal court. The operation is twofold, involving both internal and external audiences; shifts in how the plays configure London involve corresponding shifts in how the plays interact with their own theater audience. In both contexts, the theatrical space of London is limited and controlled by linking it with the social space of the court.

In labeling this theatrical space "courtly" I refer less to class and privilege than to intimacy and interdependence, factors that give the courtly audience and the crowds in the streets different stakes in the display of power. Like the inhabitants of Dekker's "Court Royall," the courtly audience does not merely observe the spectacle of power but rather participates in it—a participation reinforced by the possibility of real political repercussions for nonparticipation. Though it may be numerous, the courtly audience is never a crowd, in Elias Canetti's interpretation of the term, in that its primary identification is not with itself but with the political performance in which it participates.[30] This repositioning of the social space of the second tetralogy from spectatorship to participation moves the plays along the axis from theater to ritual, subordinating the entertainment aspect of performance to what Richard Schechner has theorized as "efficacy," the ability of performance to achieve social and political results.[31]

By way of comparison, we might turn first to Shakespeare's earlier engagements with London, in the first tetralogy. For all their emphasis on the private machinations of select noble characters, the plays of *Henry VI* are crowded in a way rarely found in the later histories. The currents of political change are often expressed through the staged movements of masses of people—not only on the battlefields of *3 Henry VI* but in the fights between Gloucester and Winchester's men (*1 Henry VI* 1.3), Jack Cade's rebellion, and the entry of "the commons, like an angry hive of bees" after the death of Gloucester (*2 Henry VI* 3.2.125). The political threat of the urban crowd extends to its role as audience as well. Talbot's description of his French imprisonment in *1 Henry VI*, "In open marketplace produc'd they me / To be a public spectacle to all" (1.4.40–41), recurs in the context of London in *2 Henry VI*, when Gloucester, imagining his banished wife enduring "the flinty streets" of the city on her journey to banishment, laments that "ill can thy noble mind abrook / The abject people gazing on thy face" (2.4.8, 10–11). For the nobility in *Henry VI*, the public space of London is typically a location of threat and vulnerability.

Richard III, on the other hand, engages with London in markedly different terms. Like *1 Henry VI* and *2 Henry VI*, the first part of *Richard III* employs urban space in various ways, most typically as a location where various characters can meet by chance. The symbolic possibilities of the royal city are noted, particularly in an explicit reference to *camera regis:* Buckingham's greeting to the young Edward V, "Welcome, sweet Prince, to London, to your chamber" (3.1.1). The Lord Mayor appears several times in his official capacity as civic representative, and the consent of London to Richard's accession is portrayed as an important political objective. The theatrical aspects of the city are also highlighted; the discussion among three citizens in the second act establishes that the drama of the court is playing out before a larger audience, and the play's urban aspect reaches its climax in Richard's false performance of piety and royal reluctance before the assembled crowd of citizens (3.7.56–247). In these respects, *Richard III* shows a principally civic picture of London, understanding it through its traditions and representative structures. This is a picture of the city also visible in the plays of *Henry VI*—and celebrated in *Sir Thomas More*, Thomas Heywood's *Edward IV*, *The Death of Jack Straw*, the Lord Mayor's shows, and citizen comedies such as *The Shoemaker's Holiday*.

At the same time, *Richard III* portrays the space of London in terms that rob it of any possible civic power. Buckingham's use of the *camera regis* trope is deeply ironic; indeed, "to your chamber" could also refer to the looming Tower of London, which will shortly become Edward's prison. The Lord Mayor is either a craven politician who connives with Richard or a coward who is intimidated by him— in either case, a far cry from the doughty mayoral figure of *1 Henry VI*, who stops the brawling of Gloucester and Winchester's factions on the streets of the city. What scenes we see or hear of the London crowd show them as powerless. Buckingham describes the crowd at Guildhall as "like dumb statues or breathing stones" that "Gazed each on other and looked deadly pale" at his oration on behalf of Richard (3.7.21–22). And Richard's theatrical performance before the civic community later in the same scene takes place entirely within the keep of Baynard's Castle, the Mayor and citizens hemmed into an aristocratic stronghold and enforced to give their consent. In these respects *Richard III* can be read as an anticivic play, one that takes pains to empty out the significance of London's symbols and space. This change could be understood as a response to the dangers of urban visibility and vulnerability observable in the plays of *Henry VI*, but it is important to note that it forms a part of the play's general perversity: after all, Richard is an illegitimate actor performing power in a world on the brink of apocalypse, and it is fitting that all tradi-tional forms of authority fall away in the process. I would suggest that *Richard III*'s principal urban effect is to demolish the civic vision of the city—a vision, as we have seen in previous chapters, that was both nostalgic and increasingly at odds with London's reality. Appropriately, the civic language of the first tetralogy does not recur in the second tetralogy—except in *Henry V*, where its choric presence is both contingent and tactical. Rather, with *Richard II*, we return briefly to the danger of the urban audience.

York's description of the parade of Richard and Bullingbrook through London in *Richard II* echoes Talbot's "public spectacle" in the marketplace and the abject urban passage of Gloucester's wife in the *Henry VI* plays; significantly, it is the sole appearance of this threatening space in the second tetralogy. Bullingbrook, capitalizing on what Richard called his "courtship of the common people" (1.4.24), is received favorably by the London crowd:

> You would have thought the very windows spake,
> So many greedy looks of young and old
> Through casements darted their desiring eyes
> Upon his visage, and that all the walls
> With painted imagery had said at once,
> "Jesu preserve thee! Welcome Bullingbrook!" (5.2.12–17)

These lines may well have inspired Dekker's description of the crowd at James's coronation (with its focus on filled windows and eyes) and suggest a similar unease. Though the reaction endorses Bullingbrook's capture of the throne, the metaphoric reframing of watching as speech indicates the active power of their gaze; the language York uses underscores the unsettling qualities of the greedy, desiring crowd, threatening to consume that which they observe. These threatening undertones come to fruition in the second part of the passage, which describes Richard's public humiliation. Ironically, Greenblatt's dictum, "Royal power is manifested to its subjects as in a theater," echoes this quite different scene of royal theatricality:

> *As in a theater* the eyes of men,
> After a well-graced actor leaves the stage,
> Are idly bent on him that enters next,
> Thinking his prattle to be tedious,
> Even so, or with much more contempt, men's eyes
> Did scowl on gentle Richard. (5.2.23–28, emphasis mine)

While the Chorus's exhortation in *Henry V* turns the theater into a city, in this passage the city is turned into a theater; stripped of his symbolic power, the crowd is free to see Richard as an actor on a stage, and a poor actor at that. But because York's description frames the scene, Richard's theatrical failure before the London crowd is also a demonstration of his theatrical power, shown in the pathos of the "gentle sorrow" with which he shakes off the rubbish thrown on him, "His face still combating with tears and smiles, / The badges of his grief and patience" (31–33).

York charts the play's turn from the public audience of the city by creating a private audience of himself and his wife—and by extension the theater audience. Phyllis Rackin has argued that while the deposition scene implicates the audience in Richard's disgraces, in this scene the theater audience is distanced from the reaction of the described audience, and thus relieved of the responsibility for the destruction of the king.[32] I would extend this insight by observing that the context the theater audience is distanced from is urban, while the context that includes them is courtly. In both cases the courtly audience connects with the royal spectacle through a privileged knowledge. York and his wife, like the theater audience, know Richard and understand his performance; unlike the "rude misgoverned" crowd in the streets (5), they know better than to consider him a poor actor. Likewise, Richard knows his audience in the deposition scene—"I well remember / The favors of these men" (4.1.167–68)—and his helplessness at the hands of the anonymous London crowd contrasts with his complete control over the theatrical (if not political) space of his abdication.[33]

While this retreat from the public space of London stands outside the tide of power and is connected with royal failure (albeit a failure that redeems Richard as martyr), in *Henry IV* the same process becomes part of the foundation of royal success. *Henry IV* re-engages with London under very different terms. The populous, crowded space of the city is absent, replaced with a city characterized by intimate and quasi-private spaces, a development reflected in a corresponding change in the ethics and mechanics of public display. The scene of Bullingbrook's triumph and Richard's fall recurs in *1 Henry IV*, when Henry, who was so greedily devoured by London eyes in *Richard II*, now declares the virtues of keeping his image private (3.2.39–59). In his rewriting of the earlier play it is Richard who "Grew a companion to the common streets, / Enfeoff'd himself to popularity" (68–69). The common populace is now no more a bellwether of political change but rather "the blunt monster with uncounted heads / The still-discordant wav'ring multitude" that Rumor associates with the theater audience at the beginning of *2 Henry IV* (Ind.18–19).[34] Despite this assertion we are given no examples of the fickleness of the population; unlike the riotous crowds in *Henry VI* and *Richard II*, the absent populace of *Henry IV* is by implication completely tractable to the project of rule. Playing to the crowd becomes not only craven but useless; though Henry claims the rebels have had their grievances "Proclaim'd at market-crosses," to "please the eye of / Of fickle changelings and poor discontents," they receive no benefit from their attempts to sway public opinion (*1 Henry IV* 5.1.73, 75–76). In effect, audience is reconfigured as poor and impotent, controlled by forces they can barely grasp; Falstaff's cynical comment on his charge of men in *1 Henry IV* could well be spoken with an eye to the theater audience: "They'll fill a pit as well as better" (4.3.66–67).

Still, London persists as a location for a different sort of royal theatricality. *Henry IV* confines London to the boundaries of the Boar's Head Tavern, within which Hal plays at beggar and king to his motley troop of followers. The theatrical space of the Boar's Head is mimetic of the court, presenting an intimate, involved audience—as Hal says, "I know you all" (1.2.195)—with a well-established hierarchy of power. On the symbolic level, this mirror of the court is parodic and potentially subversive, but Hal's complete control over its theatrical space renders the threat ineffective. Though Falstaff may occasionally attempt to assert his carnivalesque power over Hal, there is never any doubt about who is truly the master of ceremonies at this theater inn. In effect, the court encloses London, and is always available to suppress its riotous energy when it goes past the point of toleration. The perimeters of the Boar's Head are continually patrolled by the guardians of rule, and even within this constrained theatrical space Hal frequently asserts his rank in order to blunt the edge of Falstaff's disruptive ironies. *Henry IV* reverses the spatial dynamic of *Richard II;* it is in the space of the court that the public presentation of monarchy takes place, while the space of the city is characterized by a besieged privacy. London is not only less powerful than the court; it is smaller, too, and Hal's progress toward the throne involves abandoning this limited, local, sullen theatrical ground, in which he has merely played at playing, in favor of the larger, grander, international world of state politics. This movement can be described as ritualistic, in the sense that it is both symbolic and efficacious, and as Jonathan Goldberg has argued, the ideological effect of this ritual transformation is to coerce complicity from all who witness it.[35]

The position of the theater audience in *Henry IV* is complex; while *Richard II* separated the audience from the public world of London, in *Henry IV* the audience is at once associated with the local space of the city and made a participant in its rejection by Hal. The rejection itself, though it takes place on the streets of the city immediately after Hal's coronation, is presented in an explicitly courtly environment. From the stage directions it would appear that no one waits outside the Abbey but Falstaff and his friends; outnumbered by the new king's retinue of officialdom, it is Falstaff, London personified, who is vulnerable to their aristocratic gaze. Falstaff acknowledges as much; noticing the disreputable appearance of his entourage, he uneasily remarks, "'tis no matter, this poor show doth better, this doth infer the zeal I had to see him" (*2 Henry IV* 5.5.13–14). Falstaff's pitiful reaction to the dismissal, "he must seem thus to the world" (78), recalls his view of himself as "all the world" and thus impossible to banish; now this world is banished, confined, forced to shrink itself even further if it hopes to host the king's presence again (5.5.52–54).

The impoverished, inconsequential urban audience of *Henry IV* is rehabilitated in the opening lines of *Henry V*. While many critics have noted that the desired audience of "monarchs to behold the swelling scene" (1.Pro.4) is impossible, the Chorus does not belabor the point, focusing instead on the inadequacies of the stage and actors; though not royal, the theater audience is still complimented as "gentles all" (8) and as such is placed within the courtly frame of the play. The regular interjections of the Chorus render the division between public and private theatrical spaces irrelevant; all is now public, necessarily and explicitly staged to the theater audience, allegedly patriotic and involved Englishmen all. At the same time, however, London vanishes from the dramatic world of the play, save as a brief scene of departure in the second act, in which the death of Falstaff is lamented. Harry's constant staging of himself takes place not before an urban crowd or a tavern audience but in front of an army, a very different collective body with a critical stake in believing in the godlike power of their leader. In front of this crowd, the theatrical strategy relies on a conceit of intimacy and courtliness: "We few, we happy few, we band of brothers . . . Be he ne'er so vile, / This day shall gentle his condition" (4.3.60–63).[36]

It is only after the victory of this few that Harry can stage himself to the many, in the moment of public spectacle discussed above:

> But now behold,
> In the quick forge and working-house of thought,
> How London doth pour out her citizens!
> The Mayor and all his brethren in best sort,
> Like to the senators of th'antique Rome
> With the plebeians swarming at their heels,
> Go forth and fetch their conqu'ring Caesar in;
> As by a lower but by loving likelihood,
> Were now the general of our gracious Empress,
> As in good time he may, from Ireland coming,
> Bringing rebellion broached on his sword,
> How many would the peaceful city quit,
> To welcome him! (5.Pro.22–43)

In the Chorus's development of this scene we can see a new tactic for conditioning the London audience. While the initial overlap between the space of the stage world and the space of the playhouse carries the potential for the same threat that Richard faced, the lines that follow it displace the scene, removing it to a location that is both distant and gentrified. The urban crowd becomes a background to the highlighted audience for Harry's entry, "the Mayor and all his brethren," described as "the senators of th'antique Rome." As the city is idealized into ancient Rome a social hierarchy is introduced, implying a certain form of courtly (or at least gravely republican) behavior. London is removed by simile to the classical world, and the audience's firsthand participation in the scene is suspended by the historical distance. The invocation of Essex's Irish campaign, "bringing rebellion broached on his sword," ends this suspension, but the contemporary London now invoked is radically different from that at the start of the passage. Elizabeth's colonial ambitions are explicitly linked with Harry's foreign conquests, royal power is displaced into her representative, and in a tone far removed from the entreaties that began the passage the Chorus reminds the audience, no more simply a theater audience, of real-life political imperatives: "How many would the peaceful city quit, / To welcome him!" Harry's entry into London knits together historical event, classical topos, and future obligation, and in this knitting produces an absolute space of public royal display unseen since *Richard II*. The anchor of these transformations is the physical space occupied by the massed bodies of spectators in the London playhouse, but as the mental space of the imagined London is transformed a corresponding alteration takes place in the social space of the theater, redefining the audience's appropriate behavior from a directed act of dramatic imagination to a ritualized form of social submission.

As Goldberg has noted, this is the only explicit use of a contemporary royal reference in Shakespeare's work.[37] In effect, the invocation of contemporary politics represents a solution to the problem of how to place the monarch in the public city, a project abandoned in *Richard II* and inverted in *Henry IV*. If the initial overlapping between Henry V and *Henry V* threatens to make an image of the monarch subject to the theater audience's desires, the second part of the passage trumps this maneuver by making the London scene within the theater subordinate to an imagined scene on the contemporary streets of London, in which the spectators' response will not be that of paying customers but political underlings. In many ways it is the culmination of a strategy that the Epilogue to *2 Henry IV* first adopted: "I kneel down before you—but indeed, to pray for the Queen" (Epi.16–17). At the same time, there is something tenuous about this royal triumph, occurring in an unstaged urban interlude that barely interrupts the play's continental focus. Even the tactic of invoking Essex is somewhat dubious; as Annabel Patterson has observed, Essex's presence underscores the fact that Elizabeth's gender precludes her from being paraded through the London streets as a returning conqueror herself.[38] The absolute space of this triumphal entry is at best contingent, possible only through the careful orchestration of an unlocatable scene of civic endorsement.

The tensions catalyzed in this final urban scene of the second tetralogy are still present when Shakespeare returns, over a decade later and under a different monarch, to the scene of London. Contrary to some critical approaches, Shakespeare does not end his investigation of English history with the second tetralogy.[39] The play that most vigorously examines the urban contexts of rule is one located on the margins of the modern critical discourse of royal power: *Henry VIII*, the last play, stepchild of the history cycle.[40] If the spatial dynamic of *Richard II* involves working through the dangerous urban spaces of *Henry VI*, *Henry V 's* metatheatrical framing of royal power links it with *Henry VIII*, a play that pushes the issues of royal staging and urban context in new directions. In contrast to the earlier history plays, concerned above all with the problems of political instability and compromised monarchy, *Henry VIII* presents an unshakeable ruler and regime. Perhaps because the question of Henry's legitimacy (in either the political or genealogical sense of the word) needs never to be broached, *Henry VIII* is able to pay close and critical attention to the spectacular rituals that define both the symbolic structure of royal power and the theatrical structure of the play. In so doing, it overturns the *camera regis* model found in the second tetralogy, and redefines the public theatrical space of London in terms that are at once politically quiescent and spatially transgressive.[41]

THE COURT AND PARIS GARDEN

"Think you see the very persons of our noble story as they were living," commands the Prologue to *Henry VIII*:

> Think you see them great,
> And followed with the general throng and sweat
> Of thousand friends; (1.Pro.25–29)

The contrasting elements of this exhortation frame the play's treatment of spectacular power. The presentation of greatness pervades *Henry VIII;* from the Field of Cloth of Gold, which opens the chronicle, to Elizabeth's christening, which completes it, the play is arranged around spectacles of noble and royal magnificence. Charting the fall of Buckingham, the rise and fall of Wolsey, and the fall of Katherine and the rise of Anne—and foretelling the eventual rise of Elizabeth and James—the play structures itself according to the antiquated *de casibus* tradition; as the Prologue concludes the above command, "then, in a moment, see / How soon this mightiness meets misery" (29–30). Through this episodic narrative structure, which seems to consciously return to the dramatic patterns of the first tetralogy,[42] the play interleaves political, matrimonial, and religious narratives in a sequence of pageant-like falls and ascents.

Henry VIII 's theatrical effectiveness depends directly on this pageantry and visual power; in the absence of the complex characters and gripping narratives that mark the second tetralogy, it relies on an overwhelming display of regal finery to captivate its audience. This theatrical shallowness is appropriate to the apparent political tenor of the play. Unlike the earlier history plays, royal legitimacy has an easy invulnerability in *Henry VIII.*[43] Henry dominates the world of the play as the play appears to dominate its viewers, and such small conflict as the events of the play produce seems largely intended to demonstrate the providential triumph of Henry and his offspring. With political legitimacy—the crux of all the earlier history plays—thus rendered a non-issue, the staged character of Henry is flattened, rendered a static and inscrutable presence. In this atmosphere of political stability the theatrical display of greatness is presented not as a means of maintaining or extending power but as an epiphenomenon of power, an inevitable byproduct of Tudor righteousness.[44]

Such a seamless and unproblematic conception of royal theatricality begins to unravel, however, when we look at the theatrical space in which greatness is manifested, a space whose ambiguous character is revealed by the play's attitude toward "the general throng and sweat of thousand friends" that follows the persons of the noble story. The word "sweat" bothered the Victorian editor P. A. Daniel so much that he emended it to "suite," a word suggesting a more refined and well-tempered audience.[45] Such distaste is reflected elsewhere in the play itself, as in the words of the gentleman who describes the crowd at Anne's coronation, "I am stifled / With the mere rankness of their joy" (4.1.58–59)—a phrase that, with similar fastidiousness, the *Riverside Shakespeare* glosses as "very exuberance."[46] This editorial reluctance to acknowledge the sweaty, smelly bodies of the urban populace is understandable in the context of the play; "sweat" changes the tenor of the Prologue's statement, drawing attention from the noble body of the great man to the grotesque body of the crowd that surrounds him. The unpleasant corporeality of the word changes the meaning of the imagined scene from a *de casibus* exemplum to an immediate moment of theater that, in the context of an address to the audience, is inherently self-conscious.

Despite the Prologue's exhortation, *Henry VIII* is dramatically structured to avoid such conjunctions with the general throng. All moments of public spectacle in the play are quarantined offstage, conveyed only through description. Staged spectacular scenes, such as Katherine's trial or Wolsey's masque, are located indoors, taking place before small, noble audiences in locations separated from London by royal or ecclesiastical demarcation. This division in theatrical space splits the play into two discrete realms, a dyadic geography of the court and the city. Within the former the Henrician court is staged in full splendor; in the latter the regal display is only passingly visible, communicated for the most part through description and anecdote. To a court world characterized by invisible influence and hidden agendas, London represents a space of uncomfortable visibility; as the First Gentleman says to the Second, standing on the street after Buckingham's execution party has passed, "We are too open here to argue this; / Let's think in private more" (2.1.168–69). Disclosure and discovery trigger death or disgrace for many characters in the play (Buckingham, Wolsey, Gardiner), and the importance of reticence and secrecy to the intrigues of the powerful cascades through the hierarchy of characters, quelling rumor and chilling conversation. At the same time, the unseen audience of London acts as a significant context for *Henry VIII 's* courtly performances. At various points in the play the public geography of the street intrudes and makes its presence known: Buckingham's fall is occasioned by his alleged inquiries into Londoners' perceptions of the king (1.2.152), Wolsey takes public credit for the remission of a tax he himself instituted (1.2.104), and Henry must command the Lord Mayor to stamp out city rumors of his secret marriage to Anne (2.1.149). Viewed from this perspective, the inherently lopsided relationship between public and private (what is private can become public, but not vice versa) creates a hierarchy between these two realms of the play that reverses the nominal importance of each in the dramatic narrative. The street envelops the court, a larger frame of reference that always exists in the background. Whether acknowledged as such or not, London is always present. This spatial model is the reverse of the *camera regis* strategy developed in *Henry IV* and *Henry V;* while in those plays the court envelops the city, here it is London that surrounds the private and protected domains of court theatrics.

This emphasis on courtly privacy necessarily reaches its apotheosis with Henry himself, who is never paraded through the "too open" streets of London during the play. Instead, the public aspect of rule takes the form of a distributed monarchy, in which the rituals of royal investiture—Anne's coronation pageant and Elizabeth's christening— take the place of the royal presence itself.[47] While the actual cere- monies take place offstage, considerable attention is paid to the London audience of these events. In the coronation scene the crowd is manifested through vivid description; in the christening scene the crowd is almost staged, in a *coup de théâtre* found nowhere else in Shakespeare's work. As the "general throng and sweat" of the Prologue's speech reframes historical edification as a present moment of theater, so the coronation and christening scenes interrupt the cohesive inevitability of *Henry VIII 's* predestined narrative. Despite their offstage location, and their ancillary relationship to the play's larger focus on national and dynastic issues, these descriptions of jubi- lant London audiences have a theatrical impact inconsonant with the expectations of the play's historical teleology.

In both scenes we are shown an audience whose behavior clashes with the play's courtly focus. The ideal context for royal spectacle is shown in Anne's regal coronation progression across the stage, which precedes the report of the offstage coronation itself and is prefaced in the Folio text with the title, "The Order of the Coronation" and a list of all the noble and civic retinue. This numbered list follows a clear order of degree, moving from the Lord Chancellor and Mayor of London through various high nobles, all gorgeously appointed, to cli- max with the new Queen, "in her robe, in her hair, richly adorned with pearl, crowned. On each side of her, the Bishops of London and Winchester" (4.1.sd).[48] An almost identical procession closes the play, after the christening, and we are led to imagine that a similar display begins the play, in the description of the Field of Cloth of Gold in the first scene; in Norfolk's words:

> All was royal;
> To the disposing of it nought rebell'd,
> Order gave each thing view; the office did
> Distinctly his full function. (1.1.42–45)

These absolute spaces of lucid hierarchy, however, are impossible in the explicitly urban contexts of the christening and coronation. Through its wild and polymorphous crowds, London acts as a dangerous supplement to *Henry VIII 's* staging of royal power.

In the coronation scene this supplement is physically present in the person of the Third Gentleman. The first part of the scene is framed by the same two gentlemen who watched Buckingham's passage to execution, a parallel made explicit by the First Gentleman's comment, "that time offered sorrow, / This general joy" (4.1.6–7). They watch as Anne's procession from the coronation crosses the stage in high splendor and courtly order, and provide annotative glosses on the passing nobles. After Anne has left the stage the Third Gentleman arrives, providing an additional choric voice that changes the scene from a mirror image of Buckingham's execution (demonstrating the king's power to reward as well as punish) to an examination of the dynamics of public ceremony. Despite its visual impact, Anne's silent progress across the stage becomes secondary to the Third Gentleman's description of the actual coronation. He has been "Among the crowd i' th' Abbey, where a finger / Could not be wedg'd in more" (4.1.57–58), a location that foreshadows the emphasis of his report. Although he describes the coronation itself, his attention is increasing drawn to the audience, using their reaction to Anne to convey the phenomenological intensity of the event:

> when the people
> Had the full view of [Anne], such a noise arose
> As the shrouds make at sea in a stiff tempest,
> As loud and to as many tunes (4.1.70–73)

The "stiff tempest" is the spectacle of Anne, the power of her revealed image. But like an invisible wind, this spectacle cannot be perceived except through the effect it causes in the London audience. The musical phrase recalls the "still-discordant wav'ring multitude" of *2 Henry IV* (1.Ind.19), but the expression has a different meaning: not a fickle crowd, but a crowd that is inherently chaotic, unfocused, and excessive.[49] It is the excessive nature of the crowd's investment in the ceremony that anxiously fascinates the Third Gentleman. Figures of excess fill his description: "Hats, cloaks / (Doublets, I think) flew up, and had their faces / Been loose, this day they had been lost" (73–75). This image pushes past the limits of decorum: the movement from hats and cloaks to doublets and then on to faces undermines the original gesture of fealty, and underscoring the stifling character of the crowd's presence.

The intemperateness of the crowd's response is reminiscent of the scene of Bullingbrook's entry in *Richard II,* but there are crucial differences in how the crowds are described. In *Richard II,* the crowd is fixated on the body of the *de facto* ruler, focusing all their energy and attention on the singularity of the royal presence. To look at that crowd is to be always drawn back to the resplendent image of Bullingbrook on his proud horse. In *Henry VIII,* the Third Gentleman's description of the multitude indicates a different sort of crowd energy:

> Such joy
> I never saw before. Great-bellied women,
> That had not half a week to go, like rams
> In the old time of war, would shake the press
> And make 'em reel before 'em. No man living
> Could say, "This is my wife" there, all were woven
> So strangely in one piece. (4.1.75–81)

With this vivid description the spectacle of Anne's body is displaced by the strange, disturbing spectacle of the grotesque body of the crowd. On one level the image is carnivalesque, in the sense of providing an ironic reflection of the royal ceremony: the pregnant women, inappropriately out in public during the last stages of their terms and packed so tightly together that their husbands cannot differentiate them, comically reframe the context of Henry's remarriage and Anne's implicit fecundity. More important, however, is the way the energies of the image separate it from the space of the coronation. To return to the terms I introduced at the beginning of this chapter, the crowd in *Richard II* is a *setting,* existing to frame the absolute space created by the apotheosis of the new monarch. In *Henry VIII,* by contrast, we are given the *scene* of the crowd, a separate entity set in motion by Anne's coronation but possessing a prodigious momentum of its own.

As in *Richard II,* where windows and walls seem to speak, here the crowd's spatial and symbolic character associates it with the city. One of the key characteristics of the grotesque body, in Mikhail Bakhtin's analysis, is its lack of individuation, both internally and externally; it "transgresses its own confines, ceases to be itself. The limits between the body and the world are erased."[50] In the extremity of the grotesque image the division between the body of the crowd and London dissolves, creating a theatrical space in which the physical attributes of the crowd merge with the symbolic meaning of the city.

An ambiguous making and unmaking permeates the image: the "woven" women are once the fabric of the crowd and city and at the same time battering "rams in the old time of war," used to breach city walls, that "shake the press" and make the crowd "reel before 'em," disrupting and dividing that which they constitute. The confusion is reinforced on the sexual level: as phallic battering rams the women penetrate the crowd and the city, yet by virtue of their pregnant state are already penetrated themselves. This intense, bewildering tangle of symbolic structures is the heart of the spectacle of London: a shifting, anonymous, polymorphic mass characterized by monstrous fecundity and chaotic energy.[51]

The disturbing urban images of the coronation scene are ultimately contained within a courtly frame. The description of the coronation is broken off by a misnaming: the Third Gentleman makes reference to "York-place," the palace's name when occupied by the now-disgraced Wolsey, and is admonished "You must not more call it York-place, that's past; . . .'Tis now the King's, and call'd Whitehall" (95–97). The dangerous error causes the conversation to return to the intrigues of the court, with a discussion of the participants in the coronation and their political weight. But the spatial and political economy of *Henry VIII* causes this courtly frame to operate differently than in *Richard II*. There, the theater audience is included in the courtly audience, distancing it from the urban crowd. Here, the theater audience is specifically excluded; the scene ends with a gesture toward theatrical discretion as the Third Gentleman invites the other two back to the court, offering to tell them more out of the theater audience's earshot (113–17).

In the christening scene the staging of London is undertaken in a radically different manner. The rhetorical progression of the coronation scene (from the royal spectacle to the spectacle of the crowd/city and then back to the decorum and circumspection of court intrigues) does not occur in the christening scene, which opens *in media res* with the stage direction, "Noise and tumult within." No description is given of the christening, whose causal relationship to the public melee is only mentioned in passing. The only characters on stage are the Porter and his Man, acting as lower-class guardians of courtly inviolability, and the scene largely consists of their voicing their violent disapproval of the behavior of the offstage crowd. Given the way the scene interrupts the smooth culmination of the play's narrative, it is appropriate that the first and continual note is one of surprise. "How got they in, and be hanged?," cries the Porter to his Man, outraged by the intrusion of the crowd into the palace yard (5.2.17).

What offends them is the inappropriateness of the crowd's presence; "Is this a place to roar in?" roars the Porter as he beats back the crowd "do you look for ale and cakes here, you rude rascals?" (7, 10–11). The response of the gatekeepers to this intrusive presence is violence of an extreme variety: "Fetch me a dozen crab-tree staves, and strong ones; these are but switches to 'em" (7–9); "What should you do, but knock them down by the dozens?" (31–32); "As much as one sound cudgel of four foot (You see the poor remainder) could distribute, I made no spare, sir" (19–21). As the quotations indicate, none of these violent measures have any effect; they only serve to emphasize the unruly and indifferent power of the crowd. A grudging amazement at the uncontrolled and uncontrollable nature of the crowd permeates the scene; in response to the Porter's question about how the crowd got in, the Man responds, "Alas, I know not, how gets the tide in?" (17–18). This expression of the crowd's inexorability reaches its epitome when the Man says, "We may as well push against Powle's as stir 'em" (16), metastasizing the crowd into urban edifices and equating its immovable presence with the symbolic weight of London itself.

The violent antipathy of the scene frames the relationship between the crowd and the palace guard (or, in symbolic/spatial terms, the city and the court) in terms of battle: the former is seen as launching a dangerous assault on the latter that must be repelled. The female battering rams of the coronation scene multiply into a host of military metaphors: "the women . . . besiege" the palace, the crowd will not be moved "unless we sweep 'em from the door with cannons, to scatter 'em" (13–14), one man is described as "a mortar-piece to blow us" (46), and the Porter claims in defense of his inadequate defense of the palace that "an army cannot rule them" (77). Chastised by the arriving Lord Chamberlain, the Porter says, "We are but men; and what so many may do, / Not being torn a-pieces, we have done" (75–76). While the crowd in the coronation scene merely upstages the official spectacle, here it is perceived as threatening to destroy it. The violence of the crowd in the coronation scene was random and self-directed; here the target is explicitly believed to be the palace and its defenders. The martial rhetoric reaches its mock-climax with the Man's description of his sortie against the pressing mob:

> They fell on, I made good my place; at length they came to th' broom-staff to me, I defied 'em still, when suddenly a file of boys behind 'em, loose shot, deliver'd such a show'r of pibbles, that I was fain to draw mine honor in, and set 'em win the work. (53–58)

The threatening qualities of this discourse are all the more remarkable because, in contrast to the crowd scenes of *Henry VI* and *Richard II*, this crowd presents no direct threat. The people have assembled in the palace yard because they are overjoyed at the christening of Elizabeth; as in the coronation scene, their ecstatic response validates this symbolic perpetuation of Tudor legitimacy. Noting this allegiance, Leonard Tennenhouse has argued that in *Henry VIII* "the disruptive power associated with the erotic, the demonic, and the folk never constitutes a field of contention," tying this assertion to James's appropriation of popular pastimes and other carnival activities as a symbol of loyalty.[52]

Such a reading glosses over the details of James's strategic assimilation of carnival. While James's support for traditional games and potentially destabilizing social practices is well established, it is important to keep in mind the specifically *rural* character of the pastimes that received royal endorsement.[53] In the *Book of Sports*, after listing many country recreations that are lawful on Sundays, James goes on to reaffirm the unlawfulness of "Beare and Bull-baiting" and "Interludes."[54] Such prohibited pastimes are precisely the urban activities with which the London crowd of *Henry VIII* is associated: "These are the youths that thunder at a playhouse and fight for bitten apples. That no audience but the tribulation of Tower-hill or the limbs of Limehouse, their dear brothers, are able to endure" (5.3.60–63). This is a specifically urban form of carnival, one particular to London itself.[55] While James may have idealized rural folk activities as evidence of cultural tradition and political stability, as we have seen he frequently displayed considerable antipathy toward his capital and "the idle people that swarme in London streets."[56] In his speech to the Star Chamber on June 20, 1616, James complained that London's growth was "causing dearth and scarsitie through the great provision of victuals and fewel, that must be for such a multitude of people" (225). London's unhealthy and expensive rapacity is portrayed as indifferent to social barriers, drawing commoner and noble alike:

> all the countrey is gotten into London; so, with time, England will only
> be London, and the whole countrey will be left waste: For as wee now
> do imitate the French fashion, in fashion of clothes . . . so have wee got
> up the Italian fashion, in living miserably in our houses, and dwelling
> all in the Citie. (225–26)

Here the specific focus of James's concerns is the nobility leaving their country estates and flocking to London. Once in the urban swarm,

James fears, the nobility lose their aristocratic distinctiveness, becoming part of the anonymous mass of the city. But the key anxiety is expressed in symbolic terms: "England will only be London." London is portrayed as a ravenous body, consuming the country and its inhabitants, growing with a monstrous and engulfing rapidity.[57] In its urban manifestation, carnival is no friend to the Jacobean court; the growing power of London, manifested in these grotesque images, is by implication exactly what James thinks is wrong with the country.

Nevertheless, Tennenhouse is correct in saying that the London crowd of *Henry VIII* presents no threat to the political order of the play. Despite its raucous nature, the crowd does not ultimately impede or disrupt the ceremony of royal investiture. Although the gatekeepers continually assert that the crowd cannot be moved, when the time comes for the christening procession to return to the court at the end of the scene, a path is apparently cleared with little effort; the royal party seems to enter the court without hindrance. Despite its disruptiveness, this is an extremely loyal crowd. The christening scene cannot be termed subversive or iconoclastic: it contains no inversions of power, proposes no uncrownings. Unlike the public audiences of the earlier history plays, in no way is the London crowd portrayed in the play as rebellious.

Why, then, is so much anxiety attached to the loyal, though excessive, behavior of the crowd? This question can only be answered by reframing it in a way that moves beyond a dichotomy of loyalty or rebellion. Rather than asking whether or not the crowd is subversive, we should ask: What political anxieties are articulated by the insertion of the carnivalesque crowd into the theatrical economy of *Henry VIII*? The answer, I think, lies in the problematic nature of the spectacle of the London crowd, both in terms of what and how it symbolizes and in terms of its effect on the theatrical space of the play. As well as a historical practice and a cultural paradigm, carnival is also a mode of performance, and as such can be interpreted through the Lefebvrian spatial model I have been employing.[58] Carnival is an inversion of social space; by suspending the rules of everyday life, it causes a transformation in the mental space of the festive event. The effect of this spatial transformation is the deconstruction of the divisions and hierarchies that characterize the theatrical structure of *Henry VIII*. In contrast to the ideal ceremony of the Field of Cloth of Gold, an absolutely courtly space where "Order gave each thing view" (1.1.44), the coronation and christening scenes produce a theatrical space that is inherently disordered and will not respect rankings and boundaries. As Bakhtin says, "Carnival is not a spectacle seen by the people; they live in it, and everyone participates because its very idea embraces all people."[59] This participation is very different from the participation of the courtly audience in the *camera regis* models of the second tetralogy, since the carnivalesque crowd "is outside of and contrary to all existing forms of the coercive socioeconomic and political organization" (266). Unlike the controlled and limited spaces of courtly theater there can be no boundaries or limitations to carnival, which will always consume whatever stands outside it.

This consuming quality of urban carnival, lying at the heart of James's nightmare of London absorbing the countryside, also explains the spatial character of the christening scene. The christening crowd is a perfect example of what Canetti calls "the open crowd," the crowd that as soon as it exists "wants to consist of *more* people."[60] The open crowd is the "natural crowd," in contrast to "the closed crowd" caught within theaters and other auditoriums; in language that extends Bakhtin's repudiation of theatrical boundaries to urban ones, Canetti comments, "there are no limits whatever to its growth; it does not recognize houses, doors, or locks" (16). It is in the context of the unmanageable space of the open crowd that the unusual staging of the christening scene becomes significant. If the spectacle of the crowd symbolizes London within the play, the off-staging of the crowd establishes a connection with the real city, outside the theater walls, a London represented by the theater audience. Like the unstaged crowd, the theater crowd is located just offstage, and the analogies between these two masses of bodies are explicit. The play has linked these audiences since the Prologue's opening address, which is full of attempts to control the audience's emotional reaction to the events of the play. "Be sad, as we would make ye," says the Prologue (1.Pro.25), attempting to enforce a decorous and appropriate response to the material, exactly that which is lacking in the unstaged audiences of the play. The Prologue seeks to curb the behavior of the audience—to make it passive, ennoble it, instruct it on the correct and courtly form of responsive behavior—even as the play demonstrates its disruptive power. If the play will not stage the public scenes that take place before the "general throng and sweat" it is because it is already staging itself to the audience in the Globe theater; by linking these two audiences the christening scene transforms the closed crowd of the playhouse into the open crowd of the city streets. The spectacle of the christening crowd becomes the spectacle of the theater audience: the stage becomes opaque, reflecting to the audience an image of itself. Reversing the theatrical hierarchy, the two guardians of the stage become spectators themselves. Rather than the city watching the court, the court watches the city, and while at the end of *2 Henry IV* the courtly gaze overwhelmed Falstaff and his stragglers, here the court can only watch, not control.

Control is returned in the final scene of the play, of course, where yet another royal and civic procession travels across the stage; as with the coronation, the stage direction confirms the stately pomp of the spectacle:

> Enter Trumpets, sounding; then two Aldermen, Lord Mayor, Garter, Cranmer, Duke of Norfolk with his marshall's staff, Duke of Suffolk, two Noblemen bearing great standing-bowls for the christening gifts; then four Noblemen bearing a canopy, under which the Duchess of Norfolk, godmother, bearing the child richly habited in a mantle, etc., train borne by a Lady, then follows the Marchioness Dorset, the other godmother, and Ladies. (5.4.sd)

In the final scene as well is Cranmer's famous act of divine prognostication over Elizabeth, which foretells, "In her days every man shall eat in safety / Under his own vine what he plants" (33–34), a bucolic image of country life that reasserts a rural vision of the nation. In this way, the excesses of the urban play may be contained by its ceremonious conclusion. On the other hand, the relations between the two scenes run deeper than their sequential order; it would be equally valid, at least, to see the crowd scene as preemptively desacralizing the ritualistic aura of the conclusion. From the Porter's question—"you must be seeing christenings? Do you look for cakes and ale here, you rude rascals?" (5.3.9–11)—onward, the scene frames (or unframes) the ceremony with inappropriate language. Images of sexual excess crowd the scene, culminating in the Porter's exclamation, "have we some strange Indian with the great tool come to court, the women so besiege us?" (32–34). Here the christening of an infant girl, the future "Virgin Queen," is sacrilegiously transformed into an erotic freakshow.

This, of course, is exactly the sort of thing that the gatekeepers fear the scene before the palace will produce: a disruption in the stately christening procession as it returns to court, a distraction from the aristocratic splendor of this culminating royal view. As the Lord Chamberlain says toward the end of the crowd scene:

> Hark, the trumpets sound.
> Th'are are come already from the christening.
> Go break among the press, and find a way out

> To let the troop pass fairly; or I'll find
> A Marshalsea shall hold ye play these two months. (83–86)

In the event, no such disruption takes place; indeed, the participants in the christening procession make no mention of the great crowd that blocked their way, and are perhaps completely unaware of it. With this obliviousness, the two scenes seem less progressive than contrasting, offering less a developing focus than two different endings for the play. And if it is possible to read this fracture as signaling the insignificance of the city to the royal court, the reverse is possible as well. Ultimately, I would suggest, the threat of London in *Henry VIII* is less the repudiation of royal power than insularity from it. Unlike the singular focus of the royal spectacle, the spectacle of London that is revealed here is exactly that which cannot be focused on: the sublime confusion caused by an excess of complexity. Like the chaotic noise of the shrouds in the wind, making a discordant, random music, the spectacle of the crowd and the city cannot be made coherent and explicable. As the "woven women" image from the coronation scene indicates, this spectacle cannot be *known;* the density and multiform complexity of the image resists the controlling, dividing eyes of either the speaker or the peering husbands he imagines. The spectacle of London inaugurates another form of spectacular power: inchoate, directionless, but one that refuses to participate in the courtly decorum and hierarchy of *camera regis.*

It is on the geographical level that the relationship between the court and the city is most clearly articulated. "You'll leave your noise anon, ye rascals"; cries the Porter, "do you take the court for Parish Garden?" (5.3.1–2).[61] This first sentence of the scene, spoken before we even know who the Porter is addressing, is particularly ironic from the perspective of the theater audience. Paris Garden was the location of a Bankside bear-baiting pit, a type of amphitheater structurally so similar to the public theaters that early modern panoramas of London often confuse the two in their labeling. To compound the connection, Paris Garden had specific theatrical associations: the Swan theater had been erected on its site in 1595, and in 1613 the Hope theater took its place.[62] Thus, in effect, the Porter's anachronistic question is, "Do you take this for a mere amusement? Do you take this for a play?" As in the scene before Katherine's trial, where Henry decrees, "The most convenient place that I can think of / For such receipt of learning is Black-Friars" (2.2.137–38),[63] the Porter's winking question concedes the commercial frame of the event and admits that the overriding purpose of this theatrical spectacle is entertainment rather than efficacy.

These metatheatrical gestures reconfigure theater and spectacle in the context of the immediate audience, the proximity of the real city, and the real staging of royal power. Yet unlike the similarly breaching moment in *Henry V,* the theatrical space produced is not the absolute space of royal ritual, but the quotidian, material space of play-acting, where greatness is made familiar. The theatrical power of the court becomes the theatrical diversion of Paris Garden.

The rhetoric of geographic indifference litters the christening scene: "Is this a place to roar in?" (5.3.7); "Do you look for ale and cakes here, you rude rascals?" (10–11); "Is this Moorfields to muster in?" (33); "from all parts they are coming, / As if we kept a fair here!" (68–69). *Henry VIII* is structured through a number of interlocking binary oppositions: between history and performance, between the stage and the audience, between ritual and entertainment, and between the court and the city. In the christening scene, the crowd's "taking" of the court is something that crosses the barrier between these oppositions, a transgressive opening up of the space of the court into the undifferentiated mass of urban experience.[64] It would be unfruitful, I believe, to explain this dynamic in new historicist terms, as a subversion of royal power; the crowds in *Henry VIII* are emphatically loyal, and the actual power of the state, rooted in bureaucratic and juridical apparatuses, is unchallenged by the crowd's behavior. I do want to argue, though, that this emphatic loyalty is one way that the play articulates contemporary anxieties about London, anxieties that cannot be easily explained through a binary opposition of loyalty or rebellion. The problem with the crowds in the coronation and christening scenes is not that they are subversive but that they are *too much:* they offer *more* joy, *more* loyalty than is needed or desired. This idea of *more* is at the heart of how they are portrayed. Images of spatial and generative excess fill the descriptions; as the Lord Chamberlain exclaims on his arrival: "Mercy o' me, what a multitude are here! They grow still too; from all parts they are coming" (67–68). As well as drawing in all the city, relentless growth is also expressed as an internal attribute of the christening crowd; in an image recalling the grotesque fecundity of the coronation scene, the Porter exclaims, "Bless me, what a fry of fornication is at door! On my Christian conscience, this one christening will beget a thousand, here will be father, godfather, and all together" (35–38). Canetti's comment on the open crowd, that which "wants to consist of *more* people," echoes this excess, and another echo can be found in King James's gloomy prediction that "in time, England will only be London." By emphasizing the uncontrollable growth of urban crowds, the play suggests that what London has become stands outside the old technologies of symbolic power.[65] In contrast to the spatial ideology of the royal entry, *Henry VIII* reveals the scene of London as something *more* than a setting for the public display of power in early modern England.

Chapter 4

Distracted Multitude:
The Theater and
the Many-Headed Monster

At the height of his alienation from the plebeians, Coriolanus expresses his popular revulsion in terms of a paradox:

> I would they were barbarians, as they are,
> Though in Rome litter'd; not Romans, as they are not,
> Though calved i' th' porch o' th' Capitol! (3.1.237–39)

The idea of Rome is the agon of *Coriolanus,* the central conflict that determines and destroys the title character through his futile attempts to separate himself from the common people and separate them from the city. Yet the impossibility of Coriolanus's phrasing in this passage makes us pause; he attempts to estrange urban multiplicity from the city, in effect banishing the crowd from Rome. His wish might prompt a reframing of Sicinius's question: not "what is the city but the people?" but "what is the people if not the city?" This chapter addresses this reformulated question by exploring a set of symbolic correspondences between collective violence, theatrical power, and urban meaning through an analysis of the discourse of the crowd as a "many-headed monster." My central aim is to demonstrate a broad engagement with the crowded space of London across a wide variety of plays and other literature—as a counterpoint, perhaps, to the

narrow focus on city comedy that usually accompanies urban subjects. Drawing on material from many disparate locations and
traditions, and making connections between plays rarely considered
together, this chapter seeks to uncover the common anxieties about
the crowd that join them. It returns most strongly to a point made in
chapter 1, that plays stage crowds in order to negotiate their
relationship to their urban audiences.

Although in some ways proceeding from my discussion of
Henry VIII, this chapter marks a transition in my argument in several
respects. In the previous two chapters I am primarily interested in discussing the space of the crowd as it is manifested as an *event* in the
immediate, historical context of London, focusing on how the crowd
was understood in relation to the physical space of the city during the
transformative dynamics of public ritual. In this chapter and those that
follow it, I want to approach these issues from another perspective,
emphasizing the other half of the spatial equation made in the
Introduction: the *discourse* of the crowd, the ideological framework
within which the urban multitude was contextualized. Event and discourse, and their figuration in metaphor and metonymy, are of course
inextricable, but my privileging here of the second term involves a shift
in methodology of sorts. Rather than starting with how the early
modern city was understood, this chapter traces a particular species of
the figure of the crowd. My main focus is the triangular relationship
this figure mediates among the theater, the audience, and the city. The
chapter focuses on the commercial theater, following a progressive
dissocation of urban theatricality from official power over the last two
chapters: from civic pageantry, to commercial representations of royal
spectacle, to the taking of the court as Paris Garden in *Henry VIII*. The
plays considered here take us some distance from the specific context
of London, but only in terms of dramatic setting; theatrical performance, and metatheatrical reference, always has as its root the material
context of playing to London. What is at stake, then, is a dialectic
between representation and performance, and thus between defined
and undefinable understandings of the crowd and the crowded city. By
dramatically figuring urban multiplicity as a "many-headed monster"—
a label that originates in Plato and was ubiquitous by the sixteenth
century—the theater appropriated a discourse most commonly used
to attack it; this appropriation, I want to argue, allowed the theater to
register ambivalence about both its place in the symbolic space of
London and its commercial service to the crowded city.

The methodological shifts discussed above initiate a conceptual
shift, from thinking of the crowd primarily an urban *frame* (albeit a

problematic one) for official displays of power to thinking of the crowd as a space defined by *circulation*. Framing versus circulation relates to the event/discourse paradigm; the circulation of urban discourse is mimetic of the circulation of the crowd in complex ways. In this shift I also want to put more pressure on the relationship between the theater and its urban audience, repositioning the playhouse not only as a place of staging but also as a place of dissemination. The theater audience demarcates the space of drama, but it also disperses it, circulating its images throughout the urban body. This disseminating power was coded by civic elements hostile to the theater as an appropriation of urban space, an illicit infiltration of London that corrupts and pollutes the symbolic landscape of the city with an illegitimate theatrical significance.

In *Coriolanus*, the discourse of the multitude *as* a discourse is first made clear in the second act, by the Third Citizen, who responds to the Second Citizen's complaint that Coriolanus has "stuck not to call us the many headed multitude" by saying "We have been called so of many" (2.3.16–18). He then continues by offering a particularly benign gloss on the term:

> not that our heads are some brown, some black, some abram, some bald, but that our wits are so diversely colored; and truly I think, if all our wits were to issue out of one skull, they would fly east, west, north, south, and their consent of one direct way should be at once to all the points o' th' compass. (2.3.18–24)

This diversity of opinion is a central part of the idea of the many-headed monster, although it fails to capture the intense loathing that Coriolanus displays. Nevertheless, the citizen's final conjoining of "one direct way" and "all the points o' th' compass" does hint at the heart of the matter for Coriolanus in a metaphorical way. If the horrifying psychological idea of the many drives Coriolanus's hatred, it is expressed through the circulatory qualities of the crowd, their ability to disseminate. As he says in the first scene of the play:

> They'll sit by the fire, and presume to know
> What's done i' th' Capitol; who's like to rise,
> Who thrives, and who declines; side factions, and give out
> Conjectural marriages, making parties strong,
> And feebling such as stand not in their liking
> Below their cobbled shoes. (1.1.191–96)

In this image, the elite of Rome play their parts as if on a stage before the common people—a commonplace idea, but one given particular force by the unauthorized circulation that occurs. The plebeians appropriate the affairs of the Capitol, turning the governance of Rome into their private entertainment by the fire. In *Coriolanus* the power of the people is explicitly a theatrical power, but a theatricality always figured through appropriation and transformation. Coriolanus fears a decentered Rome that escapes the hierarchical structures of society, metamorphosing what "yet distinctly ranges" (3.1.205) into a grotesque intermingling of high and low through the invisible and innumerable pathways of urban communication.

The Third Citizen's wry comment, "we have been called so of many," points toward a philosophical and political discourse of the many-headed monster that stretches back to Plato. In Book IX of *The Republic*, Socrates has Glaucon imagine a strange beast, similar to "creatures like the Chimera, Scylla, Cerebus, and many others in whose natures many different kinds grow into one."[1] Socrates then further directs Glaucon's conceptualization:

> Fashion me then one kind of multiform beast with many heads, a ring of heads of both tame and wild animals, who is able to change these and grow them all out of himself.
>
> A work for a clever modeler, he said. However, as words are more malleable than wax and such things, take it as fashioned.
>
> Then one other form, that of a lion, and another of a man, but the first form of all is much the largest, and the second second. . . . Gather the three into one, so that they somehow grow together. . . . Model around them on the outside the appearance of being one, a man, so that anyone who cannot see what is inside but only the outside cover will think it is one creature, a man. (235)

This is the Platonic model of the soul: the figure of the man represents reason, the lion represents will, and the many-headed beast represents appetite. This is also the Platonic model of the city: its three general classes of guardians, militia, and commoners are identified through a respective tendency toward reason, will, and appetite within these populations. The just man, Socrates explains, would make reason and will rule the passions and appetites; he "would look after the many-headed beast as a farmer looks after his animals, fostering and domesticating the gentle heads and preventing the wild ones from growing. With the lion's nature as his ally, he will care for all of them and rear them by making them all friendly with each other and with himself" (236). Similarly, by implication, the guardians should govern the lower classes by controlling and chastising those aspects of their nature that they cannot control. As Socrates says of one whose soul "is naturally weak and cannot rule the animals within":

> In order that such a man be ruled by a principle similar to that which rules the best man, we say he must be enslaved to the best man, who had a divine ruler within himself. It is not to harm the slave that we believe he must be ruled . . . but because it is better for everyone to be ruled by divine intelligence. It is best that he should have this within himself, but if he has not, then it must be imposed from outside. (237)

Using the city as a conceptual tool, Plato both explains the allegedly inherent differences between social classes and justifies the subjection of the many to the rule of the few.

The equivalence between the soul and the city is a foundational premise of *The Republic,* which stresses, on a number of occasions, that "each of us has within himself the same parts or characteristics as the city" (100). As Socrates declares:

> When one of us hurts his finger, the whole organism which binds body and soul together in the unitary system managed by the ruling part of it shares the pain at once throughout when one part suffers . . . And whenever anything good or bad happens to a single one of its citizens, such a city will certainly say that this citizen is a part of itself, and the whole city will rejoice or suffer with him. (123–24)

With this corporeal model, Plato provides the *locus classicus* for what I have termed "the articulate city"—understanding the urban population as inextricably gathered together in a sinewed and interwoven society, each member performing the functions appropriate to his or her role and state. By extrapolating from the body, the city is made functional and organic, although not all functions are equal; as long as the many-headed monster is tended correctly, appetites will not rule the city.

Conceptually, this is a powerful model, but what is perhaps most interesting about its enactment in Plato is the lack of visual clarity it produces. If the posited equivalence between body and city has a persuasive transparency to it, when forced to actually model the political relations of the urban population Socrates must turn to a "multiform beast" that can barely be visualized, an awkward conglomeration of monstrous body parts; as Glaucon dryly comments, it is "work for a clever modeler." What the model of the single human body lacks is an effective way of figuring multiplicity. On one level, the problem is the simple numerical difference between the few who rule and the many who are ruled; on another, the problem is the sheer multiplicity of bodies that constitutes a city. The figure of the many-headed monster thus allows Plato to make sense out of the city, but it does so in terms that undermine the controlling intentions of the original model. This creates a fundamental tension in the articulation of the ideal city. Just as the philosopher must subordinate the many-headed monster within himself, and within the city he rules, so Plato must keep the monster subordinate within his model. The very name of the beast threatens the model of which it forms a part; after all, the composite beast that contains the many-headed monster is itself a many-headed monster. This, perhaps, is the biggest threat of the multitude: not to overpower the other attributes or classes by rebelling against them, but to make them one with itself. Plato's catalogue of increasingly imperfect cities in Book VIII of *The Republic* shows this process in quasi-historical action, but we can also imagine it in more theoretical terms: the many-headed monster is the Derridean supplement to Plato's civic model, both filling a lack in the original model and threatening to replace the entire model with itself.

For these reasons, as I suggested in chapter 1, the figure of the many-headed monster can be understood through the opposition Gilles Deleuze and Felix Guattari construct between arborescent and rhizomatic systems. Arborescent multiplicities work on a principle of order and articulation, while rhizomatic multiplicities work on a principle of unordered connection and metamorphosis; as Deleuze and Guattari explain:

> Arborescent systems are hierarchical systems with centers of significance and subjectification, central automata like organized memories. . . . Unlike trees or their roots, the rhizome connects any point to any other point, and its traits are not necessarily liked to traits of the same nature; it brings into play very different regimes of signs, and even nonsign states. . . . In contrast to centered (even polycentric) systems with hierarchical modes of communication and preestablished paths, the rhizome is an acentered, nonhierarchical, nonsignifying system without a General and without an organizing memory or central automaton, defined solely by a circulation of states.[2]

Plato's articulate city, modeled on the human body, is the epitome of the arborescent system; it establishes clear vertical hierarchies between different elements, linking each to each through a model of appropriate relations, a fiction of permanence and transparency. Yet it is conjoined with this other figure, a figure of motion and constant change, a figure whose plastic applications take in all these different things. The many-headed monster is intended to be subordinate, and thus arborescent, in the tripartite model of the soul and city, but the terms of the engagement make this impossible.

This threat is most visible in the scenes in which Plato explicitly stages the one against the many—the only times apart from Book VIII's historical survey that the crowded city is present in *The Republic*. Plato's explanation for the necessity of separating the young philosopher from the city is exemplary in this regard; alluding to the dangers of "sitting together in assemblies, in courts, in camps, or in some other public gathering of the crowd," he builds a picture of the malign effects of exposure to multiplicity:

> they object very noisily to some of the things that are said or done, and approve others, in both cases to excess, by shouting and clapping. . . . During such a scene what is the effect on the young man's psyche, as they say? What private training can hold out against this and not be drowned by that kind of censure or approval, not be swept along by the current whithersoever it may carry it, and not declare the same things to be beautiful or ugly as the crowd does. (149)

Clearly, the one cannot stand against the many; the repression the young philosopher must effect against his own many-headed appetites cannot take place in a context that gives too much power to the corporeal multitude. This description parallels Plato's discussion of poets; as the young philosopher risks being corrupted by the opinions of the crowd, so the poet is dangerously protean because he attempts to play to the whole multitude. In each case the threat of the crowd is expressed in theatrical terms: they are figured as an audience, one that has power over the actor before them, not the other way around. Public space in *The Republic* seems to be inherently theatrical, the location for falseness and transformation—the location of the crowd.

At the root of the figure of the many-headed monster, then, is an issue of how urban space should be perceived and represented. Plato's discourse is notoriously antiurban, and *The Republic* is persistently unsure of how to deal with the populous city. Socrates first conceives of the city with as few people as possible, based only upon necessity: "As they need many things, people make use of one another for various purposes. They gather many associates and helpers to live in one place, and to this settlement we give the name of city" (39–40). It is only after the objections of the others that he allows the topic to shift to the luxurious city, "swollen in bulk and filled with a multitude of things which are no longer necessities" (43). From the problems of this excessive, luxurious city develop many of the best known attributes of Plato's republic, particularly the banning of poetry: luxury leads to war, which leads to the need for city militia, which leads to the question of how they should be educated, which leads to the banning of poetry as corruptive and unhealthy. In other words, urban multiplicity is the problem that *The Republic* seeks to solve; to limn the ideal city, Plato must purge it of publicity and crowdedness.

We might then take two overlapping ideological discourses from Plato's use of the many-headed monster. On one level, the intent is clearly to stigmatize the common people by categorizing their stupidity and cupidity. But conjoined with this categorization is the many-headed monster as the opaque figure that threatens the articulate city, a rhizomatic multiplicity connected to scenes of assembly, dissemination, grotesqueness, and theatricality. In short, the many-headed monster is a figure for crowded urban space, the crowded city. But though it is intended as a way of visualizing urban multiplicity, it is itself fundamentally unrepresentable; even in the hands of a clever modeler the many-headed monster cannot be pictured properly, as a tree-system, because inherent to its figuration is the idea of separation and division. The many-headed monster is what all things are threatened to become in the articulate city, having a power to engulf and incorporate, a grotesque body. Deleuze and Guattari say that "rhizomatic multiplicities expose arborescent pseudo-multiplicities for what they are" (8); from Plato on, it could be said, the figure of the crowd is the rhizome that feeds on the tree of social hierarchy.

*   *   *

It is perhaps the awkwardness of this classical figure of the crowd that produces its multiform discursive presence in the sixteenth century. As noted in chapter 1, the most common application of the *topos* of the many-headed monster was to the violence of crowds and the inherent ungovernability of the populace, especially in the context of political upheaval. In Thomas Elyot's *Governor* and Fulke Greville's *Treatise of Monarchy*, for example, it is thus presented as an argument against Athenian democracy and Roman republicanism, respectively, while in Walter Raleigh's *History of the World* it appears as a figure of *vanitas*, a proof of the fragility of popularity and the necessity of a Stoic disposition.[3] In the most extensive critical treatment of the many-headed monster, Christopher Hill has argued that the ubiquity of the trope is based in real or imagined political instability; the denigration of the common populace was necessary to propping up a threatened model of social hierarchy:

> The idea that be many-headed is the same as to be headless is easier to conceive metaphorically than literally. It relates to the theory of degree, to the conception of a graded society in which the feudal household and the family workshop or farm were the basic units. The many-headed monster was composed of masterless men, those for whom nobody responsible answered. Dread and hatred of the masses were often reflected in literature.[4]

Hill is surely right to connect representations of the populace with "the fears of the propertied class" (186), but a basic equation of representation with political anxiety oversimplifies the uses to which the trope of the many-headed monster was put—uses that inevitably partake of the symbolic contradictions inherent to the Platonic model. In *Religio Medici,* for example, Thomas Browne attacks not the common people but the very idea of aggregation:

> If there be any among those common objects of hatred which I can safely say I doe contemne and laugh at, it is that great enemy of reason, vertue and religion, the multitude; that numerous piece of monstrosity, which taken asunder seeme men . . . but confused together, make but one great beast, and a monstrosity more prodigious than Hydra.[5]

In this formulation, assembly itself is a prodigious occurrence, an unnatural conglomeration of bodies, real or imagined, capable of turning men into monsters. To be assembled is to be outside of social order and outside of nature. Browne's disgust is not limited in terms of class; as he says, "neither in the name of Multitude doe I onely include the base and minor sort of people; there is a rabble even amongst the Gentry, a sort of Plebeian heads, whose fancy moves with the same wheele as these" (77). In this description the Platonic associations of the many-headed monster are reinscribed in metaphorical, rather than definitional, terms. Rather than defining a particular class fraction "composed of masterless men," many-headedness becomes a vehicle for describing certain social behaviors and social conditions. To be "Plebeian" is to lose distinction; to be controlled by social forces, moving in their wheel; to be subsumed into a larger, undifferentiated mass.

In rhetorical terms, the many-headed monster is thus an overdetermined location: it is a point at which numerous discourses meet, particularly because of the fluid contradictions inherent to the image. In the proliferation of early modern applications the idea often loses its particular figural quality; many descriptions of the crowd that emphasize the symbolic effects of the concept elide the specific image of many-headedness. In these slippages, which point up the tensions between the abstract and the manifest multitude (as in Plato), the paradoxical qualities of the image of the many-headed monster are revealed. Is it one body with many heads, a figure of division, or many heads joined together, a figure of multiplication? Does its monstrousness result from union, or disorder, or a union that is inherently disorderly, a disunited unity? Perhaps the sheer multiplicity of possible meanings that the phrase produces mirrors the image itself; in this sense (as it might apply in *Coriolanus*), the monstrousness of the idea could be found in its plasticity, transferability, and lack of demarcation.

One of the most extensive and complex appropriations of the discourse of the many-headed monster, and one that clearly shows the supplemental qualities inherent to the model, is found in George Chapman's *Andromeda Liberata,* an epithalamium published in 1614 for the marriage of Frances Howard and Robert Carr, the Earl of Somerset. Presenting the story of Andromeda and Perseus as an allegory of their marriage, the poem portrays Cepheus, the monster that Perseus slays, as the figure of the crowd:

> A whale so monstrous, and so past defence,
> That all the royall Region he laid wast,
> And all the noblest edifices rac't:
> Nor from his plague, were strongest Cities free,
> His bodies vast heape rag'd so heauily.
> *With noblest names and bloods is still embrewd*
> *The monstrous beast, the rauenous Multitude.*[6]

The "rauenous Multitude" is here both explicitly monstrous and implicitly urban, connected with the destruction of cities and described as "like a ruin'd Cittie" at its death by Perseus's hands (sig. D3v). These urban connections are strengthened in the amazing image created for the arrival of the monster at the gates of the city:

> The people greedie of disastrous sights
> And newes, (the food of idle appetites)
> From the kings Chamber, straight knew his intent
> And almost his resolu'd thoughts did preuent

> In drie waues beating thicke about the Shore
> And then came on the prodegie, that bore
> In one masse mixt their Image; that still spread
> A thousand bodies vnder one sole head
> *Of one minde still to ill all ill men are*
> *Strange sights and mischiefes fit the Populare.* (sig. C1)

Chapman emphasizes the connection between the populace and the monster through a vivid juxtaposition: the greedy people swarm around the city in "drie waues" as the prodigious monster approaches the shore, "one masse mixt [in] their Image." As in Plato's descriptions of the actions of the many-headed monster, the scene Chapman presents is theatrical in tone. As if at a Bankside theater, the crowd assembles just outside the gates of the city to watch the spectacle of the noble princess being set upon by their own double, the monster. The doubling of crowd and monster conflates this viewing of the monster's attack and the attack itself; the multitude's eager observance of the scene of Andromeda's rape is itself a sort of rape, a humiliation of the noble virgin before the eyes of the unworthy masses.

Chapman's target in the poem thus seems to be the common people, presenting in quasi-proverbial terms the theory of degree elaborated by Hill. The political context of the poem, however, complicates its rhetorical assertions. Although it begins conventionally, by banishing the populace from the place of the marriage—"Away vngodly Vulgars, far away, / Flie ye prophane, that dare not view the day" (sig. B1)—the lines that follow establish a more particular context:

> Nor speake to men but shadowes, nor would heare
> Of any newes, but what seditious were,
> Hatefull and harmefull euer to the best,
> Whispering their scandals, glorifying the rest,
> Impious, and yet gainst all ills but your owne,
> The hotest sweaters of religion. (sig. B1)

Chapman's delicate subject here is the rumors that surrounded the marriage, particularly the scandalous and sordid trial of Frances Howard during her attempts to annul her prior marriage to Robert Devereux.[7] Rather than simply vilifying the general population, Chapman's diatribe focuses on "our factious brood / Whose forked tongs, wold fain your honor sting," a construction that connects awkwardly with his attacks on "the spleens profane / Of humours errant, and *Plebeian*" (sigs. ¶3, ¶3). As in Browne, what is under attack here is less the plebeians than activities and social dynamics deemed plebeian in character. But where Browne fears aggregation and crowding, Chapman's great anxiety is dissemination and circulation: the dispersed multitude of gossip-mongers that circulate rumors about the marriage. This gossiping, of course, was hardly the province of the common people; it was primarily in the context of the court and the metropolitan gentry that the stories of Frances Howard circulated and spread. The image of the multitude thus moves away from class designations to become a stigma, a way of describing and attacking channels of movement and dissemination that elude direct observation. Chapman's many-headed monster could clearly be described as rhizomatic, as it proceeds from principles of acentered interconnection, illicit appropriation, and unauthorized communication.

Similar themes and tensions are visible in the *Iustification, of A Lately Pvblisht and most maliciously misinterpreted Poeme*, which Chapman felt compelled to publish the following year. Apparently responding to complaints about the focus of his attacks, Chapman begins his vindication of *Andromeda* by claiming that he presented

> the vulgare onely in their vnseuerd herde; as euer in antient tradition of all autenticall Aucthours they haue beene resembled: To whom they were neuer beholding for any fairer Titles; than the base, ignoble, barbarous, giddie multitude; The Monster with many heads.[8]

Through the invocation of "autenticall Aucthours," especially Plato, Chapman authorizes his diatribe and attempts to restrict its range of targets. The frame of the allusion widens and shifts again, however, when he turns to discussing the reception and circulation of his poem:

> For the violent hoobub, setting my song to their owne tunes, haue made it yeeld so halfhand distastefull a sound to my best friends, that my Integritie, euen they hold affected with the shrill echo thereof, by reflexion, receuing it the mouthes of others. (sig. *4–*4v)

"The violent hoobub" crosses the boundaries of Chapman's philosophical distinction, figuring both the "vnseuerd herd" and the readers of the poem, who have appropriated its structures and transformed its meaning. As in the scene described outside the city walls, representation collapses into its reception: as Andromeda was threatened with defilement by the "monstrous beast," so *Andromeda* has been ravished by its entry into the marketplace of rumor. Chapman describes the maligning of his poem as a thread spread "into the eares of the manie . . . where multiplying and getting strength it was spred into an Artificiall webbe, to entangle my poore poeticall flie" (sig. *4v). In this image, what the "eares of the manie" produce is multiplicity; the thread of rumor becomes many threads, tangled together, in which the author finds himself helpless. Chapman's twin works demonstrate a continual process of falling into the multitude, of being forced to move with its wheel, through an intertwining of theatricality and dissemination. The noble princess is attacked by the monster; this spectacle is greedily watched by the urban crowd; the poem's censuring presentation of this theatrical dynamic becomes fodder itself for the multitude. In the poem, Cepheus threatens to destroy the city, but the behavior of the populace demonstrates that the city is already destroyed and cannot be saved by Andromeda's sacrifice; as the poem's subsequent circulation confirms, the city of Andromeda and *Andromeda* has wholly been given over to the many-headed monster and its debasing entertainments. By publishing his poem, Chapman has himself staged the monster to the multitude. Rather than stopping the city's devouring of Frances Howard, his intervention has only increased its violent appetite.

In this conjunction of base theatricality, the alleged appetites of the common people, the urban circulation of rumor, and the threatened destruction of the city, Chapman's deployment of the many-headed monster bears a remarkable resemblance to the use of the trope in contemporary attacks on the theater. The antitheatrical discourse is the location of some of the most explicit and intense invocations of the many-headed monster as a violent mass. The theaters were, of course, often the site of actual crowd violence. But the attacks made on the theaters around the figure of the violent multitude suggest something more at stake—something specifically related to the idea of the city. Antitheatrical writings have attracted a great deal of critical attention, but what has often been overlooked is the extent to which they frame their discourse in urban terms.[9] What the antitheatricalists do, I want to suggest, is analyze the crowded city through the language of theatricality; the figure of the theater stands as a symbolic representation of the crowded city. As in Chapman's mimetic opposition between the drama of the monster and the monstrous crowd that watches it, the antitheatrical discourse creates parallels between the theater as a physical location for crowds and as the dramatic performance that catalyzes the rhizomatic dynamics of the crowded city. And as in Chapman's account of his poem's entry into these dynamics, what is produced is a range of issues surrounding gathering, circulation, dissemination, and violence.

At times the civic discourse presented in the antitheatrical tracts is explicitly Platonic. I.G., in *A Refutation of the Apology for Actors*, notes that, "Plato disputing of the true perfection of a Citty, would haue Poets banished from that society, as enemies to the Cities full perfection," a note also struck by Stephen Gosson in *The Schoole of Abuse:* "Plato . . . gaue them all Drummes entertainment, not suffering them once to shew their faces in a reformed common wealth."[10] But less specific urban contexts are also frequently employed. In *Plays Confuted in 5 Actions*, Gosson opines, "The fayrest citie in the worlde may bee ouerthrowen, with lesse charge, lesse labor, lesse time, than it can bee builte," later offering a historical example of the same: "The noble *Scipio Nasica* perceiuing that the Citie cannot longe endure whose walles stande and manners fall, when hee sawe the whole Senate bent to builde upp Theaters, and set out Playes, with earnest persuasion drewe them from it."[11] In *A Mirrour of Monsters*, William Rankins employs the prophetic language of the Jeremiad and the imagery of Jerusalem's fall and the Babylonian captivity, figuring virtue as an urban edifice leveled by the catastrophe of theatrical folly:

> Where humaine mindes might easilie behold Vertue dismembered, her Towers throwne downe, her bulwarks battered, her walls wasted, her stately buildings beaten downe with these barbarous minded mates: her Treese bereft of leaues, and now against Nature inhabited rather by beasts of the field, and foules of the ayre, then by the mindes of men, such enmitie is there sworne betweene Vertue and Follie.[12]

This civic attack on the theater is often put forward in more corporeal language, in terms of various sources of contamination or uncleanness in the urban body. The theaters, says the *Refutation*, reside in the suburbs because "the honorable Citie of London hath spued them out from within her Walles," rejecting them from the body of the city (sig. A4v). Gosson's *Schoole of Abuse*, which includes a letter to the Lord Mayor of London urging him to ban the playhouses, also employs bodily language in its image of the walled city: "I cannot thinke that Cittie to be safe, that strikes downe her Percollices, rammes up her gates, and suffereth the enimie to enter the posterne."[13] In this sodometrical image the theater is portrayed as an ejected presence that threatens to return to commit a preposterous and defiling violence on the city. *This Worlds Folly* imagines the theaters as "menstruous rags" that "besoil and coinquinate" the "whole vesture" of the city.[14] Here the associations between the theater and the crowded city are made apparent, for what is the pollution trapped by the theater except the bloody filth of its citizenry? While Thomas Heywood argued in his *Apology for Actors* that the theater is "an ornament to the Citty,"[15] the antitheatricalist discourse suggests that the theater is a blemish or contaminant, a prodigious mark on the urban body that threatens its destruction.

It is the urban *bodies* of the theater audience, however, that receive some of the strongest attacks. The *Refutation* suggests that it is "in generall the vulgar sort" who "runne madding vnto playes" (sig. I1), while in the *2nd and 3rd Blast of Retrait from Plaies and Theaters*, Anthony Munday describes the audience in monstrous terms:

> They are alwaies eating, & never satisfied; ever seeing, and never contented; continualie hearing, & never wearied; they are greedie of wickednes, and wil let no time, nor spare for anie weather (so great is their devotion to make their pilgrimage) to offer their penie to the Divel.[16]

As Jean Howard has shown, the primary attack made against the theaters is that they corrupt and alter their audiences with the complementary sins of idleness and falseness.[17] The disparaging tone that the antitheatricalists take with the playhouse audiences could thus be understood as refuting the basic contention of apologists such as Thomas Nashe or Heywood, that plays instruct their audiences in correct social behavior and position. *This Worlds Folly* offers an assessment of the lessons available at the theater: "More haue recourse to Playing houses, then to Praying houses, where they set open their eares & eies to suck vp variety of abhominations, bewitching their minds with extrauagant thoughts" (sig. B1v). Indeed it is often the theater crowd itself that is deemed to pervert the possibility of learning. For the author of *This Worlds Folly*, it is the multitude in the audience who call the tune; speaking of the actors, he writes, "and by howe much more exact these are in their mimicke venerean action, by so much more highly are they seated in the Monster-headed Multitudes estimation" (sig. B2–B2v). The *Refutation* makes a similar judgment: "when that great maister the multitude is added also, and the whole company swarming on euery side vnto vices, then chiefly are wee infected with depraued opinion, and drawne from our very expresse nature" (sig. F1v). In more moderate language, the *2nd and 3rd Blast* explains the apparent problem:

> the opinions of the rude multitude are not alwais the soundest, which are mooved with unconstant motions, where by manietimes they like

of that which is most hirtful; and dislike that which is most profitable.
(sig. D6)

Yet the complaints about the multitude at the theaters can also be understood, as Munday's image of the multitude "mooved with unconstant motions" suggests, within the rhizomatic model I have been sketching. Munday's focus on the movement of the crowd correlates to their "swarming on every side," their "venereal action," and even their "extravagant thoughts"; this conjunction of images of illicit motion limns the dynamics of gathering and dispersal that underlie the rhizomatic understanding of multiplicity.

It thus was not only the evils of theatrical *display* that animated the tract writers, but the evils of theatrical *crowding* as well. In discussing the scene of the playhouse—what Gosson calls a "Gordians knot of disorder," where, as Munday writes, "the people disperse themselues" and "the whole multitude reuel it out"—the antitheatricalists continually emphasize the grotesque and violent nature of the crowding that takes place.[18] For Gosson, plays are the work of the devil and "drag such a monstrous taile after them, as is able to sweep whole Cities into his lap" (sig. B6–B6v) "Truly," says John Northbrooke, "you may see dayly what multitudes are gathered togither at those Plaies, of al sortes, to the great displeasure of almighty GOD, and daunger of their soules."[19] The tracts resound with the descriptions of "Th'usuall flocking and gadding . . . to these Play-Houses and ydle places of entercourse," where "you shall haue them flocke thether thicke and threefolde," where "people in heapes daunce to the diuell."[20] Theater and collective violence are inextricably linked in these descriptions, not only through the spread of sedition and the instruction in vice, but also through the very act of gathering the multitude together. In the view of the antitheatricalists, violence is the inevitable outcome of theater in both real and symbolic terms because the institution of the theater exemplifies and heightens the unsettling and disorderly dynamics of the rhizomatic urban populace. The theater is a magnet that gathers people, and that gathering together is the source of social disorder.

In *Plays Confuted in 5 Actions,* Gosson explicates the contradictory dynamics of the urban crowd through the explicit citation of the many-headed monster:

The rudest of the people are sometime ravished with every giewgawe, sometime so heavie, that they runne together by heapes, they know not whither; and lay about with theire clobbes, they see not why. Which thing the auncient Philosophers considering called them a monster of many heades. If the common people which resorte to Theaters being but an assemblie of Tailors, Tinkers, Cordwayners, Saylers, Olde Men, Yong Men, Women, Boyes, Girles, and such like, be the judges of faultes there painted out, the rebuking of manners in that place, is neyther lawfull nor convenient, but to be held for a kinde of libelling, and defaming.[21]

Two ideas are juxtaposed in this passage. In the first part, Gosson uses the idea of the multitude to justify his association of theater and violence; the gewgaws of the theater catalyze a chaotic energy inside the multitude so that they "runne together by heapes" and break out into random, disordered violence. In the second part, what is emphasized is the corresponding circulatory aspect of the urban crowd, the idea that the theater disseminates to the population an inappropriate knowledge, revealing or inventing things about the elite that should not be aired in this environment. The idea of application, the allusion to contemporary events, was of course one of the most vexed issues for the theater, and one of the few circumstances where playwrights could get into serious trouble. But the circulatory and disseminating power of the theater was not just condemned on those grounds. The *Refutation* complains of "the multitude, who chiefly run flocking to the Play-house, that they might make mirth of such folly and laugh at it, and that they might tell it to others when they come home, to make more fooles laugh for company" (sig. D3). Phillip Stubbes's *Anatomie of Abuses* makes the same case in more perverse terms:

> marke the flockyng and runnyng to Theaters and Curtens, daylie and hourelie, night and daie, tyme and tide, to see Plaies and Enterludes, where suche wanton gestures, such bawdie speeches: suche laughyng and flearyng: suche kissyng and bussyng: suche clippyng and culling: such wincking and glauncing of wanton eyes, and the like is vsed, as is wonderful to beholde. Then these goodly Pageantes beeyng ended, euery mate sortes to his mate, euery one bringes an other homewarde of their waie very freendly, and in their secrete conclaues (couertly) they plaie the Sodomite, or worse.[22]

Stubbes's sodometrical imagery is striking, but what is even more significant is that theatergoers *play* the sodomite; deviant theatricality is imagined as continuing beyond the theater into the city, infiltrating its nooks and crannies, persisting in the movement from public stage to secret conclaves.

As *This Worlds Folly* declares, "what voice is heard in our streets? Not but the squeaking out of those . . . obscene and light jigs, stuffed with loathsome and unheard-of ribaldry, sucked from the poisonous dugs of sin-swelled theatres" (sig. B1v). In this portrayal, the theater is everywhere in the city, an ineradicable disorder distributed throughout the urban space by the movement of the multitude. The *Mirrour of Monsters* says, "Players by sticking of their bils in London, defile the streetes with their infectious filthines" (sig. C2). This language of infectious theater persistently recurs, particularly in symbolic forms. John Rainoldes, in *Th'Overthrow of Stage Plays,* offers a curious story out of Lucian, describing the fate of the city of Adbera:

> Where, when at midsummer, in very hott weather, *Andromeda* (a Tragedie of *Euripides*) being played, manie brought home a burning ague from the theater: about the seuenth day folowing . . . all . . . did fall into a strange distemper and passion of a light phrensie. The which exciting them to say & cry aloude such things as were sticking freshly in their memorie, and had affected most their minde, they grewe all to Tragedie-playing. . . . So that the whole citie was full of pale and thinne folke, pronouncing like stage-players, and braying with a loude voice. (sig. Q1v)

The scene is comic, perhaps more so than Rainoldes intended, but the image it conjures up is disturbing in its implications. Like Chapman's poem, this *Andromeda* disseminates from the scene of its performance through the entire city; as the plague of the theater spreads, each citizen becomes a stage-player, turning the entire space of the city into a confusing cacophony of random performances. In a way, we are taken back to the territory of Plato's republic, where the metaphor of theatrical performance characterizes the corrupting effects of urban multiplicity; here, instead of the Platonic articulate city, we have a city that feverishly articulates shreds and patches of theatrical speech. Plato imagines a city purged of random, anonymous multiplicity, though the banning of poetry and the rule of the wise. The antitheatricalists look out on a city completely polluted and infected by the theater, a city that could only be rendered articulate through a Platonic ban.

*　*　*

It is perhaps to be expected that such attacks on the crowded city would be found in the antitheatricalist discourse, pursuing a Platonic dream of urban purification. What is more striking is the congruence between these attacks and the representations of crowds in early modern drama. We might consider the language employed in

Hamlet, at the sole moment where the public world appears ready to inundate the private space of the play:

> *Messenger.*   Save yourself, my lord!
> The ocean, overpeering of his list,
> Eats not the flats with more impiteous haste
> Than young Laertes, in a riotous head,
> O'erbears your officers. The rabble call him lord,
> And as the world were now to begin,
> Antiquity forgot, custom not known,
> The ratifers and props of every word,
> They cry, "Choose we, Laertes shall be king!" (4.5.99–108)

In this hysterical description the discourse of the many-headed monster is invoked, showing the crowd as the mindless, rebellious common herd ready to throw off the constraints of order and custom, to forget history and rebel against authority. The messenger's evocation presages a new world and a new ending to the play, a breach in the paranoiac bounds of the palace. Such a breach does not occur, of course. Laertes bursts into the room with his followers, then sends them away before he addresses Claudius; after a brief and somewhat comical protest, the crowd leaves to "keep the door" and allows the play to revert to the doubled family romance that governs its actions. Nevertheless, this brief appearance concretizes the *Hamlet's* muted concern with the multitude, if only in ironic terms. Claudius's response to the intrusion is both to gird himself with the pieties of royal invulnerability—"There's such divinity doth hedge a king / That treason can but peep to what it would / Acts little of his will" (4.5.124–26)—and to explain his lack of action against Hamlet through another crowd, "the general gender" (4.7.18), described earlier as "the distracted multitude" that "like not in their judgment, but their eyes, / And where 'tis so, th'offender's scourge is weigh'd, / But never the offense" (4.3.4–7). This was a theatrical commonplace, of course; Samuel Daniel's *Philotas*, for example, sounds a similar note: "Here shall you see how th'easie multitude / Transported, take the partie of distresse; / And only out of passions doe conclude, / Not out of iudgement of mens practises."[23] The underlying point is Platonic, as the power of emotion to cloud reason is a prime argument for banishing poetry.

However, the metaphorical theatrical implications of the "distracted multitude" in *Hamlet* are connected to the immediate context of playhouse practices by the echo of Hamlet's earlier punning response to the Ghost, that he will remember him "while memory holds a seat / In this distracted Globe" (1.5.96–97). In his analysis of the role of memory in the liminal dynamics of Shakespearean epilogues, Robert Weimann argues that this image of the "distracted Globe" carries strong implications of the commercial or mercantile business of the stage, the necessity of disseminating the memory of the play beyond the event, producing thereby a return to the theater. He suggests that the epilogues involve "the underlying circulation of authority, including the authorization of spectators to recollect, discuss, and reappropriate the performed play after its theatrical transaction is over."[24] This insight provides a way to begin to understand the theatrical dynamics inherent in dramatic treatments of the multitude.[25] In *Hamlet,* the distracted multitude is the invisible offstage audience who watch the events in the palace, who necessarily misinterpret (in Claudius's view) the progress of the story, who rise up unexpectedly with the arrival of Laertes and disappear just as quickly. But the distracted multitude is also connected to Elsinore's double, the city that the tragedians have been forced to leave because of "innovation" (2.2.332), where "the general" feed on plays and reject them if their sallets are not savory enough, and where the fickleness of the crowd and the dangers of popularity have a commercial and quotidian background. Play and performance thus merge, and the problem of satisfying the distracted Globe crosses with the representation of political authority.

The implications of *Hamlet's* engagement with the multitude become clearer through their rewriting in Francis Beaumont and John Fletcher's *Philaster: or, Love lies a-bleeding. Philaster* depends on *Hamlet* for many things, especially its portrait of Philaster as a melancholy and possibly unstable prince, disinherited from his rightful patrimony; the points of contact between the two plays' treatment of the larger public world that surrounds them are highlighted in the denouement of *Philaster,* where the city rises against the usurping King of Calabria and his accomplice, the Spanish prince Pharamond. Pharamond, having "gone to see the city / And the new platform" (5.3.2–3), has been taken prisoner by its citizens, who now storm toward the palace "led by an old gray ruffian who comes on / In rescue of the lord Philaster" (116–18). Panicked, the King releases the imprisoned Philaster to go and calm the city. In the next scene the mutinous citizens take the stage with their captive Pharamond, whom they threaten with extreme violence: "I could hulk your grace and hang you up cross-legg'd like a hare at a poulter's" (5.4.30–32). The language of "hulking," or disemboweling, intensifies as the scene progresses, with the "old gray ruffian" instructing his followers to "branch me his skin in flowers like a satin, and between each flower a mortal cut. Your royalty shall ravel. Jag him, gentlemen. I'll have him cut to the kell, then down the seams" (38–41). This corporeal unraveling of the prince reaches its climax in a lengthy projected dismemberment of Pharamond's noble body:

1 Cit.   I'll have a leg, that's certain.
2 Cit.   I'll have an arm.
3 Cit.   I'l have his nose, and at mine own charge build a college and clap't upon the gate.
4 Cit.   I'll have his little gut to string a kit with, for certainly a royal gut will sound like silver.
Pha.   Would they were in thy belly, and I past my pain once.
5 Cit.   Good Captain, let me have his liver to feed ferrets.
Cap.   Who will have parcels else? Speak.
Pha.   Good gods, consider me! I shall be tortur'd.
1 Cit.   Captain, I'l give you the trimming of your two-hand sword and let me have his skin to make false scabbards.
2 Cit.   He had no horns sir, had he?
Cap.   No sir, he's a pollard. What woulds thou do with horns?
2 Cit.   Oh, if he had had, I would have made rare hafts and whistles of 'em; but his shin bones, if they be sound, shall serve me. (58–75)

In this extraordinary passage, the trajectory of dismemberment is made clear; Pharamond's body, figured first as a dressed beast in a merchant's shop and then an unstitched royal fabric, now metamorphoses into site for commercial scavenging, with his skin used for scabbards, his bones for whistles, his guts for string. The imagery is less of destruction than of appropriation. The body of the prince circulates into the economy of the city; through dismemberment, Pharamond is rendered functional.

With this *urbs ex machina* climax *Philaster* answers *Hamlet*, showing the urban crowd appropriating the space of the stage and writing their own ending to the play; we might say that the fear expressed at the end of *Henry VIII* here comes to pass, as the citizens burst past the barriers and stand on the platform itself. In this regard, the actions of the crowd reflect larger social issues, of course; the intermittent violence of apprentices was well known, and the treatment of the Spanish prince reflects contemporary attacks on Spaniards during the period, such as the mobbing of the Spanish nobleman during the 1617 Lord Mayor's Show, noted in chapter 2. Still, despite these historical contexts the principal dynamic of the crowd's appropriation is theatrical. Visiting "the new platform" in the city—perhaps visiting a new theater?—Pharamond encounters the crowd, who have followed the plot of *Philaster* from the outset and are now determined to end it in the manner they desire. In this determination, the denouement resembles nothing so much as Beaumont and Fletcher's first collaboration, *The Knight of the Burning Pestle,* in which common theatergoers leap on stage and demand a play more to their liking.

Facing the crowd, the King in *Philaster* declares: "How they swarm together! What a hum they raise! Devils, choke your wild throats" (5.3.152–53). In descriptions such as these we see the play's fundamental ambivalence toward the city that it stages. Although the entry of the crowd saves *Philaster,* the action of the crowd is largely presented in terms of chaos and confusion—even by Philaster himself, who echoes the messenger in *Hamlet:* "let me stand the shock / Of this mad sea-breach, which I'll either turn / Or perish with it" (185–87). If in the actions and voices of the urban crowd we see the city of *Philaster* articulating its desires, the terms in which that articulation takes place are remarkably disarticulated, from the perspective of those that observe them. Put another way, the articulation of the city's multiplicity is always subtended by its disarticulating tendencies— here shown most explicitly through the prospective disarticulation of Pharamond. In Chapman's *Andromeda* the rhizomatic patterns of urban circulation are represented as a savage physical attack on the noble body of Frances Howard; *Philaster* implies something similar through the subsuming of Pharamond's body into the mercantile processes of the city. This representation shows the "distracted multitude" in the full range of meanings that "distracted" had in the early modern period: not only fickle or mad, but also divided, dispersed, and *dismembered;* in other words, the rhizomatic urban crowd with which the theater must engage.[26]

If this eruption of extreme comic violence into the stately context of Beaumont and Fletcher's play is unusual in early modern drama, the impulses behind it are ubiquitous in contemporary stagings of the crowd. In this regard we might take *Philaster* as paradigmatic of concerns that can be seen across a wide variety of plays. In the following selective inventory of dramatic invocations of the many-headed monster, I want to suggest that the deployment of the figure of the crowd always functions metatheatrically, doubling the playhouse audience in order to comment on the purpose and practice of urban playing. What we see in these portrayals of the crowd is not simply the prejudices of the age, or the commonplace rhetoric of kings and nobles, but a specific and deliberate attempt to link the space of the play with the space of its performance—a linkage, as I will go on to argue, that not only dramatizes the circulation of theatrical authority but engages complexly with the crowded city upon which the theater depends.

Self-referential language about the many-headed monster pervades early modern drama, both through direct appeal and indirect allusion. Near the beginning of John Marston's *The Malcontent*, Altofronto blames the discordant multitude for his political fall:

> the crowd
> Still lickerous of untried novelties,
> Impatient with severer government,
> Made strong with Florence, banished Altofront. (1.1.217–20)

His return to power is partly effected by the crowd as well; Celso, his deputy, keeps close watch on "that beast with many heads / The staggering multitude," and informs Altofronto when popular opinion has returned to his side (3.1.93–94). The dovetailing of the action of the play and the attitudes of this unseen multitude almost suggests, as in *Philaster*, that this populace is watching *The Malcontent* and changing its judgments on its rulers accordingly. Similarly, the curse of the imprisoned Appius on "the Hydra-headed multitude, / That only gape for innovation" (5.2.2–3) in Webster's *Appius and Virginia* suggests the possibility, as in *Hamlet*, of a theatrical and commercial valence to "innovation" as well as a political one—a connection emphasized and strengthened by his following lines:

> The same hands
> That yesterday to hear me conscionate,
> And Oratorize, rung shril Plaudits forth
> In sign of grace, now in contempt and scorn
> Hurry me to this place of darkness. (10–14)[27]

In Thomas Middleton's *Mayor of Queenborough*, Vortiger begins the play by crying out "Will that wide-throated beast, the multitude, / Never leave bellowing?" (1.1.1–2), complaining that "this forkèd rabble, / With their infectious acclamations, / Poison'd my fortunes for Constantine's sons" (6–8).[28] These introductory lines of the play, positioned in the liminal space between the dramatic narrative and its theatrical manifestation, strongly indicate the incorporation of the playhouse audience into the frame of the play: a request for silence from the chattering playgoers modulates into the political pretext for the action of the drama. A different sort of theatrical incorporation is perhaps visible in Rumor's prologue to *2 Henry IV*, which reports the circulation of misunderstood tales of Shrewsbury, the battle that ended *1 Henry IV*. In taxing the theater audience, "the blunt monster with uncounted heads" (Ind.18), with similar misunderstandings, and describing this urban gathering as "my household" (22), Rumor's description might figure the extra-theatrical circulation of the earlier play, taken out of the control of the players and spread through the city in multiple and imperfect forms.

These plays show a consistent use of the discourse of the many-headed monster to frame and reflect the theatrical performance of the play. Often the conspicuousness inherent to the theater (and on which the theater relied for its business) is represented through the dangerously visible space the main characters find themselves in. At the start of Thomas Dekker's *Lusts Dominion*, the Moor Eleazar complains to his lover, the Queen Mother of Spain, that "I cannot ride through the Castilian streets / But thousand eies through windows, and through doors / Throw killing looks at me," and accuses her of arming "this many-headed beast" through her profligate actions (sig. C7). As the play progresses, Eleazar and the Queen turn this urban space of extreme visibility to their advantage; the Queen tells her agents to "tickle the ears of the Rude multitude, / With Eleazar's praises" and accusations of bastardy against her son Philip, heir to the throne (sig. C7). After the agents speak these libels to the crowd in the marketplace of Seville, a "rout of Stinkards" (sig. D12v) attack the palace, causing the Queen to echo the messenger in *Hamlet:* "the madde people / Tempestuous like the Sea, run up and down, / Some crying kill the bastard, some the Moor" (sig. E2v–E3). Eleazar responds haughtily:

> I rusht amongst the thickest of their crowdes
> And with a countenance Majestical
> Like the Imperious Sun disperst their cloudes;
> I have perfum'd the rankness of their breath,
> And by the magick of true eloquence,
> Transform'd this many headed *Cerebus,*
> This py'd-Camelion, this beast multitude,
> Whose power consists in number, pride in threats;
> Yet melt like snow when Majestie shines forth
> This heap of fools, who crowding in huge swarms,
> Stood at our Court gates like a heap of dung,

> Recking and shouting out contagious breath
> of power to poison all the elements;
> This Wolf I held by'th eare, and made him tame,
> And made him tremble at the Moors great name. (sig. E3)

The marketplace circulation of stories about royal affairs turns into a scene of theatrical crowding, with the palace as the stage, surrounded by a "rout of Stinkards" who display all the characteristics of theater audiences commonplace to satirical accounts. Eleazar, in response, positions himself in Orphic terms, taming "this many headed *Cerebus*"—an image that perhaps foreshadows his eventual fall, as Orpheus was dismembered by the riotous Maenads. Political readings of the myth of Orpheus were commonplace in the Renaissance, interpreting Orpheus as a figure for civility and urbane eloquence opposing itself to the savagery of the common people; we might recall the words of the author of *Apologie of the Cittie of London*, discussed in chapter 1, who describes the city as a place where men "are withdrawn from barbarous feritie and force to a certaine mildnes of manners."[29] The main context here, though, is a sort of theatrical brinkmanship: Eleazar, the villain of the play, asserts his ability to lord over the citizens of both Seville and London, to cow the opposition he might find in the theater audience, to overpower the rank breath of the London crowd with true eloquence. Where is Lust's dominion? Beyond the usurped state of Spain, perhaps it is exactly where the antitheatricalists would place it: the space of the theater, and the space of the crowded city.

The first part of Dekker's *Sir Thomas Wyatt*, which chronicles the drama surrounding Lady Jane Grey and Queen Mary's accession, revolves around a series of political spectacles staged for the multitude—who, like the multitudes of *The Malcontent*, "gape for noueltie" (2.2.17). In the third act, set in the Tower of London, the imprisoned Jane gestures at the crowds outside her cell, probably in the direction of the theater audience, and echoes the earlier comment: "Out of this firme grate, you may perceiue / The Tower-Hill thronged with store of people, / As if they gap'd for some strange Noueltie" (3.2.11–13). Guildford amplifies her comment:

> see you how the people stand in heapes,
> Each man sad, looking on his aposed obiect,
> As if a generall passion possest them?
> Their eyes doe seeme, as dropping as the Moone,
> As if prepared for a Tragedie.
> For neuer swarmes of people there doe tread,

> But to rob life, and to inrich the dead
> And shewe they wept. (3.2.23–30)

The spectacle of punishment and the spectacle of the theater cross here; stage and scaffold become interchangeable, as the tragedy of Jane's impending execution is figured as the play that it is. The second part of the play focuses on Wyatt's rebellion against Mary because of her proposed marriage to King Philip of Spain. Instructed to lead the city's defense against Wyatt, the "sword and Buckler-men of London" (4.2.20) decide instead to join the attack on London because "Wyat is up to keepe the Spaniard's down" (44); as their leader says, "Wyat for rising thus . . . is worthy to be hang'd—like a Ieuell in the Kingdomes eare, say I well my Lads?" (33–35). When they all reach the city gates, however, the Earl of Pembroke appears "vpon the Walles" to block Wyatt's entry:

> Auaunt thou Traitor, thinkes thou by forgerie
> To enter London with rebellious armes?
> Knowe that these gates are bard against thy entrance
> And it shall cost the liues of twentie thousand
> True subiects to the Queene before a Traytor enters. (4.3.19–23)

Faced with this setback, the London crowd deserts Wyatt, leaving him alone on the stage to lament: "O London, London, thou perfidious Town, / Why hast thou broke thy promise to thy friend" (44–45). In this narrative we are given a double picture of London. The keeping of the city walls against Wyatt, a scene that might have been taken from Heywood's *Edward IV,* portrays the city in patriotic terms, as demonstrating its arborescent integrity by holding off an external invader; against this, the crowd that first supports and then abandons Wyatt is the rhizomatic city, described with the stigmas of the many-headed monster. This dramatic supplement allows Dekker to solve the problem of the play's reception—how does one present a popular, anti-Spanish hero as a villain?—by putting the problem itself on stage; the pattern of the city's loyalty to Wyatt and then its rejection of him traces the path that the play must follow with its own audience, leading them from sympathy for the play's hero to estrangement from him. But more could be at stake. Surely in dramatizing the crowd's abandonment of Wyatt the possible fate of *Wyatt* may be signaled: will memory hold its seat in this distracted Globe?

The explicit context of all these multitudes is clearly political, of course, and it is thus correct on one level to see these plays as working through the dynamics of political hierarchy identified by Hill. Such linkings of political visibility and theatricality are commonplace in the period, and certainly one available reading of these scenes would be as an exposure and implicit critique of the theatrical basis of the display of state power. In Philip Massinger's *The Emperor of the East,* the theatrical metaphor is expressed in terms that recall the antitheatrical attacks on protean shapeshifting:

> O the miserable
> Condition of a Prince! who though hee varie
> More shapes then Proteus in his minde, and manners,
> Hee cannot winne a universall suffrage,
> From the many-headed monster, Multitude. (2.1.95–99)[30]

The foundation of this exclamation is Plato's argument against popular government: to govern effectively one must ignore the populace, because no one ruler can be all things to all subjects. As its appearance in *Coriolanus* suggests, the trope of ephemeral political popularity is a commonplace; the drama of the period is full of those who rise and fall on popularity, or are alleged to. However, the dynamic introduced by framing these discussions in the context of the many-headed monster suggests that the source of the theatrical power of the state, as I have been arguing throughout the preceding chapters, comes from the audience, and furthermore suggests a population for whom the line between political and commercial theatrical displays, between ritual and entertainment, is blurred. And in this blurring is the possibility of reversing the metaphor, and imagining political power as an analogue for the shifting and unstable power and position of the theater in the city. In the figure of the giddy, many-headed multitude we can see the theater's urban audience, who misinterpret, who continually judge by emotion, who are wayward, who make demands, who gape for innovation, who show no reason in their theatrical appreciation.

As Richard Helgerson and others have argued, the theater was engaged in a process of defining its place in the national culture and the city, and it is possible to construe negative portrayals of the rude multitude in terms of social class, a desire to purge out the common herd in favor of the privileged judicious spectator.[31] This was certainly a rhetorical tactic always available, as in *Hamlet,* to explain a theatrical failure. But given the necessity of staging to the common multitude in the large amphitheaters, I think that the real dynamic at play is the theater's relationship not to its *immediate* audience but to the larger urban multitude, the absent and imaginary audience that cannot be grasped, that have the power to make or break a theatrical venture. Rather than simply a present crowd, the many-headed monster is the rhizomatic city, at once itself and the principles of infinite connectability and acentered communication that characterize the movement of information in the metropolis. In this formulation, the relations between the city, the theater, and the crowd become more complex, less about their actual conjunction in the space of the city and more about the symbolic relationships that can be established between them. We might imagine the theater, as both a cultural and commercial institution, as being caught between the ideal, articulate city and the random, disarticulate mass of people that manifest the city in the playhouse; to stage or invoke this mass is to mediate between these terms.[32]

This idea of negotiating between theater, crowd, and city is especially visible in Marston's *Histriomastix,* which, as noted in the first chapter, contains a great attack on the city by "this common beast the multitude" (5.4.29).[33] This attack culminates in a scene of great confusion, one that echoes *2 Henry VI* and other plays:

> Enter all the factions of Noblemen, Peasants, and Cittizens fighting: the ruder sorte drive in the rest and cry a sacke, a sacke, Havoke Havocke, Burne the Lawiers bokes; teare the Silkes out of the shops: in that confusion: the Scholler scaping from among them, they all go out and leave him upon the Stage. (s.d. 5.7)

The play's estates satire here turns into pitched battle, resulting in the sack of the city; since the nobles and citizens are central, named characters and the peasants are anonymous extras, the scene further involves the wresting of the stage and the play from the hands of its principals. Chrisoganus, the "Scholler" who escapes from this urban catastrophe, occupies a liminal position in the drama; he describes the effects of the entry of the multitude to the theater audience:

> Witness the present Chaos of our Sceane,
> Where every streete is chain'd with linckes of spoile,
> Heere proud Ambition rides; there Furie flies,
> Heere Horror; and there ruthlesse Murder stalkes,
> Led on by Ruine, and in Steele and fire,
> That now on toppes of houses; now in vaults,
> Now in the sacred Temples; heere, and there
> Runnes wilde. (5.7.17–24)

The chaos of the scene recalls the *topos* of the "Triumph of Death" that Michael Neill has discussed in the context of plays like

Tamburlaine—with Ambition, Horror, and Fury taking control of the streets and Murder figured as stalking Tamburlaine himself—but it also represents a parodic inversion of the symbolic architecture of civic pageantry and the royal entry: the linked streets hold back urban spoils, not the urban crowd, the city is transformed not into *camera regis* but into a civic conflagration, destroying all.[34]

The "rude multitude" that brings in such wreckage is clearly rural in character; at the start of Act Five, War commands Fury to "goe now and fill / The trunck of Peasants with thy dangerous breath, / Inspire them with the spirit of Mutiny" (5.1.14–16). Despite this ascription, however, the sort of opposition between urban order and rural disorder that frames plays such as *The Death of Jack Straw* is problematic here. Part of the problem is that "the multitude" of *Histriomastix* seems to comprise more than just these ravening peasants. In Act Two, Philarchus, in retort to Chrisoganus's attacks on the idle behavior of the nobility, quotes, "Tis still safe erring with the multitude" (2.1.61), establishing the term as a commonplace and proverbial wisdom; later, Pryde stings the wealthy citizens by saying, "Are you not Lawyers, from whose reverend lippes / Th' amazed multitude learne Oracles?" (4.1.37–38), clearly indicating something other than the peasantry. In response to Chrisoganus's attacks on their repertory, the player Gutt says, "Will not our owne stuff serve the multitude?," to which Chrisoganus replies, "Write on, crie on, yawle to the common sort / Of thickskin'd auditours" (4.4.10, 11–12). As in Chapman, the narrow class identifications of the multitude shift and widen, incorporating within them the language of cultural dissemination and circulation.

It is the relation of the players to the rampaging multitude that is most interesting. The players are a poor sort of rude mechanicals who have turned to traveling players because of the peace and plenty that rule the land. This catalyst strangely parallels some of the antitheatrical attacks; in the *2nd and 3rd Blast*, a similar story is told of Rome:

> For in those daies everie part of the Romane empire was in health and sound . . . citizens did abound in wealth and pleasure, so that it was verie hard in such aboundance of al things, for religion to continue pure, and manners uncorrupt. Then everie where Autors of filtie pleasure were cherished; for in al places men were fat. (sig. C3v–C4)

Histriomastix similarly charts the movement from Peace and Plenty to War and Ruin, and the eventual return of Peace after a purgatorial time of poverty and repentance. The description of the players' rise and fall seems like an origin myth or potted history of the English theater; we see them begin as country bumpkins crying plays in the marketplace, meet with success in playing noble houses, and eventually make their way to the city. In this movement from the rural to the urban, the trajectory of the theater matches that of the "rude multitude" who destroy the city, turning it into a scene of theatrical violence. With this parallel, we might wonder how much culpability is being ascribed to the theater. As war erupts in the city, the players are pressed into the army; immediately before the entry of the multitude described above, one soldier says to the players, "Sirha is this you would rend and teare the Cat / Upon a Stage, and now march like a drown'd rat? / Looke up and play the Tamburlaine: you rogue you" (4.6.4–6). The moment is comic, but the commonplace image of playing Tamburlaine amidst urban destruction ties this exchange to Chrisoganus's description of the ruined city, and ties the violence of the stage to the violence in the streets. Distinct boundaries between theater, audience, and city are fictive. On the one hand, the players are always on the outskirts of the action, always considered insignificant, always the playthings of fortune. On the other hand, the exile of the players immediately precedes the reentry of Peace and Plenty at the end of the play; although the point is not made explicitly, the city apparently needed to be purged of the theater before it could be rectified.

Before the sack of the city, we see the citizens fearing the impending approach of the multitude. Upon hearing that "the rude commons in disseverd troupes / Have gathered dangerous head" (4.5.13–14) the merchant Velure replies:

> Faith, I am ignorant what course to take,
> Wee i' th Citty heere are so distracted
> As if our spirits were all earth and ayre,
> I know not how. (16–19)

The "disseverd troupes" of the multitude are here opposed to the "distracted" city; the entry of the first causes the second. Why is the relation between the crowd and the city dramatized in this manner? Where can we locate the theater itself in this dynamic? Two possible answers emerge. Perhaps in this attack the city stands for itself, and the supplement of the crowd, achieved through the vehicle of the theater, renders the city distracted. Or perhaps the city stands for the theater (the stage is the space of the city, invaded by a crowd from elsewhere); the assault of the crowd causes the theater itself to be

distracted, pulled apart, disseminated. In some ways, these two readings collapse into each other, since the theater can only be the city in
the terms suggested by the antitheatricalists, as the contamination of
the urban body and destruction of the articulate city. The paradoxical
alignment of theatrical and antitheatrical views of the distracted multitude relates at least in part to the conjoining of symbolic and mercantile issues. The antitheatricals highlight the theater's dissemination
of itself in the urban community, but this dissemination was the
absolute necessity of the companies, the basis for their continued existence. In portraying the crowd, the theater does not rebut the
antitheatricalist position; rather, it appropriates it, incorporates it,
mimicking its tenets and demonstrating its effects. At the heart of this
maneuver, I would suggest, is a fundamental ambivalence about the
place of the theater in the city, and a fundamental ambivalence about
its service to the many-headed monster.[35]

* * *

In the usual reading, *Histriomastix* initiates what has come to be
known as the War of the Theaters, in which Ben Jonson battled
Dekker, Marston, and Shakespeare through the medium of the
stage.[36] Rather than seeing this altercation primarily in personal
terms, as has traditionally been the case, I would like to suggest that
the War of the Theaters can be understood as an engagement with the
sorts of issues I have been discussing in this chapter, principally
the negotiation of the urban role (and urban space) of the theater.[37]
Most of the plays usually associated with the War have an urban setting, at least in part; most directly engage, at least in passing, with
issues of theatrical audiences. By focusing on the drama of others,
these plays estrange the theater from its immediate context, creating a fictive distance between their performance and their object: a
distance that allows a tacit self-exploration.

These generalizations are particularly true of Jonson's plays, which
repeatedly engage with the question of the theater's relation its city
and audience. The terms of this engagement, however, are markedly
different from the plays I have been discussing, due to their satirical
underpinning. The satirical city, as I suggested more specifically of
city comedy in the first chapter, is always a version of the articulate or
arborescent city; as Gail Kern Paster has argued, it might perhaps be
best described as the mirror image of the ideal civic city of the pageants and proclamations.[38] In this way, satire is the mode in which the
arborescent system attempts to heal itself, a dynamic always present in

the plays of Jonson. The master metaphor for Jonsonian satire is anatomy, but of a particular sort, presenting a body *in extremis* but not dismembered. As Asper declares at the outset of *Every Man Out of His Humor*, observing "this thronged round" (Ind. 51):

> Well I will scourge those apes,
> And to these courteous eyes oppose a mirror,
> As large as is the stage whereon we act:
> Where they shall see the time's deformity
> Anatomized in every nerve and sinew. (117–21)[39]

This is the necessary role of the stage for Jonson; it takes the undifferentiated "thronged round" and reflects back to it a deformed yet articulate body, with "every nerve and sinew" shown in order to demonstrate the true, arborescent connections between all things. In this approach to the city Jonson particularly follows Horace, the preeminent source for early modern satire. While Horace does invoke Plato's "many-headed monster" in his first Epistle, *belua multorum es capitum,* his treatment of the figure is substantially different from Plato's: this monster is not a figure of impenetrability but a figure of knowledge. Where Plato sees the many-headed monster as the indescribable multiplicity of the city, for Horace this multiplicity is fully describable; indeed, the Satires and Epistles are devoted to a detailed itemization of the behaviors and practices found in the urban labyrinth, a tracing of urban depravity in the hopes that it might be corrected.[40]

Jonson is often seen as quintessential urban playwright of the early modern period; as Martin Butler writes, "the urban experience was the single most determining factor of his career."[41] He is also often seen as the playwright most interested in the problem of common audiences and public playing. Less frequently discussed are the conflicts and tensions that these twinned preoccupations presented— tensions particularly evident in the space in which they meet, the theater. Jonson's cities are never anonymous; almost every character is named or otherwise identified not long after taking the stage. With the exception of *Sejanus,* which I will discuss in the next chapter, Jonson avoids the crowded, distracted, anonymous city as if threatened by it—as perhaps he was.[42] As Asper fulminates away at the outset of *Every Man Out of His Humor* (immediately before he discovers he is in a theater), Mitis chastens him: "Contain your spirit in more stricter bounds / And be not thus transported" (Ind. 46–47); Cordatus agrees, "Unless your breath had power / To melt the world, and mould it new again" (48–49). What lies beyond the space of the stage? How can the "bound" of the stage be extended? What effect can it have on the populous city that surrounds it? If these are the questions that animate Jonson's drama, they also point to the fears that undermine it. Herbert Blau, in his study of the concept of the audience, writes of Jonson:

> He hoped to diminish the gross physicality of theatrical form by throwing the emphasis on the disembodied words, assertive and retiring at once, disappearing in the utterance, the very entrance being an exit. Precisely what he liked about words turned out, one might have guessed, to be a problem with the audience.[43]

This seems inadequate as an assessment of Jonson's engagement with words, an engagement always marked by exactly this "gross physicality," as Bruce Boehrer and others have demonstrated.[44] But as an assessment of Jonson's engagement with the audience it is exactly right. "What was really there," Blau remarks, "with its tawdry seeming substance, so disenchanted Jonson that he sought transparency elsewhere" (289). The audience is opaque, not transparent; it is both physical and disembodied, present and absent, a fiction. In *Every Man Out* the stage is imagined as a mirror where they shall see time's deformity, but what does it reflect? "The audience"? "The public"? "The city"? All are illusions, in a way; only population is real.

Early in his treatise, Blau engages with this disturbing aspect of the theater:

> In the system under suspicion, there is the fantasy of a public. . . . For all the reassuring presence . . . of any representative figure, what we feel in reality is the vaporization of authority, along with identifying concepts of class and status. . . . There is in all this a dematerialization of the political, which by a kind of suction upon the social, swallows its identity, leaving it dumb and anonymous, without a name. (8)

Blau's context is modern theater, "the system under suspicion," but I would suggest that we can see the same issues at play in the early modern theater, and particularly in Jonson's varied engagements with the theater audience. Jonson flatters his audience in direct address, he preempts its judgment by revealing the action of the play in the prologue, he doubles it by placing judicious spectators on the stage, he tallies the economic purchase of its wit, he grids it, abstracts it, systematizes it—but virtually never acknowledges it as the distracted multitude, dumb and anonymous, without a name. This recognition only appears in the context of *other* plays, the estranged theater of other writers, which he excoriates in literary prefaces and collected opinions. This recognition also occurs in the "Apologetical Dialogue" that closes *Poetaster*, where Jonson for the first time engages directly with the crowd, figuring it as "the barking students of Bears' College" (32), emblematic of a debased theatricality—and then in terms identical to those employed by Chapman in *Andromeda Liberata*, as the multitudinous monster that taxes others for its own crimes and is turned to stone by the Persean force of Jonson's invective (50–55). It is in this closing apology as well that Jonson, disgusted that the "multitude of voices" (193) should laud the abused theater of his rivals, forecasts his own abortive turn toward tragedy and the city of the crowd in *Sejanus*.

Jonson's complex engagement with the distracted multitude is especially shown in *Poetaster*, which we might see as caught between the horns of a dilemma: how can the play define the public role of theater without engaging with what the crowded city is?[45] How can poetry articulate the *polis* and yet evade the Platonic ban? In part, the play attempts this through a careful finessing of the location of the populous city. Prior to the exasperated rupture of the "Apologetical Dialogue," the place of the multitude in *Poetaster* is obscure. We do not find it in the theater audience, whose uniformly gracious "shine" offends the sight of Envy in the Induction (Ind. 11); Envy hopes for some contaminating heterogeneity in the form of poets, but if in attendance, they do not respond to her call. Nor are any crowds present in the play itself. We have a dyadic geography of city and court, as in *Henry VIII*, but the city is clearly the articulate city, as it is in all of Jonson's plays; indeed, the urban scenes might have come out of one of his city comedies. The multitude does lurk somewhere on the fringes of the play, as the audience of the common players and writers, but it is given no theatrical presence. The possible metatheatricality of characters such as Tucca and Lupus complaining of being made ridiculous on the public stage seems to have no purchase; its irony lies in the inherent ridiculousness of the characters, but the joke does not produce the sort of *mise en abyme* that we might expect.

It is in Act Five that the multitude finally enters the play, an entry catalyzed, significantly, by the establishment of Caesar as the focus of the drama. The presence of the multitude builds through a series of increasingly specific rhetorical figures. First, Caesar defends poetry as that which can immortalize the city, setting up a contrast between "Rome and her monuments" and the "innovating dust" that might threaten them (5.1.24). Similarly, Horace says that rulers other than

Caesar are "hosted to their thrones / By fortune's passionate and disordered power," a description that again seems to evoke the many-headed monster without naming it (47–48). Horace then declares his own separation from the contaminations of the city, "this grave of sin," and then judges Virgil to be similarly "refined / From the tartarous moods of common men" (89, 102–03). He also declares that the seating of Virgil above Caesar is a "particular" case, separate from "the vast rude swing of general confluence" (5.2.40), a judgment that reconfirms Caesar's uniqueness; in doing this he is "distinct" from those whom "custom rapteth in her press"—"press" having a double meaning of urgency and crowdedness (45). In all of these cases, what is established is singularity: of Horace, of Virgil, of poetry, of Caesar. The multitude acts as a necessary supplement to these figurations; as in Plato, the one is defined in opposition to the many.

There is a trajectory visible in these images, as the multitude is gradually concretized in the movement from the metaphors of "innovating dust" and "disordered power" to the more direct references to the city and "common men," and finally to "the press" and "the vast rude swing of general confluence." As the act progresses, these rhetorical descriptions become more explicit. Next is Virgil's description of Fame, clearly a figure for the many-headed monster in its urban form, affrighting "cities and towns of most conspicuous site" (5.3.95). Its multitudinous tongues and ears connect it to the prologue Rumor in *2 Henry IV*, drawn from the same passage in the *Aeneid*; its circulatory love of libel and scandal connect it to Chapman's *Andromeda*; and both these qualities connect it to Spenser's Blatant Beast (perhaps the principal source for this widely popular image), whose escape at the end of Book VI signals the abrupt conclusion of the *Faerie Queene*, halfway through its journey. Virgil says, "This monster—," and is interrupted by "shouting offstage" that heralds the entry of Lupus with his charge of treason against Horace. Lupus, set on by the player Histrio, has found an emblem in Horace's papers of a bird of prey feasting on a dead animal, and interprets it as an attack on Caesar: "Is not here an eagle? And is not that eagle meant by Caesar?" (5.3.65–66). Horace defeats this charge with the final invocation of the multitude in the body of the play, which completes the "imperfect body" of the emblem—not with Caesar, but with a proverbial wisdom recognizable in *Hamlet, Histriomastix, Philaster,* and most of the other plays under discussion:

> "Thus, oft, the base and ravenous multitude
> Survive, to share the spoils of fortitude." (67–68)

On one level, the intention of this gloss is clear: Virgil's invocation of Rumor becomes an actual rumor, which is exposed as the product of the common stages that threaten true poetry—as in the "Apologetical Dialogue"—and the imperial glory of Caesar's court that it supports. The player is whipped, and the playwrights who spread the rumor are purged. But the frame also works in the other direction; if the spread of rumor through common plays is the overt subject of the engagement, this illicit circulation parallels the poisonous world of courtly eavesdropping.[46] The world of the court, the principal scene of *Poetaster*, has become like the crowded city, moving with the same rhizomatic dynamics. Attempting to fix his drama in a location firmly separated from the many-headed monster, Jonson finds no safe place left.

The figure of the ravenous crowd both creates the scene and rectifies it, filling out the imperfect body of the emblem, changing the eagle into a vulture (or perhaps revealing that the eagle was always a vulture). In a way, we might parallel this invocation of the multitude to the supplemental entries of crowds in other plays: it produces the intended resolution for the drama. But in producing this resolution, it threatens the whole gimcrack structure of authority Jonson presents. If the bird in the emblem can be both eagle and vulture, Caesar can substitute for the multitude; after all, the play shows us Caesar similarly thriving on rumor and hearsay, the circulation of information. With this ambiguity, the distance between Horace and the crowd, and Virgil and the crowd, is also undermined, since their separation occurs through the example of Caesar, "distinct" from the "general confluence." And thus the separation between *Poetaster* and the common stages it spurns is revealed as fictive. The play is subsequently described in the "Apologetical Dialogue" as "the most abstracted work, opposed / To the stuffed nostrils of the drunken rout!" (194–95), but this cannot be sustained; as Alan Sinfield has commented, the play "is itself a market product. . . . As much as any of Jonson's work, *Poetaster* keeps falling back—vividly and intriguingly—into the market vulgarity from which it purports to separate itself" (84). In this context we might return to the Prologue of the play, which speaks out against "base detractors and illiterate apes" and "that common spawn of ignorance / our fry of writers," describing rival playwrights and players (70, 79–80). In these descriptions of common ignorance it seems the multitude is present as well, brought in by their factors the playwrights. As in the body of the play itself, the rival poets thus represent the circulative aspects of the crowd and the distracted city. If it is the work of other dramatists and the conduits of theatrical display that have most conspicuously rendered Jonson's plays meat for the multitude, his plays have never truly escaped this reality in the first place. As Dekker's response in *Satiromastix* makes clear through its denial of special place to Jonson's theater, *Poetaster* collapses in on itself; attempting to indicate difference, it ends up suggesting sameness. In this regard, we might consider further the threat implicit in the moral Horace provides for the emblem. In contradiction of Caesar's claim that poetry can preserve the arborescent city against the "innovating dust" of the many-headed monster, the emblem suggests what Jonson most fears: it is not poetry but the ravenous multitude that survives, a way of happening, a mouth.

In some ways, it is especially fitting that Jonson would figure the multitude as the *gloss,* not the emblem itself, as this stands in direct contrast to the usual deployment of the figure of the crowd. The city of satire is particularly opposed to the crowd because the populous, rhizomatic city is opaque and needs interpreting. The function of the satirist is to see all—whether this capacity derives from an inborn greatness and separation from the herd like Horace, or a tireless investigator of vice like the Belman of London—and to see it clearly. But the populous theatrical cities that appear in this chapter are never transparent; the meaning that they carry always needed to be divined. The crowds that gather outside of Jane Grey's cell, the crowds that gape for innovation or novelty, the "disseverd troupes" that attack the city: all are tokens, signs of something else, tangible signifiers of a level of meaning that requires explication and is never sure or certain. Unlike the transparencies of the articulate city and its satirical complement, the crowded city is both inarticulate and disarticulated, distracted, dismembered—if a body at all, a body without organs.[47] Because of this lack of anatomical cohesiveness, the crowded city always bodes. In chapter 5, I argue that this boding can be best understood through an early modern expression, one we have seen applied to the many-headed monster numerous times in this chapter: the crowded city is *prodigious,* in all the senses that the word carries. And as I will argue in the context of *Julius Caesar* and *Sejanus,* this prodigious city, this illegible epitome of the complex and heterogeneous disorder of London, linked in the popular discourse with images of dismemberment and violence, was dramatized as both inevitable and disturbing.

C H A P T E R 5

"ROME, ETC.": *SEJANUS, JULIUS CAESAR*, AND THE PRODIGIOUS CITY

Silius. *What wisdom's now i'the streets? I'the common mouth?*
Drusus. *Fears, whisperings, tumults, noise, I know not what.*

(Sejanus *2.492–93*)[1]

This chapter takes as its focus the relation between dramatic space and theatrical space as it is negotiated in two plays, Shakespeare's *Julius Caesar* and Jonson's *Sejanus his Fall*. In a number of ways it continues the work of the previous chapter, extending the argument that with the staging of crowds plays sought to negotiate their relationship to their urban audience, the distracted multitude. In place of the fairly straightforward dynamics discussed in chapter 4, however, both *Julius Caesar* and *Sejanus* present the relationship between drama, theater, crowd, and city in complex and even contradictory terms. Although both plays manifestly connect what takes place on the stage to what takes place in the theater, an easy parallel between dramatic crowd and urban audience is never sustained. Rather, exploring the links between stage and crowded city leads to a complex consideration of not only the social and symbolic place of the theater in the city, but also the dramatic cohesion and integrity of the play. There are a number of reasons for this complexity of vision, not least the skill of the two dramatists, but I would suggest that the most significant is their common subject and setting: Rome. The critical discourse on the importance of Rome to both Jonson and Shakespeare is long and extensive, particular in terms of the philosophical, ethical, and political discourses embodied in the ancient city.[2] Rather than rehearsing this broad subject, my intention in this chapter is to look at *Julius Caesar* and *Sejanus* less as part of an intellectual tradition and more as part of a popular theatrical movement, one that produced dozens of plays in the period.[3] In this way, we can position the two plays as within a commercial category, representatives of a larger urban fascination with Rome that is fundamentally related to issues of urban legibility.

My title for this chapter is lifted from Brutus's impassioned apostrophe to an invisible city, as he reads the cryptic messages that Cassius has arranged to be thrown through his window:

> "Shall Rome, etc." Thus must I piece it out:
> Shall Rome stand under one man's awe? What, Rome?
> My ancestors did from the streets of Rome
> The Tarquin drive when he was called a king.
> "Speak, strike, redress!" Am I entreated
> To speak and strike? O Rome, I make thee promise
> If the redress will follow, thou receivest
> Thy full petition at the hand of Brutus! (2.1.51–58)

The "etc." in the letter Brutus reads is supplemental, signifying both a lack in Rome that Brutus must piece out, and an addition, the supplement of purging violence that will make Rome pure again. But the Rome of both *Julius Caesar* and *Sejanus* can also be thought of as supplemented by London.[4] The metaphorical relationship between Rome and London within the worlds of both plays provides a useful distance and displacement within which certain themes and issues—in particular the figure of the violent urban crowd—can be broached without fear of censure. Classical Rome, put simply, is where one may (or perhaps must) talk about the crowd, a fact confirmed by the presence or discussion of urban crowds in the majority of the Roman plays performed in the period. In part this is due to the significance of the common populace to the politics of the ancient city, especially in the days of the republic and the civil wars that ended it. But the significance is more than just political; the matter of Rome, in many ways, is population—and the threat that population poses to urban legibility. In this regard, Rome provided important classical examples for modern instances.[5] Geoffrey Miles notes that constancy was "the defining virtue of the Romans . . . [and] is central to [Shakespeare's] reconstruction of the ethos of ancient Rome," going on to argue, "this ancient virtue was being revived by contemporary writers as a cure for present-day problems."[6] The point, I think, can be extended from the ethical to the urban. Beyond personal virtue, Rome itself was supposed to be constant, eternal, and fixed—even if its history constantly demonstrated its mutability and metamorphosis.[7]

In the act of staging, Rome connects with London in still more complex ways, in the context of the urban multitude and the position of the theater as an institution. For Shakespeare, Jonson, and other dramatists, Rome could be understood in (at least) two opposing yet complementary ways.[8] Ancient Rome was, in Gail Kern Paster's phrase, "the archetypal earthly city," the touchstone of urban meaning, the classical locus, the urban space organized into ideal urban existence, the necessarily legible city.[9] On the other hand, ancient Rome was also an early modern gallimaufry, a hodgepodge of unconnected and disparate accounts, a classical source imported into inappropriate locations, a theatrical plethora and dramatic stock-in-trade, in the context of which famous Roman lines (including those invented in Elizabethan London) were parodied as stale commonplaces.[10] In other words, Rome is always a supplemented location in early modern London, an over-significant space whose staging was necessarily a very self-conscious act.

Although *Julius Caesar* and *Sejanus* date from toward the beginning of this engrossment of Rome in London,[11] they share in this theatrical self-consciousness and double vision. On one level, both plays mirror contemporary London to a considerable degree, relocating issues and problems to ancient Rome in ways that highlight their critical significance in the context of the city. On another level, both are extremely concerned with the act of staging and with the theater's self-conscious role as an urban institution that not only reflects, but also produces, urban meaning.[12] These concerns—and the relationship between city and theater that informs them—are articulated through the engagement each play has with the prodigious city. The word "prodigious" carries a host of meanings that reflect the range of the early modern concern with the abnormal. The most immediate meaning of prodigy in the two plays is an unnatural occurrence or manifestation that must be interpreted in order to divine its significance. Prodigy also carries other significances, such as political manipulator, or a mark of abnormality on the body, the stigma of the scapegoat that must be driven out of the community—a meaning of obvious, if perhaps ironic, significance to both plays. But the most important definition of prodigy in this context is as sign or omen. As I suggest at the end of chapter 4, the prodigious always bodes, always means something, even if that meaning is unclear and needs interpretation. Both *Sejanus* and *Julius Caesar* contain an extensive amount of supernatural phenomena, most of which is manifested in an urban setting and witnessed by the general populace. In Shakespeare's play, the prodigious principally augurs the central action of the drama, the assassination of Caesar; in Jonson's play, it is the imminent demise of Sejanus that causes Rome suddenly to become prodigious. In this way the prodigious helps to frame the action of the play, giving it greater and more fatal significance. In both plays, however, the supplement of the prodigious—closely connected with the crowded city—operates to frustrate its apparent purpose of underscoring dramatic meaning. In these two plays we see the Derridean supplement working in its full complexity. The "etc." to Rome, to the ideal space of the city, is that which completes it, undermines it, opposes it, threatens it, and replaces it. *Julius Caesar,* it might be said, presents a tension in the relation between Rome and "etc.," between the ideal and the corporeal, between dramatic and theatrical spaces. *Sejanus,* on the other hand, in refusing to present an ideal city in any form, presents a world where "etc." has substituted for Rome, where the city is purely supplemental, where the theatrical supplants the dramatic and destroys it.

A further supplement to the Rome of *Julius Caesar* and *Sejanus* could be noted as well. It was to Rome, time and time again, that the antitheatricalists returned, either to praise rulers who had driven out players or to condemn the theatrical excesses of emperors such as Nero. The *Mirrour of Monsters* notes approvingly that "Players were banished from Rome for theyr beastlie enormities."[13] In *Plays Confuted in 5 Actions,* Stephen Gosson details a long list of Roman theatrical abuses, concluding, "Sithince you soe even by the examples of the Romans, that playes are Ratsbane to the governement of commonweales."[14] In the *Schoole of Abuse,* his example becomes contemporary: "Compare London to Rome, and England to Italy, you shall finde the Theaters of the one, the abuses of the other, to be rife among us."[15] Roman theatricality, in other words, produces Italianate depravity in London. As quoted in the previous chapter, the *2nd and 3rd Blast of Retrait* includes a lengthy picture of an abundant and idle late Roman empire sliding into decay because of the theaters.[16] The most extensive Roman example can be found in the *Refutation of the Apology for Actors,* perhaps because Heywood had relied so heavily (and so inexpertly) on Rome in his defense of playgoing. There the author delivers a lengthy history of the fall of the Roman republic and argues *post hoc propter hoc* that the theater was to blame: "a while after the institution of Stage-playes, ensued those most lamentable civill warres that were the overthrow of the Cities state."[17] The passage climaxes in a nightmarish vision of the city as victim of both civil war and the theater: "the whole Cittie, Streetes, Market-places, Temples, and Theaters themselves, were filled with dead carkasses" (B3).[18] The parity suggested between the scene of theater and the scene of violence, and the portrayal of a literally dismembered theatrical public, recalls the discussion of the distracted city that dominated chapter 4. It also resonates in interesting ways with the dynamics of both *Sejanus* and *Julius Caesar.*

Both plays, of course, climax in scenes of popular dismemberment, although in both cases the dismemberment produces somewhat anticlimactic effects. The tragic grandeur of Caesar's assassination is undercut, in various ways, by its farcical echo in the collective dismemberment of Cinna the Poet, which both duplicates the miscalculations that informed the first killing and mocks the aristocratic pretensions of the noble assassins. Sejanus's death at the hands of the Roman crowd is told by Terentius, who begins his narrative by exclaiming:

> O you, whose minds are good,
> And have not force all mankind, from your breasts;
> That yet have so much stock of virtue left,
> To pity guilty states, when they are wretched:
> Lend your soft ears to hear, and eyes to weep
> Deeds done by men. (5.743–47)

And yet—as this speech, which seems to rebuke as much as entreat its audience, indicates—pity is almost impossible to produce at the end of *Sejanus,* despite the appalling events that Terentius relates. Both plays display remarkable ambivalence toward tragic pathos. While in *Julius Caesar's* case this has often been interpreted as an effect of its austere dramatization of *romanitas*—and in *Sejanus's* case as part of the play's overall failure as a dramatic piece—this mutual uneasiness with the affective power of the theater connects to a broad range of cultural and political issues relating to the plays' relationships to their audience and the theater's relationship to London. Chapter 4 argued that the language of dismemberment or distraction implicates the illegible crowded city, and that Hamlet's distracted Globe catalyzes a range of associations between theatrical performance and urban dissemination. These Roman plays preserve these associations, and extend them: if Rome is the archetype of urban legibility, what is the early modern London that stages this archetype but Rome dismembered? But as the issue of pathos indicates, they also use dismemberment for somewhat different purposes. In both plays, dismemberment makes the space of the city prodigiously significant, but like the plays' ambivalent deployment of affective power this significance is not stable. *Julius Caesar* links prodigiousness to multiplicity, opposing prodigious, populous Rome to the legible city that Brutus imagines—the city at the moment of being purged of extraneous meaning; for the play to achieve coherent meaning it must flee the space of populous Rome and relocate in the heroic forum of the battlefield. In *Sejanus,* more radically, the entry of the prodigious occasions a crisis of interpretation, changing the interpretive bases of the play in such a way that coherent meaning seems impossible. Rather than acknowledging the play's urban setting as a location of significance, the play uses the interpretive impasse it establishes to force the action from the Roman stage into the English theater, in which the play's performance is met by the crowded city's popular rage.

Julius Caesar: "Prodigious Grown"

As discussed in the third chapter, the public world of London returns to the history plays in *Henry V,* with the imagined return of King Harry to London:

> But now behold,
> In the quick forge and working-house of thought,
> How London doth pour out her citizens!
> The Mayor and all his brethren in best sort,
> Like to the senators of th' antique Rome,
> With the plebeians swarming at their heels,
> Go forth and fetch their conqu'ring Caesar in. (5.Pro.22–28)

The scene represents an unusual and iconic weaving together of the dramatic space of the play, the theatrical space of the playhouse, and the urban space of London. London is both realized and idealized through the invocation of the metaphor of Caesar, suggesting the identical qualities of the Roman triumph and the Elizabethan royal entry, the absolute space that creates the city as the chamber of its ruler. Caesar here stands as the classical example, the conventional truth through which the space of London and the space of the theater are brought together and made inseparable. The ritual of possession is given a theatrical valence that acts to confirm, celebrate, and solidify the unity of the moment. This might be described as the supplementing of London with Rome, not the reverse: Roman ritual becomes a frame whereby the space of London is organized and given an emblematic clarity it usually lacked.

Julius Caesar, in all likelihood Shakespeare's next play after *Henry V*, opens under profoundly different dramatic terms: "Hence! home, you idle creatures, get you home!" (1.1.1).[19] The first scene of this play presents the event, not the example, of welcoming the return of "the conqu'ring Caesar," but the celebratory unification of city and theater that we see in the earlier play here completely dissolves. In this shift from Rome as symbol to Rome as a stage presence, urban space, dramatic space, and theatrical space are all portrayed as contested territory. James R. Siemon describes the tonal shift between these two scenes by suggesting, "metaphoric continuities and certainties give way to the interpretive disjunctions and difficulties of historical metonymy."[20] In urban terms, Rome moves from metaphor to metonymy, and complementing this movement is a refiguring of the urban crowd, now a dispersed multitude whose unity necessarily equals disunity. In Caesar's Rome, the transformation of the city into a theatrical space by gathering the crowd together to see the body of the great produces not synthesis but distraction. Most pointedly, the swarming of the plebeians is not celebrated as an act of cultural memory but stigmatized as an act of cultural forgetting:

> O you hard hearts, you cruel men of Rome,
> Knew you not Pompey? Many a time and oft
> Have you climbed up to walls and battlements,
> To tow'rs and windows, yea, to chimney tops,
> Your infants in your arms, and there have sat
> The livelong day, with patient expectation,
> To see great Pompey pass the streets of Rome:
> . . .
> And do you now cull out a holiday?
> And do you now strew flowers in his way
> That comes in triumph over Pompey's blood? (36–51)

The scene of crowded Rome thus contrasts not only to the world of Shakespeare's last play but to the recent past of his current one; at the heart of Marullus's complaint is the illegitimacy of Rome framing Caesar as it once did Pompey. The crowded space is put forward not as a frame with which to glorify the ruler but as an illicit gathering that must be dispersed, lest the gods send "the plague / That needs must light on this ingratitude" (1.1.54–55).

The most obvious way to explain this disparity, of course, is that the plays present very different cities. The London of *Henry V* is a city unified behind its bold hero, participating and glorying in his grand expansion of English sovereignty. The Rome of *Julius Caesar* is a city riven with class conflicts, repressive attacks on the common people, internecine struggles among the elite, and a restive and violent population. In this, however, it resembles contemporary London more than the ideal and rhetorical London of *Henry V* does, which as I have suggested previously could only be created *entr'acte*, framed on both sides with the foreign glories and spoils of Agincourt. A further point could be offered: by the time *Julius Caesar* was in performance it was obvious that the Irish campaign of Essex, *Henry V's* modern "conqu'ring Caesar," was an irredeemable disaster.[21] In these ways, and others, the Rome of *Julius Caesar* bears many resemblances to the conflicting ideas of London examined in this book. As with London, there is a great concern with the changing nature of the city, an urban locality in the process of becoming something new. "What trash is Rome?" asks Cassius (1.3.107); his point is rhetorical, and aimed at his fellow aristocrat Casca, but on another level the question could be taken as real, and aimed not simply at the noble Romans but at the city as a whole—specifically at the engrossed, populous Rome that so threatens its former glory. The descriptions of Rome offered by the urban commentators in the play bear out this idea; Rome is trash, the citizens are rocks and stones, chaff, rags and tags, weak straws, and "offal," with the double meaning of chips of wood and of viscera: literally, a dismembered multitude.[22]

It is well known that Shakespeare changed his sources when it came to the crowd of *Julius Caesar*. Plutarch, although no friend to the common populace (and although sharpened in this regard by North's translation), does not portray a multitude entirely unaware of Caesar's ambitions, does not have the crowd turn their favor from Caesar to Brutus to Antony in the oration scene, and does not have them deliberately murder a man they know is innocent. In earlier criticism, these changes were often taken to demonstrate Shakespeare's aristocratic and antidemocratic leanings; more recent commentary has tried to position this as a pessimistic phase in his considerations of the popular voice.[23] Leaving aside such imponderables, I want to suggest that the changes can be best understood as the insertion into the text of a contemporary conventional wisdom, an example of the pervasive discourse about the multitude as fickle, irrational, and prone to sudden random and inexplicable violence. A discourse, furthermore, that as I have argued was increasingly finding its determinants and applications in the context of London in general and the theater in particular. The crowd of *Julius Caesar* is thus an Elizabethan supplement to the play, framing Rome but also threatening to become it. As David Kranz has noted, *romanitas,* the stolid and stoic self-sufficiency that will go uncomfortably beyond parody in the figure of Coriolanus, is constructed in *Julius Caesar* through an opposition to the crowd; the presence of the distracted multitude, the Elizabethan cobblers and carpenters that swarm around and change their minds continually, provides the foil by which the steadfastness of the true Romans can shine.[24] The play undercuts this construction, of course; Caesar gives his most powerful speech of self-sufficiency, as one "constant as the northern star" and "Unshak'd of motion" just as the other noble Romans swarm around him for the kill. What separates the noble Romans from the many-headed monster is their lack of multiplicity: their small numbers and their individual names.[25]

It is appropriate, then, that Flavius's opening interrogation of the cobbler should ask after his trade, not his name:

> What, know you not,
> Being mechanical, you ought not walk
> Upon a laboring day without the sign
> Of your profession? Speak, what trade art thou? (1.1.2–5)

For an audience aware of the urban chaos and repeated bans on public assembly in recent years, Flavius's opening lines would have much resonance. Flavius and Murellus's inquisition of the carpenter and cobbler follow the pattern of behavior seen in the official response to the violent manifestation of London's multitude, and draw a strong connection between Rome and London as disordered cities. Without sign of their occupation, the assembled crowd carries the potential of masterlessness; the illegibility of the crowd makes this an illicit gathering. This immediate allusion to the disordered state of London has a complement in the way in which the play reinvents the theatrical parameters of *Henry V.* The inversion of the scene of civic triumph mirrors a corresponding shift in the play's theatrical attitude. In place of the fawning Chorus of *Henry V,* who carefully places the scene for the theater audience and entreats its participation in the theatrical invention, *Julius Caesar* uses the opening scene to establish an alienating and problematic relationship with its audience. Like the plebeians, the theater audience has gathered together today (and culled out a holiday?) to see Caesar, to create him as a theatrical figure, and it quickly discovers from the tribunes that this is a mistaken and idle activity.[26] Flavius and Murellus speak in the puritanical tones of antitheatricalists, condemning those who would interrupt the quotidian life of the city in order to gather in crowds and create theater. The first word the audience gathered together in the Globe hears is "Hence!": go from here, disperse, go to where you belong.[27]

Dispersed by Murellus and Flavius, the crowd has gathered again by the next scene, belying the tribunes' trust in the efficacy of their rebukes: "See whe'r their basest mettle be not moved. / They vanish tongue-tied in their guiltiness" (1.1.61–62). The action is fundamentally rhizomatic; like the crowds criticized in the proclamations against assembly, *Julius Caesar* presents a city composed of dispersed multitudes, able at any moment to grow to head. On another level, this ebbing and returning points to a fundamental spatial tactic of the play. Crowded, populous Rome generally dominates the first act of the play; the phantasmagoric third scene imagines a city crowded with people and portents, in Casca's report that "there were drawn upon a heap a hundred ghastly women, / Transformed with their fear, who swore they saw / Men, all in fire, walk up and down the streets" (1.3.23–25). The crowd then disappears from Act Two (concerned with the conspirators' plans) and returns in full force in the catastrophic events of Act Three. This rising and falling action, setting up contrasts between public and private spaces, provides extensive points of contact between the stage crowds and the theater audience, until the stage crowds finally disappear in Act Four, when the play finally escapes the bounds of the prodigious city.

Throughout its course *Julius Caesar* plays with the reactions of the theater audience with great skill and remarkable antagonism. In the opening exchange, the comic responses of the cobbler invert the appropriate response to the figure of authority, encouraging the audience to laugh with the quick-witted commoner against the officious tribune. This comedy is quickly brought to a halt with the mention of "Caesar," which both places the scene for the audience (who, for the first thirty lines of the play, would know only that they were watching an urban crowd) and radically changes its dynamics. One can imagine the theater audience responding as the plebeians do to Murellus's impassioned rhetoric: chastened, "tongue-tied in their guiltiness," ashamed for laughing at serious matters. A similar effect is produced in the funeral orations, where the crowd is made to sway from Brutus's chilly ethical defense of the assassination to Antony's carefully orchestrated appeal to the emotions, which climaxes in the display of Caesar's body. The theater audience is clearly led to see the crowd's stereotypical fickleness in satirical terms, a perspective strengthened by Antony's cynical comments on his speech after the maddened crowd departs. And yet the same stratagems were employed against the theater audience in the previous scene, where Antony, alone on the stage with the body, begs forgiveness of "thou bleeding piece of earth / That I am meek and gentle with these butchers" (3.1.254–55), and prophesizes on Caesar's wounds in an impassioned soliloquy. In that scene the audience is captivated and moved; in the scene in the marketplace it watches others watching, and is distanced from the effect. More to the point, in the marketplace scene the theater audience sees its own, directed reaction to Caesar's dismembered body derided. Pathos is repackaged as theatrical oratory, and in this reframing the enthralling of the crowd through emotion is mocked and made to seem base and dangerous.

If *Henry V* found a solution to the problematic power of the theater audience and the problematic position of London as a frame for the royal presence by portraying the latter in a theatrical context explicitly subordinated to a contemporary political power, *Julius Caesar* reconfigures this dynamic by creating an urban space in which neither political power nor theatrical power are legitimate. As John Drakakis has observed, *Julius Caesar* has no king, no central and controlling locus of power.[28] Instead, the play presents (at least) two constellations of potential authority in the play—Caesar and the crowd versus the noble Romans—each of which serves to render the other suspect as a location for interpretive truth or sympathetic investment. In urban terms, the implication of this dynamic is that no overriding symbolic authority possesses the symbolic space of the city. Instead, we see the city presented as an appropriable frame of significance.[29] Cassius's image of "Rome indeed and room enough, / When there is in it but one only man" (1.2.157–58), a direct reference to the concept of *camera regis* that plays so crucial a role in the second tetralogy, is here a complaint that Caesar has inappropriately taken Rome.

One way in which this dynamic works is as a potential critique of political power and the theatrical mechanisms that enforce it; the whole action of the play, in some ways, is about producing strategic theatrical effects in the context of the city, with the intention of producing a particular legitimating response from the easily manipulated people. This, of course, is not true merely of Caesar and Antony; seen with a sceptical eye, Brutus's stage-planning of the assassination—"so appearing to the common eyes, / We shall be called purgers, not murderers" (2.1.179–80)—fits this pattern, as does his inspired, if disturbing, improvisation after the killing:

> let us bathe our hands in Caesar's blood
> Up to the elbows and besmear our swords.
> Then walk we forth, even to the market place,
> And waving our red weapons o'er our heads,
> Let's all cry "Peace, freedom, and liberty!" (3.1.106–10)

Bringing the death of Caesar to market, to sell while they can, the conspirators turn the killing into a spectacle, one intended to move the marketplace crowd in a particular direction.[30] As in chapter 4, however, I would like to reverse this dynamic and suggest that the driving force of the play is theatrical, not political, power. As the deep associations between the marketplace and the theater in the last passage suggest,[31] *Julius Caesar* stages theatricality, and not only in the sense that all of the play's protagonists are Roman actors, playing their noble parts with great posturing. It stages theatricality as a manifestation of the theater itself within the play, as a place of gathering and dispersing, a commercial venture beholden to the whims of its urban populace, a place that spins out compelling fantasies for a fickle audience. The play articulates its anxiety about these issues in their urban context by both flaunting its dramatic power, its ability to move its audience through words and images, and simultaneously disparaging these actions as anarchic and scurrilous.

In this dynamic the play incorporates the antitheatrical description of the many-headed multitude and the polluted theatrical city, not to rebut it but to use it to articulate anxieties about the theater's place in and effect on the city and to explore its relationship to the urban crowd—a series of intractable issues that remain indefinitely unresolvable in the course of the play.[32] *Julius Caesar* redeploys the antitheatricalist connection between the theater, urban violence, and the disordered, contaminated, and illegible state of the city, and then redoubles this paradigm by establishing an antagonistic relationship with its own urban audience that emphasizes its own use and abuse of theatrical power. It would be possible to see Caesar as not just the figure of a consummate actor, but the figure of the theater itself. In making this suggestion I do not mean to say that we can read the ambitions of Caesar as an allegory of the theater, as representing, for example, a fantasy of the theater attempting to dominate London and usurp control of the city from its legitimate governors—although such an application would not seem ridiculous to the author of the *Refutation of the Apology for Actors,* who warns, "As concerning publique Magistracy, Players have no authority in their enter-ludes . . . Players assume an unlawful office to themselves of instruction and correction" (sig. H2). Rather, the parallel comes from the dramatic function and theatrical significance of Caesar's role in the city: the locus around which the distracted multitude builds its energy and then disperses its mayhem through the city, the contaminating and disseminating presence in the play and the city. This is never more true than in his final material manifestation as the epitome of theatrical enthrallment, the dismembered body on the stage.[33]

The relationship between Caesar, the crowd, and the space of the city is first concretized at the end of the first scene, when Flavius instructs Murellus,

> let no images
> Be hung with Caesar's trophies. I'll about,
> And drive away the vulgar from the streets;
> So do you too, where you perceive them thick.
> These growing feathers pluck'd from Caesar's wing
> Will make him fly an ordinary pitch. (1.1.68–73)

The obvious referent for the "growing feathers" in the final sentence is the statues of Caesar decked with "trophies" or "ceremonies," the image supplemented with a particular significance. But by interrupting the thought with a further instruction, and thus paralleling the act of disrobing the statues to the act of clearing the streets, Flavius confirms that the crowd is another supplement to Caesar. Two kinds of stripping away are here put in conjunction: making the statues bare and making the streets empty. The physical space of the city corresponds to the monumental symbolism of the statues, and in both cases the intention is to purge the symbol of extraneous and dangerous meanings. The crowd in *Julius Caesar* is, like Caesar himself, a contaminating presence in the city, something that clogs the streets and must be driven out. This "driving" recurs in Brutus's invocation of his ideal memorial city, the moment of urban purification around which he bases his identity; while auguring the "etc." of Rome by the light of its "exhalations," he exclaims, "My ancestors did from the streets of Rome / The Tarquin drive when he was call'd a king" (2.1.53–54). Brutus's imagined city is not a stable past but an instant of time, an antitriumph, Rome at the very moment of being purged and cleansed; with cleansing comes legibility, the ability to read the city.

The link between the city and Caesar is made more ominous, literally, in the third scene of the play, where the space of the city becomes a nighttime world of terrible and confusing significance. For Casca it is not the individual omens but their confluence and mixture that makes them significant: "When these prodigies / Do so conjointly meet, let not men say, / 'These are their reasons, they are natural' " (1.3.28–30). For Cassius, of course, the unnaturalness of the night has a clear, if somewhat obscurely expressed, meaning:

> A man no mightier than thyself, or me,
> In personal action, yet prodigious grown,
> And fearful, as these strange eruptions are. (76–78)

What does it mean to be "prodigious grown"? Responding to Casca, Cassius makes a sly connection between two applications of the word, the unnatural omens in the night and a political prodigy, the Machiavellian and protean manipulator who illegitimately rises to political power through secret ambitions and popular posturing. Yet as the word "grown" suggests, and as the conversation between Brutus and Cassius in the previous scene emphasizes, prodigious carries here another meaning as well. To be prodigious grown is to have grown colossal, the image of Caesar supplemented by the crowd, epitomizing the "monstrous state" (71) of the city. Cassius's construction of Caesar as a prodigy himself suggests a further act of interpretation is necessary; as the equivalence established in the first scene between the decked statues and the swarming streets suggests, it is the crowded space of Rome that is prodigious grown, that has changed from its ordinance, nature, and preformed faculty to monstrous quality (66–68). It is in the space of the crowded city that prodigies are manifested, and it is the crowd that also manifests them—the most significant omen of the play, "Beware the Ides of March," is first heralded out of the body of the crowd: "Who is it in the press that calls on me?" (1.2.15). Yet in the context of the theatrical double-vision I have been arguing the play produces, in which affect is both employed and undermined, the prodigies are also a dramatic convention: unnecessary, superfluous, a theatrical effect. The supplement of the many-headed multitude creates Rome in a contradictory fashion: both significant and insignificant, needing to be read and illegible, ungraspable except in fantasy, and disturbingly and redundantly ominous.

The conspirators' solution to the problem of Roman multiplicity— to purge the city, to return it to its fictive originary ideal—is undermined at the moment of its enactment, in the exchange of Cassius and Brutus:

> *Cassius.* How many ages hence
>   Shall this our lofty scene be acted over
>   In states unborn and accents yet unknown!
> *Brutus.* How many times shall Caesar bleed in sport,
>   That now on Pompey's basis lies along
>   No worthier than the dust! (3.1.111–16)

Beyond its obvious ironies, this much-noted conversation has produced a great variety of readings: a counterritual, an example of theater as the making of history, the demonstration of the theatrical core of political absolutism.[34] But there is a potential transition between Cassius's and Brutus's questions that has been generally overlooked. Cassius, responding to the sanguinary ceremony of purification that Brutus has just proposed, speaks in the language of ritual, imagining an infinitely repeatable and translatable scene of cleansing power, a cultural heritage that will endure and spread into unimagined realms. Brutus's responding question, however, is extra-dramatic in a different way, a question about serial repetition, not *translatio.* Especially with the jarring note struck by "bleed in sport," Brutus's question could be taken a real and quotidian question, a question about the power of the play to draw and enthrall the urban multitude. How many times will Caesar bleed in sport? How many days will this drama play? How have we moved you with this deed, done for "pity" (3.1.171)? In this connection the play's dramatization of the cleansing of the prodigious city turns against itself at its apotheosis through a connection to the necessary disseminating of theatrical power. In this moment the play asserts the theater's inextricable relationship with the many-headed multitude even at the point where its prodigious circulatory power is apparently quenched.

The result, of course, is exactly what the antitheatricalists would have suggested: ravished by the spectacle of Caesar's body, the distracted multitude run together in heaps and lay about with their clubs.[35] The imminent demise of Cinna is the final Roman scene of the play, the last view of the prodigious city.[36] It portrays dismemberment as an act of willful misinterpretation, the crowd construing Cinna after their fashion. In displaying this vulnerability, the scene reverses the dynamic of theatrical power found in Caesar's body; if Caesar dismembered is the apex of theatrical power, capable of controlling all audiences through its mute eloquence, the death of Cinna allows the crowd to dismember and disseminate the weak body of the poet and the play. The crucial line of the scene, "Pluck but his name out of his heart" (3.3.33–34), evokes many of the events of the play, from the plucking down of the ceremonies on the images by the tribunes to Brutus's musings on separating Caesar's spirit from his body to, of course, the assassination itself, especially as reimagined by Antony, where Caesar's heart burst after Brutus "pluck'd his cursed steel away" (3.2.177). Yet at the same time it codes itself as inconsequential; as the Second Citizen says, "It is no matter" (3.3.33). As such, it seems a sort of urban echo, characterized by both insignificance and horrific excess.

The image of Rome that the scene of collective violence leaves us with is not the city as signifying center but as eccentric, out of its orbit, spinning away from the play ("turn him going" (34)) so that a dramatic resolution of sorts can be found somewhere else, away from the urban monster. With the scene removed to the plains of Phillipi, the city no longer watches the city and the claustrophobic doubling of the urban play recedes. Absent in dramatic speech after the messenger's report that Brutus and Cassius have "rid like madmen through the gates of Rome" (3.2.269), the word "Rome" returns in Act Five as only a name, plucked out from its local habitation. Although the first reappearance of the word might suggest an ominous return to the beginning of the play—"if we lose this battle, / You are contented to be led in triumph / Thorough the streets of Rome?" (5.1.107–9)—Brutus's immediate negative response closes off that dangerous possibility of reengaging with the theatrical space of the multitudinous city. With this gesture, foreshadowing the tragic resolution of the play, Rome is safely returned to the past, with the prodigious supplement of London's many-headed monster kept at a distance. Brutus can eulogize Cassius as "the last of all the Romans" without the risk that the plural form will conjure up the urban multitude (5.3.99). Put another way, *Julius Caesar* must be relocated outside the crowded, prodigious city in order to achieve an ending. The necessity of this movement becomes clear when considering what happens in *Sejanus,* a play that through its disgusted embrace of the crowded city shows the impossibility of the final words ever ending anything.

SEJANUS: "THE COMMON MOUTH"

The advent of the prodigious city causes *Sejanus* to open up its boundaries and admit the space of the crowd. For most of its length, *Sejanus* is an extremely closed play, operating almost entirely within the confines of the imperial court and the Senate—a panoptic theatrical location where the virtuous Germanicans watch the rise of Sejanus and marvel and curse at his power.[37] In many ways, the structure of the play is congruent to that of *Poetaster,* Jonson's previous play, though with a profoundly malign valence: instead of the superficially benevolent authority of Augustus we have the poisonous manipulations of Tiberius, whose physical absence after the second act counterpoints Augustus's late appearance in the former play, thus decentering rather than reinforcing the symbolic frame. *Sejanus* also repeats *Poetaster's* split between a maladjusted aristocratic society and a marginal, invisible multitude, except that the multitude are now, in some ways, given greater presence; in contrast to the strictly rhetorical entry of the multitude that marks the last act of *Poetaster,* the crowd bursts into *Sejanus,* destroying and dismembering Sejanus in an act of violent excess kept at bay only in being reported rather than staged. Given these points of contact, it is possible to read *Sejanus* as a rethinking of the questions of the populous, theatrical city first broached in *Poetaster* (most explicitly in the "Apologetical Dialogue")—and, further, to read the different approach of *Sejanus* as evidence of Jonson's dissatisfaction with the answers he previously proposed.

Sejanus has often been compared with *Julius Caesar,* and it seems clear that Jonson builds his play, in part, as a response to the world Shakespeare had created. The Rome invoked in *Sejanus* is typically the past Rome of Brutus and Cassius—not the actual Rome portrayed in *Julius Caesar,* but the one Brutus apostrophizes in the "shall Rome, etc." scene: the perfect republican realm wherein the city's meaning was transparent and it was possible to be a true Roman. This imaginary Rome, however, is unrecoverable even as a space of fantasy in *Sejanus.* The "true" Romans of this play, as many critics have noted, are absolutely impotent, functioning only as satirical commentators, without power and with only a partial understanding of the political game; they invoke the Rome of the past not to imagine its return but to lament its passing. The historian Cordus connects to Brutus in that he similarly describes Cassius as "the last of all the Romans" (3.392), but as his trial for that statement demonstrates, playing Brutus in this Rome cannot lead anywhere besides the bonfire and the carceral. Making the city clean—purging it, as Brutus imagined—is thus not only impossible in *Sejanus:* it is not even present as an impossible desire. With the absence of this desire, the idea of Rome as the archetypal, legible city disappears; it can only be invoked *as* absence, as something irrelevant to the Rome of Tiberius and Sejanus.

This elision of Shakespeare's ideal Rome at the dramatic level counterpoints a theatrical revision of the urban space of *Julius Caesar.*

As discussed, Shakespeare's play offers a fairly simple alternation of scenes of public display and private conversation; if these two theatrical spaces occasionally border each other—as when Cassius's seduction of Brutus in the second scene juxtaposes the offstage marketplace theatrics of Caesar and Antony—the divisions between them remain clear. The result of this structure is that the politics of display are represented in explicit terms; we see the response of the crowd to the performances of power—and, as I have discussed, the metatheatrical effects of these responses are clearly marked. Jonson's play, in contrast, avoids easy parallels between political action and theatrical performance. On one level, the dominant space of the court mirrors the space of the playhouse, in that the court is a location of both actors and audiences; on another level, the theater audience led to understand that the court as a whole is like a stage, watched by Rome. But there are no scenes that make this latter staging manifest, no scenes in which the crowd watching the public performance of power is performed; indeed, exactly *what* this unseen Rome sees in the first four acts of the play is never made clear. Like Julius Caesar, Sejanus apparently engrosses himself with public acclaim, but the play never shows this engrossment; the populous city that inaugurates *Julius Caesar* is always absent in *Sejanus*. In contrast with *Poetaster, Sejanus* shows a much more explicit engagement with the crowded city, but in contrast with *Julius Caesar* it shows a constant refusal to give theatrical presence to corporeal Rome. Even within the play's dramatic narrative, the only time Sejanus is put into direct contact with the crowd is when they dismember his body.

This populous absence attenuates the binary economy of the politics of display. Unlike in *Julius Caesar,* political actor and public audience are kept away from each other in *Sejanus,* quarantined until the last act, when the latter destroys the former. The moment of direct contact between Sejanus and the crowd—what might, given the example of *Julius Caesar,* be called the moment of urban theatricality—is thus the moment of destruction, for both Sejanus and *Sejanus.* A second, related effect of this absence is to put the problem of knowledge, specifically urban knowledge, at the heart of the play. As I have suggested, *Julius Caesar* can be understood as staging a confrontation between two Romes: the ideal, legible city to which Brutus and Cassius aspire and the crowded, prodigious city manifested around them. By both eliminating the desire for urban legibility and deferring the arrival of the prodigious city until the final act, Jonson creates a Rome that is inherently unsignifying, neither legible nor manifest. Midway through the action, Arruntius says of Tiberius's

open praise of the sons of Germanicus, "I am not Oedipus enough /
To understand this Sphinx" (3.64–65). On one level, the metaphor
draws a clear comparison between Tiberius and the monstrous captivity of the city of Thebes (and additionally suggests the unheroic
character of the Germanicans), but reading further into the narrative
of the myth suggests an implicit association of the city and knowledge:
to be Oedipus enough would not just be to understand the Sphinx
but to understand the subsequent riddle of the plagued city that leads
Oedipus to self-knowledge. The Rome of *Sejanus* is as much a cipher
as Tiberius is, with the crucial difference that the opacity of Tiberius
is vested with enormous power while that of Rome is a sign of a scattered and fragmented public.

I want to approach *Sejanus* in the context of these dramatic
imperatives—the problem of urban knowledge and the attenuation of
urban theatricality—which do much to explain some of the difficulties
the play has presented to critics. The central interpretive puzzle of
Sejanus has been how the play seems to undermine the moral messages
it propounds.[38] Echoing a long critical tradition, John Sweeney comments that "there is a discrepancy between intended meaning and dramatic action, a confusion of dramatic perspective," and goes on to say
that the play "manipulates its audience in uncomfortable ways, excit-
ing responses in order to reject them and soliciting judgements that go
unsupported by the dramatic action."[39] This tension is especially acute
at the end of the play, where the Germanicans offer a pious retelling
of the crowd's destructive actions as the work of Fortune—an interpretation fundamentally at odds with the Machiavellian power struggle that the play has presented. Similarly, the omens and auguries
abruptly introduced in the final act of the play seem designed to be
unconvincing, existing in an indeterminate position between supernatural intervention and awkward theatrical convention.

Sweeney interprets these sorts of maneuvers and frustrations
as Jonson's subconscious refusal to "give the play over to his
audience" (48). This is an astute reading of Jonson's possible motives,
but I would argue that the implications are less psychological than
thematic, and concern Jonson's engagement not only with the theater audience but with the complex theatricalities of the crowded city.
Jonson's reluctance to "give the play over" mirrors the attenuated
urban theatricality discussed above and through this metatheatrical
technique we are forced to evaluate the final events of the play not
only in the context of the rest of the play but in the context of
the play's urban performance. The first critic to do so was Jonson
himself, of course; in the dedicatory epistle to the published play,

he says:

> If ever any ruin were so great, as to survive; I think this be one I send
> you: the *Fall of Sejanus*. It is a poem that (if I well remember) in your
> Lordship's sight, suffered no less violence from our people here, than
> the subject of it did from the rage of the people of Rome.[40]

Jonson thus connects the dramatic space of the play to the theatrical space of its performance, with the purpose of framing his creation: the figure of Sejanus is the figure of the play, a work of integrity set before the common herd, who reject it for its unsavory sallets—a spectacle observed, as in the commendatory poems in the quarto text, by the elite playgoer, who recoils at the barbarity and stupidity of the multitude. This is the theater of the judicious spectator, self-differentiated from the mob; through an appreciation of the play's integrity one demonstrates one's own.

The poor reception of the play (it apparently had but one performance), and Jonson's reaction to it, has been discussed extensively, generally in the terms Jonson provides in his address to the readers: "Nor is it needful, or almost possible, in these our times, and to such auditors, as commonly things are presented, to observe the old state and splendor of dramatic poems, with preservation of any popular delight" (2:234). *Sejanus* clearly did become something of a marker of taste among the better-educated playgoers, and it is doubtless a central text in Jonson's vexed and conflicted attempts to reconcile the work of an author with the demands of popular entertainment.[41] I want to suggest, however, that to read the play and its reception in these terms—as if the reaction of the audience in the Globe theater was confirming Jonson's portrayal of them in the play—is to read it backward. The play cannot be separated from its reception because the play that we now have comes *after* that reception, and was (according to Jonson) significantly altered by the elimination of the original collaborator. Given Jonson's self-consciousness about the reception of his plays, it seems reasonable to assume that his rewriting of *Sejanus* proceeded with its initial staging in mind. And if this is the case, performance is necessarily conflated with text: what happens to Sejanus might be best seen as a commentary on what happened to the play.[42] Jonson stages the destruction of *Sejanus* through the figure of Sejanus.[43]

On one level, then, what is really at stake in *Sejanus* is the question of what happens when a play *is* "given over": how can the interface between the cohesive dramatic text and the fragmented, circulatory city be understood? Correspondingly, the play is also concerned with *what* it is given over to. *Sejanus* undermines itself in order to show the inability of the theater to represent what the crowded city is. As the prefatory quotation to this chapter suggests, there is no wisdom "i'the streets," no knowledge to be gained, only tumults, whispers, and violence. With no imaginary ideal to give it fictive coherence, the Rome of *Sejanus* always falls apart, is always already dismembered. In this way, I would suggest that *Sejanus* sets itself an impossible dramatic task: coherent meaning is not possible in the crowded city, but in this play there is no other location in which it may be vested. In order to portray the city in this way, the play must fail, must be sacrificed.[44]

Jonson deploys the figure of the crowd with great tactical skill in the first four acts of *Sejanus;* although it rarely presents a multitude that is necessarily real, a careful escalation of references gradually implies that a large, crowded city watches the world of the play, preparing for the catastrophe of the final act. These references are balanced within the structure of *Sejanus,* counterpointing the theatrical spaces presented in an alternating fashion, so that the first and third acts are paired against the second and fourth. Although set almost entirely in the dangerously exposed space of the palace, Act One is virtually without invocation of the crowded city. The closest approach is Sabinus's comment that Sejanus now "disposes every dignity" that once "Rome's general suffrage gave" (1.220, 223), a lament that places the "general" Rome in the past, not the present. Some hint of what is to come might be found in the placing of Sejanus's statue in Pompey's Theater, but the import is more Roman honor than popular display; at this point in the play, this location is clearly more a house of fame than an actual theater. Act Three, though focused around the spectacular trials of Cordus and Silius in the Senate, similarly contains little in the way of popular invocations. At issue in both trials is the performance of *romanitas* in a corrupt and fallen age, but unlike *Julius Caesar* this corruption is not expressed through the vehicle of the populous city. Cordus's defiant *apologia* touches the matter when he asks if he with Brutus and Cassius "Did . . . Incense the people in the civil cause / With dangerous speeches" (3.449–52), but the point is that no such action took place.

Paradoxically, then, when *Sejanus* is most public and most theatrical there is little reference made to the crowd. In contrast, Act Two, dominated by closet scenes and conspiracies, begins to introduce the idea of the invisible population that surrounds the world of the court—though principally through Sejanus's claim to Tiberius that Agrippina, the widow of Germanicus, puts on "popular presentings" for her sons, Nero and Drusus:

> Whilst to their thirst of rule they win the rout
> (That's still the friend of novelty) with hope
> Of future freedom, which on every change
> That greedily, though emptily, expects. (2.213, 235–38).

This is the first explicit reference to the multitude in the play, and although the terms of the reference are conventional—as in the plays examined in chapter 4, the common mouth is hungry for novelty—the manner in which it is put forward is significant. It is in some ways a suspect invocation; Sejanus's desire to manipulate Tiberius and frighten him with the possibility of "future freedom" drives the assertion, perhaps leaving it uncertain as to whether such popular presentings in fact occur. Similar descriptions are found in Act Four, as when Sabinus relates how Sejanus sets Nero and Drusus Junior against each other by telling each "how bright he stands in popular expectance" (4.209). Within the report, the populace and its affections are a mystery (requiring the interpretation of Sejanus to be understood), but in Sabinus's retelling it becomes a clear fiction: what is rumored abroad is not the actual popularity of Agrippina's sons but Sejanus's assertion of such. It is clear that the prime purpose of these assertions is tactical, not descriptive. Like Sejanus's rumor that Agrippina "with popular studies gapes for sovereignty" (2.359), what matters is not the crowd but those who might use it; the multitude is a slander, a tool for other, more important agents.

This strange displacement of the urban crowd from event into discourse has several effects, prompting the question of what sort of public Rome the play presents. In the first place, it ties the crowd to conversation, conspiracy, and rumor rather than to display and assembly. Like the distracted multitudes examined in chapter 4, the populous Rome of *Sejanus* is rhizomatic, associated with dispersal and dissemination; it is the "common mouth" of the city (2.492), the opaque pathways of urban information, which speak only in indecipherable whisperings. More directly, it is also an unknowable Rome; if the theater audience's chief connection to the crowded city is through the rhetorical gambits of Sejanus then it is given only a tenuous connection to the actual Rome of the play. Finally, it presents a Rome that is necessarily insignificant—insignificant not only in its lack of political power but in being unnecessary to the politics of display. The Rome of the first four acts of *Sejanus* cannot act as a legitimating frame for the actions of the elite; its lack of substance places it outside of the play's signifying structures.[45]

Sejanus's use of the crowd as a manipulative fiction receives a response of sorts at the end of Act Four, in the news of Tiberius's ambiguous letters, which first favor and then disfavor Sejanus and his supporters; Lepidus claims that Tiberius wants to make Sejanus

> odious
> Unto the staggering rout, whose aid (in fine)
> He hopes to use, as sure, who (when they sway)
> Bear down, o'erturn all objects in their way. (4.469–72)

This passage gives a multitude that is something more than a fiction; foreshadowing the last act of the play, the crowd materializes into an urban audience, sliding from a tactical discourse toward a tangible reality. This crowd is still not an assembled body, however; their confluence (and swaying) is presented proverbially, not descriptively. Even at this point, moreover, the crowd is kept separate from the actual theater audience. We in the audience have not been swayed to the obviously malign Sejanus, or been influenced by Tiberius's popular studies; we know almost nothing of Agrippina, and can barely distinguish Nero and Drusus Junior as characters in the drama. If, as I argued above, *Julius Caesar* manipulates the theater audience into an alternating connection and disconnection with the affections of the onstage crowd, *Sejanus* makes any sort of connection impossible. Whoever the "we" who see (or perhaps more importantly, read) this play are, we are not part of the Roman multitude.

These theatrical frameworks change abruptly in the fifth act of the play, in which the city simultaneously takes center stage and becomes the location for a terrifying plethora of prodigies. Beginning with Sejanus's equation of himself with Rome—a fevered meditation that begins, appropriately enough, with the words "Swell, swell" (5.1)— the scene quickly changes with the sudden entry of Terentius:

> I meet it violent in the people's mouths,
> Who run in routs to Pompey's theatre,
> To view your statue: which, they say, sends forth
> A smoke, as from a furnace, black and dreadful. (27–30)

The play returns to the figure of Pompey's Theater, now clearly a place for public assembly and strange sights; Satrius and Natta shortly arrive to say that the head was taken off the statue, and a "great and monstrous serpent" leapt out of it (37). As the scene continues, the portents multiply; Terentius reminds Sejanus of the recent collapse of his bed from the weight of too many suitors, and of the death of his servants, shouldered down the cliff of the Gemoines by the bustling crowd following Sejanus in the street (59–61). This is the first time in the play that such crowds have been described in the context of Sejanus, and it is significant that only on the eve of his destruction is such an association made. This scene is also the first time that the word "prodigy" appears in the play; Sejanus says dismissively of the statue, "I think you mean to make it a prodigy" (49), which Terrentius emphatically affirms. The implication is that Rome is now, suddenly, prodigious; it has become the portentous space that presages the downfall of Sejanus, as a betrayal of the gods for having dared climb so high. As in *Julius Caesar*, to be prodigious grown is to be grown populous; Rome is now for the first time directly described as a crowded, corporeal city, full of people "run[ning] in routs," speaking violence and boding ruin. The supernatural frame and the populous city are tied to each other, so that the advent of one necessitates the presence of the other. In *Sejanus*, prodigies are theatrical displays produced for the credulous multitude to gawk at— "thousands are gazing at it, in the streets" (214)—and yet the city itself is also prodigious; like those in the play, the theater audience witnesses its rising and predicts its significance.

On the other hand, as many readers of the play have commented, these prodigies seems barely believable as such, contrivances that fit awkwardly with the profoundly material world the play presents.[46] To a much greater degree than *Julius Caesar*, the political implications of a "prodigy," a Machiavellian manipulator, remain powerful in these scenes, as when Macro calls Sejanus "thou prodigy of men" (687) and when Arruntius predicts that Macro will become "a greater prodigy in Rome" than Sejanus (742). This reiteration partially grounds the references to supernatural prodigies, emphasizing the political world inhabited in the first four acts of the play. Nevertheless, the play also refuses to remain on this level; instead, it grants an apparent significance to Rome as the theater of divine retribution that is alien to its construction in the rest of the play. Sejanus, by implication, blames Macro for the omens, and indeed some of the prodigies seem more like political stunts than the messages of the gods—such as the pestering of Sejanus's statue with smoke, snake, and hangman's noose. But what are we to make of the ball lightning that hangs before "the amazed wonder of the multitude" (221), or the idol of Fortune turning her face, causing the Flamen to exclaim, "Avert you gods / The prodigy" (185–86)? The tension between the political and the supernatural in these events remains unresolved, unbalancing the play and making it difficult to understand what, exactly, is being presented. Or, to put it another way, the *fact* of presentation is highlighted by the play's open embrace of awkwardness—an embrace particularly relevant to its treatment of the crowd. As *Sejanus* cannot be both supernatural and materialistic in its framework, so the crowded city cannot be both prodigious and meaningless—and the play's refusal to resolve this conflict foregrounds the problem of its own cohesion as dramatic text and theatrical performance.

In this context, we might wonder who it is that Sejanus addresses when he exclaims, alone upon the stage:

> By you, that fools call gods,
> Hang all the sky with your prodigious signs,
> Fill earth with monsters, drop the scorpion down
> Out of the zodiac, or the fiercer lion,
> Shake off the loosened globe from her long hinge,
> Roll all the world in darkness, and let loose
> The enraged winds to turn up groves and towns;
> When I do fear again, let me be struck
> With forked fire, and unpitied die. (390–98)

Sejanus here invokes the gods, who are not in fact gods, though vested with enormous power, which he then repudiates. What is the register of this speech, which passionately invokes something the speaker does not believe exists? I would argue that here we find ourselves, for the first time in *Sejanus,* in the space of the play's performance—the "loosened globe" echoing the "distracted globe" of *Hamlet,* the "prodigious signs" of the zodiac indicating the constellations "fretted with golden fire" on the canopy of the Globe Theater.[47] At the level of a play's performance, it could be said, the "supernatural" equates to the "theatrical," as an imposition of an extradramatic frame beyond the control of agents within the drama. On this level, the play itself threatens Sejanus's downfall—like Macbeth, he refuses to submit to the narrative resolution he fears is closing in upon him—and the theater provides the scene of his destruction. As the antitheatricalists repeatedly emphasize, it is the theater that is filled with monsters, that hangs prodigious signs before the population, that exerts a malign force upon the city; through the working of the theater that city becomes infected with prodigious display. Or, to play upon Sejanus's phrasing, the theater is "loosened" and set free, producing an eccentric, rolling momentum that will destroy all in its path.

The "loosened globe" that is the theater might also be interpreted in another sense: not shaken loose, but dilated, moved from closed to open, made permeable and penetrable. I began this section by noting how abruptly the play changes in the final act, how the play is opened up to the signifying context of the prodigious city. This dramatic shift can be understood as a theatrical loosening; the final act enters the space of the theater, a space in which the play acknowledges its urban surroundings—an acknowledgment that makes both Sejanus and *Sejanus* vulnerable. These two realms of the play, however, are fundamentally incommensurable. As the political prodigy opposes the supernatural omen, so the court opposes the crowded city and the closed text opposes the open performance; what transpires in the crossing from one to the other is dismemberment.

⋅That the space of the crowded city is the space of the theater is made clear in the long description Terentius gives of the death and dismemberment of Sejanus, which begins by establishing a clear context for the actions of the crowd:

> The eager multitude, who never yet
> Knew why to love, or hate, but only pleased
> To express their rage of power, no sooner heard
> The murmur of Sejanus in decline,
> But with that speed, and heat of appetite,
> With which they greedily devour the way
> To some great sports, or a new theatre,
> They filled the Capitol, and Pompey's cirque;
> Where, like so many mastiffs, biting stones,
> As if his statues now were sensive grown
> Of their wild fury, first, they tear them down. (5.749–59)

Here the crowd resembles nothing so much as a grotesque depiction of the "barking students of Bears' College" castigated in the apology to *Poetaster*,[48] the common mouth biting at the statues of Sejanus in a confusion of representation and reality that underscores the power of the theater to elide such differences. There has been some preparation for this scene in the first part of the play; the attack, and especially its mixture of flesh and stone, echoes the assertion of Drusus, when he tells Sejanus that he will "advance a statue / O' your own bulk" on the cross, where he will "crack those sinews" of pride (570–71, 73). In this case, as in *Julius Caesar,* the crowd doubles what has already happened, a common echo to the elite threat or action.

A similar presaging of the dismemberment of Sejanus is found in Arruntius's threat, made against the possibility that Sejanus might seek the imperial throne:

> If I could guess he had but such a thought,
> My sword should cleave him down from head to heart,
> But I would find it out: and with my hand
> I'd hurl his panting brain about the air,
> In mites, as small as *atomi*. (1.253–57)

This intention, however, is marked by its focus on the pursuit of knowledge; Sejanus must be dissected and dispersed in order to discover what truth lies beneath his dissembling surfaces.[49] The dismemberment of Sejanus by the Roman crowd, in contrast, produces no revelation, only dissemination:

> These mounting at his head, these at his face,
> These digging out his eyes, those with his brain
> Sprinkling themselves, their houses, and their friends;
> Others are met, have ravished thence an arm,
> And deal small pieces of the flesh for favours;
> These with a thigh; this hath cut off his hands;
> And this his feet; these fingers, and these toes;
> That hath his liver; he his heart: there wants
> Nothing but room for wrath, and place for hatred!
> What cannot oft be done, is now o'erdone.
> The whole, and all of what was great Sejanus,
> And next to Caesar did possess the world,
> Now torn and scattered, as he needs no grave,
> Each little dust covers a little part:
> So lies he nowhere, and yet often buried. (5.808–22)

As in Arruntius's threat, the brain of Sejanus is atomized, but is significantly sprinkled over both the crowd and the physical fabric of the city. If the dismembered body is the crowd, figuring the dispersed multiplicity and heterogeneity of the urban populace, it is also the city itself; Sejanus now pervades Rome, lying nowhere and everywhere, made to circulate almost invisibly through the streets and alleys. The spatial dynamics of the description highlight its rhizomatic motion as well: at the start the crowd gathers, pressing itself close to the body of Sejanus, at the end the body is dispersed to multiplicity. As I have discussed, this dynamic of assembly and dissemination is the movement the theater produces in its bodily relationship with the crowded city, gathering the distracted multitude to display and then dispersing them through the body of the city. The scene itself is the theater as the antitheatricalists saw it: rather than infinite riches in a little room, there is "nothing [wanting] but room for wrath."

"What cannot oft be done, is now o'erdone"; in effect, Jonson takes the trope of Cinna's dismemberment and pushes it to the limit, figuring collective distraction as something that renders the body particulate, without dimension, dispersed to dust, mimicking the Brownian motions of the rhizomatic city. Although the fate of Sejanus has classical and theatrical antecedents beyond Cinna—in Seneca, in Ovidian *sparagmos,* in Actaeon, in *Dr. Faustus*—its principal frame is clearly urban and popular, as the inadequate moralizing of Lepidus presages: "Who would depend upon the popular air, / Or voice of men" (5.695–96). Here again is the paradox of the prodigious city. In his imagined excavation, Arruntius is after the meaning that Sejanus hides, the significance he holds. We might therefore describe the actual dismemberment—in the loosened, metatheatrical space of the final act—as a parallel search for the significance of *Sejanus.* Yet none is forthcoming; the movement from imagination to demonstration, from aristocratic *romanitas* to popular Rome, effects an emptying out of significance. The scene of dismemberment must bear the burden of the play, as the closing colloquy among the Germanicans makes clear, but nothing can be learned here; if Cinna makes the actions of the crowd insignificant by being the wrong man, Jonson shows that even the right man is the wrong man. And the crowded city, the necessary stage for the play's revelation, is made both meaningful and meaningless.

These paradoxes, as I have been suggesting, stem from the terms of the play's engagement with the issue of the crowded city. If, as I argued at the outset, we should view the fate of Sejanus as commentary on the reception of *Sejanus,* and not vice versa, we see the complications enforced upon Jonson. In order to stage the self-destruction of the play, Jonson had to open up the space of the play, loosen the Globe, admit that which is outside it. Or perhaps the reverse: in order to engage the crowded city, Jonson had to dismember his play. Dismemberment, after all, is what happens to plays when they are given over to the crowd; what was whole and cohesive is spread, disseminated, modified, misinterpreted. And yet, in a sense, the play refutes even this modeling of the relation between the one and the many. As is often noted, Jonson emphasizes the historical "integrity in the story" in his address to the readers and in his marginal glosses, principally with the intent of discouraging those "whose noses are ever like swine spoiling and rooting up the Muses' gardens" by demonstrating the transparency of his account.[50] This transparency, however, is occluded at the very climax of the play, in the long description of the dismemberment quoted above. As Tacitus's account of the fall of Sejanus is missing, Jonson's historical source at this point in the play is Dio's *Roman History*, which merely records in a terse manner that by the Senate's order Sejanus "was executed and his body cast down the Stairway, where the rabble abused it for three whole days and afterwards threw it into the river."[51] To describe Sejanus's dismemberment, Jonson turns to a completely different source and a completely different event, the death of the tyrant Rufinus in Claudian's *In Rufinum*—an addition Jonson does *not* acknowledge in a marginal gloss.[52]

There are a number of ways to interpret Jonson's supplemental account—most obviously, that he was attempting to bow to the pressures of the public theater. It would also be appropriate to say that the working through of his larger vision of the distracted city required a dilation on urban dismemberment: Jonson needed to bring the crowd into the play in a way he did not find in his sources. Still, it seems striking that at the very moment when the published play means to demonstrate its superiority to the common herd by the dramatic example of its protagonist and double, the text turns false, migrates to an undisclosed narrative, lies to us. What is conflated here is not just the events of the play and their performance, but the text of the play as well; Sejanus, in effect, is already dismembered, severed from his historical integrity, patched together from the odds and ends of Jonson's reading. Rather than framing the play in a particular manner for publication— as a noble ruin that survives popular rage—we might view Jonson's comments as drawing the apparatus of publication into the body of the play as well. These parallels suggest a further range of possible meanings for Jonson's deployment of the urban crowd. Sejanus is sequentially dismembered: textually, dramatically, and theatrically—and further dismemberment of the published play is threatened by Jonson's fears of those who would disseminate it, turning it to political applications and circulating libels. The author dismembers his historical account of Sejanus; the Roman crowds rush to the theater to dismember Sejanus again; and the London crowds rush to the theater to dismember *Sejanus* yet again; the published play has dismemberment at every stage, a constant feature of every aspect of the play—and has already faced further dismemberment in the circulations of the press, and may face even more in the uses to which it is put. Dismemberment becomes the controlling metaphor of the entire cultural production of the work, from author's pen to theatrical performance to popular estimation to printed publication and dissemination.

The last view of the Roman crowd shows them repenting, and wishing Sejanus "collected, and created new" (5.877). Repentance is obviously crucial to Jonson's metatheatrical framing of *Sejanus;* the fickleness of the crowd confirms not only their baseness and typicality, but also the judgment of the judicious spectator, who never wavers in his appreciation of the play. And it would be possible to read this passage as a corollary to Brutus's "How many times shall Caesar bleed in sport" speech; the next night at the theater the audience will again raise Sejanus and again destroy him. The fact, though, that there was no next night for this play suggests that "collected, and created new" refers not simply to the serial repetition of performance but to the process of transformation that the play went through in the movement from performance to published text—a process that signals not the final repair of *Sejanus* but its continuing dismemberment. Sejanus is recollected and dispersed many times; text, play, performance, and quarto all meet at the moment of their destruction by the urban crowd. In these motions of gathering and destruction we divine the operations of circulatory processes we only glimpse in the metamorphic movement of the body of *Sejanus* from one mode to another.

I began this chapter by asserting the special meaning of Rome in the early modern theater. In a way, though, both *Sejanus* and *Julius Caesar* take us to a point where Rome has no special meaning. In *Julius Caesar,* the noble idea of Rome, the imaginative trope and figure of desire so powerful that it can "move" the constant Romans who invoke it, exists only in a vacuum; its integrity is demonstrated through its opposition to, and separation from, the crowded city that it ultimately falls prey to. As I have discussed, the play relocates itself to a battlefield where "Rome" can be largely forgotten and "Roman" can remain significant: "I had rather be a dog and bay the moon / Than such a Roman" (4.3.27–28); "If that thou be'st a Roman, take it forth" (103); "Then like a Roman bear the truth I tell" (188); "This is a Roman's part" (5.3.89); "The last of all the Romans" (99); "This was the noblest Roman of them all" (5.5.68). *Sejanus* has no such escape, and remains at the location of the prodigious, theatrical city. Rather than retreating from the city, Jonson empties it of meaning. The play closes with Sejanus's widow Apicata bewailing the murder of her children "As might . . . make the old / Deformed Chaos rise again, to o'erwhelm / . . . all the world" (857–60), but this apocalyptic scene directly at odds with the certain knowledge that nothing will in fact change in Rome as a result of these tragedies. If Rome is an apocalypse, it is, paradoxically, one without end.

Both of these approaches to the prodigious city are important in considering Shakespeare's return to the urban scene of Rome almost a decade after *Julius Caesar*.[53] *Coriolanus* might even be seen as responding to *Sejanus* in the same way that *Sejanus* responded to *Julius Caesar*, in that it takes the central fact of the prodigious, unidentifiable city and deliberately uses it to despoil Coriolanus of the Roman identity he so carefully crafted. *Coriolanus* ends with a scene of urban theater, a parade to welcome the unconquering hero, that turns into a dismemberment—one that recalls both plays in its combination of political assassins and the people's beastly rage. Even more pointed is the language that Coriolanus uses earlier as he prepares to assuage the crowd through a debasing performance:

> Yet were there but this single plot to lose,
> The mould of Martius, they to dust should grind it
> And throw't against the wind. To th' marketplace! (3.2.102–4)

The marketplace in *Coriolanus*, as in *Julius Caesar*, is both the place of theater and the place of exchange, both the place of gathering and dispersal. But in *Coriolanus* the theatrical idea being expressed is overcoded with the personal, Coriolanus's pathological concern with his own identity as a Roman citizen. Like *Sejanus*, *Coriolanus* differs from *Julius Caesar* in that no escape is offered from the crowded theatrical space of the city, despite the play's frequent retreat from Rome. Although Coriolanus moves through many cities, he finds the same prodigious audience in each, a monstrously disintegrating and anonymous space that offers him no stable foundation on which to base his urban self. Urban identity, in both the sense of personal identity and the identity of the city, is one of the issues that occupy the final chapter.

C H A P T E R 6

"A Kind of Nothing": Plague Time in Early Modern London

Haue not we made an Idoll *of this Citie, which hath stood 2733 yeares, and being infected with the number of our people* Dauids sinne: *boasted of the multitudes of heads, riches, buildings:* that *this was the* Imperiall *Citie of the Kingdome,* Chamber *of the King, that with* Laodicea *wee were rich, encreased with goods, and had need of nothing: that with* Tytus *our Citie hath beene replenished, the haruest of the time her reuenue, a ioyous Citie: her* Merchants Princes, *her Traffique the Honourable of the earth. Haue not Parents gloried in the number of their children, and set too much their hearts vpon them?*

(*Samuel Price,* Londons Remembrancer)[1]

Sicinius. *What is the city but the people?*

(Coriolanus *3.1.197*)

In 1603, plague killed one in five Londoners in the space of a few months.[2] Over thirty thousand died, and thousands more fled the city, causing London virtually to stop. Its streets were deserted, except for the dying and the dead. Houses were boarded shut with the infected and their families inside. Heaps of bodies were buried in shallow graves, or left to rot in the streets and the fields. In the words of Thomas Dekker, the preeminent Jacobean plague writer, to be in London at this time was to be hung in "a vast silent Charnell-house," surrounded by a thousand fresh and decaying corpses.[3]

The scale of this calamity is hard to grasp, and in this incomprehensibility lies the traditional meaning of the plague. It is this image of plague as an inexpressible, cataclysmic wrenching of a society that causes Antonin Artaud, echoing many early seventeenth-century commentators, to imagine plague as a social purge, "after which nothing remains except death or an extreme purification."[4] For Jacobean London, however, plague was less cataclysm than context. In the early seventeenth century, London's plague was not a calamitous singularity but a constant presence, ebbing and flowing throughout the year and the years but never disappearing. In 1609, John Davies commented:

> Time neuer knew since he beganne his houres,
> (For aught we reade) a Plague so long remaine
> In any Citie, as this Plague of ours:
> For now six yeares in London it hath laine.
> Where noone goes out, but at his comming in,
> If he but feeles the tendrest touch of smart,
> He feares he is Plague-smitten for his sinne;
> So, ere hee's plagu'd, he takes It to the heart:
> For, Feare doth (Loadstone-like) it oft attract,
> That else would not come neere.[5]

Davies' observation establishes not only the persistence of the plague, but also the mental effects of this persistence on the urban population.[6] The fear of plague, Davies, intimates, is itself like a plague, roaming through the city—and, through a conjoining of the mental and the physical, is as potentially deadly as the disease itself. Even after 1612, when plague deaths in London dropped to a handful a year, the psychic presence of plague did not leave the city, as reports of plague elsewhere in the country and in Europe repeatedly presaged its imminent return.[7]

The advent of plague means the death of the festive life of the city: pageants and ceremonies are canceled, theaters closed, fairs suppressed, and the gathering of crowds forbidden. The standing plague orders make clear the extent of these restrictions: "That all Plaies, Bearebaitings, Games, Singing of Ballads, Buckler-play, or such like causes of Assemblies of people, be vtterly prohibited, and the parties offending, seuerely punished, by any Alderman or Justice of the Peace."[8] James's coronation entry, discussed in chapter 3, was long delayed because of the 1603 epidemic. Given the importance of all of these events to the legible meaning of the city, it could be suggested that in plague time London ceases to exist. As the author of *Lachrymae Londinenses* ventriloquizes the city:

> I *London*, that haue beene styled by Strangers, *Emporium celeberri-mum totius Orbis; The most famous Citie and Marketplace of the whole World.* By others styled, *Trinobantum*, I. *Troynovant* or *New Troy:* by others, *Augusta*, I. An Imperiall Citie, by all, euer held, *Camera Regis,* I. The *Imperiall and Royall Chamber of the Kings of this Nation, the Metropolis of this Land* . . . I *London,* I say againe, that yesterday also enjoyed all my Childen the Citizens their presence, with free Commerce, Merchandizing and Trading with all Merchants of Christendome; yea, I may say, of the whole World, am now become the most forlone place of the whole Kingdome.[9]

In this speech, as in the chapter epigraph, are many of the symbolic structures that shaped the idea of London: Troynovant, metropolis, marketplace, and above all *camera regis,* the designation "by al, euer held" that most defined the city's symbolic space and with which this study began. All are wiped away with the advent of plague. In view of this erasure, it may seem perverse to link plague time with the official and commercial representations of the city that dominate the earlier part of the book. My intention, however, is more than a palinodic repudiation of urban significance. Like the official processions through the streets of London, plague is both inside and outside the city: at once alien and (through implication and calendrical repetition) inherent to urban experience. In a different manner, plague also performs the city, troping quotidian urban existence into something horrifying and strange. Artaud notes the connection: "In the theater as in the plague there is a kind of strange sun, a light of abnormal intensity by which it seems that the difficult and even the impossible become our normal environment" (30). In *The Triumph of Death,* Davies uses a theatrical image to convey the intensity of London's suffering: "how yet the Plague doth rage / (With vnappeased furie) more and more, / Making our Troy-nouant a tragicke Stage / Whereone to shew Deaths powre, with slaughters sore" (sig. L1). Theatrical and ceremonial metaphors similarly pervade Dekker's plague-ridden pamphlets. In *The Seuen Deadly Sinnes of London,* Dekker describes the sins that bring the plague as "Actors in this old Enterlude of Iniquitie," going so far as to list them in a *dramatis personae* at the beginning of the pamphlet.[10] These sins enter the city in triumphal processions that bear more than a passing resemblance to the civic pageantry of the Lord Mayor's Show. Like civic pageants, plague organizes the city into a symbolic landscape, a theatrical *mise en scène* imbued with profound ritualistic meaning.

This chapter examines the presence and persistence of plague in early modern London as it is manifested in the urban literature of the period. My particular focus, unsurprisingly, is the overdetermined association between the plague and the urban crowd; as I argue in more detail below, the crowd occupies a complex and contradictory relationship with the plague, figured as both antithesis and source of urban infection. The first part of the chapter examines the negotiations that Dekker makes with the plague in his prose pamphlets, exploring how the discourse of the city and the discourse of the plague interact and become interchangeable. I then reposition my analysis within the theatrical space of *Coriolanus*, Shakespeare's most forceful examination of urban crisis. *Coriolanus*, perhaps surprisingly, is a signal text in early modern plague literature. Although plague does not appear in the play, due to Shakespeare's elision of certain parts of Plutarch's narrative, plague imagery and rhetoric is pervasive, infecting all aspects of the play.

In treating these works, my aim is to explore how the significations of the disease interact with symbolic structures of urban meaning, especially in relation to the crowd. Dekker and Shakespeare both link the idea of the city to the plague in the bodily context of the urban populace; in both the discourse of the city and the discourse of the plague interact and ultimately become interchangeable. What this merging indicates, I will argue, is that the presence of plague mirrors the crisis of urban meaning catalyzed by London's prodigious population growth. Although, as we have seen, this semiotic and spatial crisis was visible well before the death of Elizabeth, my primary focus here is on the Jacobean plague, for a variety of reasons—not least that it is only after 1603 that early modern plague literature becomes recognizable as a genre, in the sense of a popular commodity with a particular set of determinants and conventions.[11] Rather than focusing expressly on the 1603 plague or on its equally lethal 1625 counterpart, however, this chapter also concentrates on the time between these two bookends of the Jacobean period and on the symbolic problem of the disease's endurance. If plague signifies urban catastrophe, a vertical slice across the horizontal trajectory of normal existence, how can its long-term presence be understood? What does the persistence of plague do to the meaning of the city? Something of the complexity of this question can be seen in a passage from Dekker's 1608 pamphlet *The Dead Tearme,* in which London says to

Westminster of the plague:

> Sicknesse hath dwelt a long time in thy Chambers, she doth now walke still in a ghostly and formidable shape uppe and downe my streets. . . . Shall our faire bodies never recover of this Disease, which so often and often hath run all over them, and doth nowe againe beginne to bee as a plague unto us?[12]

This passage plays in interesting ways with the imagined geography of the plague, as it moves from the private space of "thy Chambers" to the public realm of "my streets," reversing and culminating in "our fair bodies," a space at once public and private, symbolic and material. This transgressive and transformative movement through and between the cities' material and symbolic spaces produces a figural slippage: plague itself becomes quasi-metaphorical, "as a plague," troping itself. In reaching for appropriate terms in which to describe the persistence of the disease, Dekker's uncanny language demonstrates both the inescapability and slipperiness of plague as an urban signifier.

This slipperiness occurs in other registers of meaning as well. As the quintessential urban malady, plague is a spatial disease; it refigures the livid and symbolic space of the city, altering and transforming the urban aspect. At the same time its resonances are temporal, recalling and recycling a long historical and literary tradition of urban dissolution. The plague city is always plural: London under plague is haunted by Florence, Rome, Jerusalem, Athens, Thebes, Nineveh, the cities of the plain. In *The Arke of Noah,* the preacher James Godskall strings together a number of common comparisons:

> we weepe, when we remember thee O London; we hang vp our harpes, and the pleasantnesse of the countrey cannot stay our teares, remembering you that are afflicted, as if we were afflicted our selues, weeping for the Citie, as Christ did for Ierusalem, Luk.19, and not onely for you, but for our selues, Luk.23.28. How could we feast, while the yron enters Iosephs soule in the Citie? We are not Nero, singing and triumphing when Rome is on fire, but as Abraham prayed for Sodome, and the Prophet for the peace of Ierusalem, so we for the peace of London.[13]

Establishing biblical antecedents to current situations is a standard sermon practice, but the plethora of associations Godskall brings to bear on London suggests the difficulty of finding an effective frame of reference, a language that will accurately represent the complexity and intensity of the plagued city. The opening of Davies' poem addresses this difficulty:

> The obiect of mine outward Sense affords
> But too much Matter for my Muse to forme;
> Her want (though she had words at will) is words,
> T'expresse this Plagues vnvtterable Storme! (Sig. I5)

"Too much matter" is indeed the problem, an expression that seems to have (at least) a triple significance: too large a subject to encompass, too much sensory material to process, and most viscerally, too much corporeal matter—the heapes of corpses filling the streets, the city grotesquely made flesh.

Davies' nominal solution is to simply tell what he sees, in an unadorned fashion: "Fancie thou needst not forge false Images / To furnish Wit t'expresse a truth so true" (sig. I5). The truth of plague, however, can never be unadorned or unornamented, can never simply mean what is experienced. In *Illness as Metaphor,* an analysis of the social and literary meanings of tuberculosis and cancer, Susan Sontag writes that "any important disease whose causality is murky, and for which treatment is ineffectual, tends to be awash in significance. . . . The disease becomes adjectival."[14] Plague shares this adjectival significance, but its transgressive spatial and historical dimensionality makes "metaphor" an inadequate word to explain its productions of meaning. *The Wonderful Year,* Dekker's retelling of the 1603 visitation, famously presents the plague as "like a Spanish Leagar, or rather like stalking *Tamberlaine,*" who "hath pitcht his tents . . . in the sinfully-polluted Suburbes" (sig. D1). In this complex image, Tamburlaine is both invader and theatrical role, the London suburbs at once the staging ground for the invasive infection and the staging ground of Marlowe's play.[15] The plague is therefore figured both as a historical conqueror and as a locus of urban theatricality. Both levels of interpretation mix the metaphoric with the material; we are caught between seeing the plague's suburban slaughter as like that of the actual Tamburlaine in other cities, or seeing it as a making-real of a theatrical representation actually present in this specific location. Similarly, plague literature almost always occupies a strange middle ground between the historical and the literary: Dekker's prose fiction is not unique in its clinical fantasies, its combination of lurid storytelling and detailed medical reports of morbidity and infection.

Most of this chapter is focused on the local meaning of plague in early modern London. But I want to begin by discussing briefly

"The Theater and the Plague," Artaud's provocative and idiosyncratic meditation on visceral transformation in the plagued city and in the theater. Artaud's short essay is useful not only because of its evocations of two millennia of plague literature (a quality endemic to the genre; writing about plague, it seems, is always reading about plague as well), but because of Artaud's overwhelming concern with the psychosocial character of the disease. In making this conjunction I do not want to suggest that Artaud understood the plague in exactly the same way as early modern writers, thereby implying that discussions of plague form a universal, timeless discourse uninflected by the specifics of historical context.[16] I do want to suggest, however, that the discursive practice of plague inevitably *tends* in this direction. As the frankly fantastical tone of Artaud's essay indicates, to write about plague is to desire the overarching, the universal, the unconditional.

Central to Artaud's understanding of the plague is his belief that it is not spread by physical means alone:

> Whatever may be the errors of historian or physicians concerning the plague, I believe we can agree upon the idea of a malady that would be a kind of psychic entity and would not be carried by a virus. If one wished to analyze closely all the facts of plague contagion that history or even memoirs provide us with, it would be difficult to isolate one actually verified instance of contagion by contact. (18)

This odd insistence, relying half-heartedly on Artaud's reading of plague material (as much literary as documentary) for its evidence, provokes several observations. Before analyzing Artaud's motives in repudiating the medical etiology of the disease (an explanation that, by the time of his writing, had the status of scientific fact), it is worth noting the interpretive power of the idea of a psychic contagion. Artaud objects to the insufficiency of the medical explanation in illuminating the social, cultural, political, and psychological impact of plague. If, following Sontag's perspective, we misunderstand Artaud as speaking metaphorically, his "kind of psychic entity" seems to operate akin to what Stephen Greenblatt calls "the circulation of social energy."[17] Though the plague itself is only vectored through fleas carrying *yersina pestis,* the multiple effects of the disease reverberate through all the pathways of the society, "infecting" all with their messages.

But Artaud means something more than metaphor. For Artaud, the effects of the disease *are* the disease; the social and psychological chaos that plague inaugurates is as much a direct product of the disease as is the somatic chaos of buboes, fevers, lesions, and death.[18]

In his opposition to the reductive compartmentalization of modern scientistic medicine and psychology, Artaud refuses to make a separation between body and mind or between the body of a citizen and the body of the city. For this reason a purely medical (i.e., purely physical) explanation of plague is anathema. Noting that the plague microbe was isolated in the late nineteenth century, he comments, "Personally, I regard this microbe only as a smaller—infinitely smaller—material element which appears at some moment in the development of the virus, but in no way accounts for the plague" (21). The bacillus, "one of those round-headed, short tailed tadpoles which only a microscope can reveal" (21), is the wrong sort of secret knowledge, a clinical diminution of the plague's power that threatens to rob it of its dramatic potential for carnivalesque social mayhem.

Like Davies' assertion that fear of the plague is "Loadstone-like," drawing the disease to where it would not otherwise have gone, Artaud's analysis is predicated on the radical inextricability of mental and physical processes. Similarly, his insistence on what he calls the plague's "spiritual physiognomy" (24)—mixing the bodily and the spiritual, the profane and the sacred, in typical fashion—echoes the views expressed by many other early modern plague writers, especially those who felt threatened by the material explanations for the plague that were overtaking traditional theological explanations.[19] "God hauing smitten our Citie with the Pestilence," wrote Henoch Clapham in 1603, "Behold, booke vpon booke, prescribing naturall meanes as for naturall maladies, but little said of spirituall meanes, for spirituall maladies."[20] A survey of the extant plague literature suggests otherwise; as common as medical nostrums are "antidotes" and "approved medicines" that consist of prayer and repentance. Clapham himself seemed unwilling to completely ignore the corporeal aspects of the plague; in *Henoch Clapham His Demaundes and Answers touching the Pestilence,* published the following year, he answers the question of whether the plague is infectious in terms that Artaud would recognize: "The first causes which breed the Pestilence, are so vnknowen, so invisble, and so strange to all our sense, that we are altogeather ignorant of them . . . Necessarily so it followeth, that som thing in this plague be *Supernaturall,* and somwhat *Naturall.*"[21] In *Newes from Graues-ende,* Dekker titles one section "The cause of the Plague," and his conclusion (after rebutting all other possible etiologies) mines the same vein: "every man within him feeds / A worme which this contagion breedes," and the plague "sucks virid poyson from our soule."[22] Plague mystifies, and from this mystification a morality of the plague is drawn. "No one can say why the plague strikes the coward who flees it" (22), says Artaud, echoing a long tradition that perhaps reached its apotheosis in Dekker, who obsessively returned to the subject of urban runaways in pamphlet after pamphlet.[23] The statement is manifestly false; people have always fled the plague, and those that flee have higher survival rates than those who remain. But plague is inevitably perceived in moral terms, as if there were an overarching plan to its spread through the city.

This desire for purposiveness in plague can be understood in spiritual terms, but there is also a particularly urban aspect to its formation. The idea of contagion in the city leads to a consideration of the complexity of the circulation of urban bodies. Although plague has always been known, on empirical grounds, to be contagious in some manner, Artaud's reluctance to attribute the spread of the disease to contagion alone can be seen across the spectrum of plague literature. In *Newes from Graues-ende,* Dekker writes:

> Can we believe that one mans breath
> Infected, and being blowne from him,
> His poyson should to others swim:
> For then who breath'd upon the first? (Sig. D1v)

Dekker scores a debating point through this tactic of *de nihilo nihilum,* but his rhetorical question opens the unsettling possibility that the path of the plague *could* be traced back through the marked bodies of the urban populace. The disfigured bodies plague leaves in its wake make circulation at once visible and deadly. But at the level of circulation there is no meaning, no spiritual pattern to be discovered: significance must be found on the level of the community, not its members. To do otherwise would be to dive into the mysteries of urban circulation: tangled and invisible genealogies of bodily contact so complex that they become a buzzing swarm.[24]

This reluctance suggests a division in the discourse of plague, a division specifically related to its urban character. To frame this division we need to return to Michel de Certeau's opposition between the conceptual image of the panoramic city and the practiced space of the city's walkers:

> The networks of these moving, intersecting writings compose a manifold story that has neither author nor spectator, shaped out of fragments of trajectories and alterations of spaces: in relation to representations, it remains daily and indefinitely other.[25]

Plague as theater operates on the level of the panoramic city, showing a fiction of unity and horrific purpose. Plague as circulation or narrative (for de Certeau, to walk in the city is to construct a story) opposes these encompassing structures of urban significance. Plague literature is drawn to the narratival, to the particular and the circulatory, but it cannot sustain itself there. The interaction of these two modes of signifying plague can be seen throughout Dekker's work. In *The Wonderful Year,* Dekker breaks off in the midst of tracing personal plague narratives by saying "My spirit growes faint with rowing in this Stygian Ferry, it can no longer endure the transportation of soules in this dolefull manner: let vs therefore shift a point of our Compasse"— a shift that leads immediately into the description of the plague as a stage Tamburlaine that I quote above (sig. D1). Dekker's narratives can never keep themselves going; the text is punctuated by breaks, shifts in focus, movements to the theatrical level of meaning. The dichotomy is shown clearly on the title page for *The Wonderful Year,* which describes what follows as first "the picture of London, lying sicke of the Plague," followed by "certain Tales . . . cut out in sundry fashions." Here and elsewhere in Dekker's plague writing there is a movement back and forth between these two levels of representation, between "pictures" and "tales."[26] This fluctuation between theatrical and narratival modes, I would suggest, relates in part to the difficulty of finding a way of representing the impact of plague on London.

*   *   *

Despite the mortality caused by the plague, London continued to grow rapidly in the Jacobean period. Except for a brief drop in 1609, the number of christenings in the city continued to rise inexorably each year, evidence that the plague was having no long-term effects on the growth of the city.[27] This was especially true after the disaster of 1603. Although the rest of the country was still heavily infected, London rebounded quickly—no doubt in large part due to massive immigration from the countryside.[28] The quick renewal of commercial activity, coupled with the deaths of many apprentices, caused a substantial labor shortage, solved by large increases in apprentice enrollments over the next few years.[29] Trade and commerce resumed with vigor, the streets became crowded again, and in 1604 the delayed coronation entry of James took place. "The Streetes seemde to bee paued with men," said Dekker of this event, observing that

> hee that should haue compared the emptie and vntrodden walkes of London, which were to be seene in the late mortally-destroying Deluge, with the thronged streetes nowe, might haue belieued, that

vpon this daye, began a new Creation, & that the Citie was the only Workhouse werein sundry Nations were made.[30]

In this instance Dekker treats the reconstitution of London as a miracle performed by the arrival of James. In *The Seuen Deadly Sinnes of London*, however, he is less sanguine about the recovery. In the introduction he castigates London for becoming again what it was before:

[God] hath ten-fold restor'de thy lost sons and daughters, and such sweete, liuely, fresh colours hath hee put vpon thy cheekes, that Kings haue come to behold thee, and Princes to delight their eyes with thy bewty. None of these favours (for all this) can draw thee from thy wickednes. (Sig. A3v)

London's ability to remake itself, to create more and more people, to generate something from nothing, was deeply troubling to Dekker. The plague comes and goes, and London goes on, driven by a fecundity and motive force that could not be understood. Although the diminishing of plague was a time for rejoicing, to Dekker's eye such a quick resurrection felt unnatural: too similar in its rapid and inexplicable spread, I would argue, to the plague itself.

The effects of this doubling of plague and urban growth are especially evident in the relationship of the plague to the crowd. The city under plague is a depopulated city; the author of *Lachrymae Londinenses* echoes many writers when he exclaims, "I can no longer forbeare mee to borrow the very words of the Prophet Ieremies Complaint. *How doth the Citie sit solitarie that was foll of people?*" (sig. B3v). Dekker writes of London's "emptie and vntrodden walkes," and "still and melancholy streets" during plague; in *A Rod for Runaways,* he comments: "The walkes in Pauls are empty: the walkes in London too wide . . . Cheape-side is a comfortable Garden, where all Phisicke-Herbes grow."[31] William Muggins, writing in 1603, asks, "Where are our solemn meetings and frequent assemblies; men stand afar off; the streets and highways mourn: traffic ceaseth."[32] As evidence of the return of normalcy, crowds were therefore a welcome sign of the city's vitality; in *The Seuen Deadly Sinnes of London*, Dekker approvingly notes how

in euery street, carts and Coaches make such a thundring as if the world ranne vpon wheeles: at euerie corner, men, women, and children meete in such shoales, that postes are sette vp of purpose to strengthen the houses, least with iostling one another they should shoulder them downe. (Sig. E1–E1v)

But if crowded streets are the symbol of the healthy city, the vibrant city, London as it should be, they are also the harbinger of the plague and thus of London's destruction. The chapter epigraph makes explicit one connection between population growth and plague: London has delighted in its "multitudes of heads," as David did when he numbered Israel and Judah; as a result God has again sent a pestilence to chastise this prideful sin.[33] Growth thus always carries within itself the threat of its own destruction.

At the same time, to be "infected with the number of our people" connotes not only pride but also contagion, as the plague was closely linked to London's overcrowding. Crowds in the streets and crowded living conditions were considered prime causes or exacerbations of the plague, as the plague orders make clear:

> Forasmuch as nothing is more complained on then the multitude of Roagues and Wandering Beggers, that swarme in euery place about the Citie, being a great cause of the spreading of the infection, and will not be auoyded, notwithstanding any order that hath beene giuen to the Contrary: It is therefore now ordered, that such Constables and others, whome this matter may any way concerne, doe take speciall care, that no wandring Begger be suffered in the Streetes of this Citie.[34]

As Margaret Healy has commented, "A rhetoric of social division expressing anxiety about the 'unruly poor' was clearly gaining ground in this period, and by the early seventeenth century it was heavily impregnated with pestilence language and associations."[35] James's 1603 anti-building declaration echoes the claustrophobic language of earlier proclamations denouncing London's crowded space, but stresses such associations:

> Whereas . . . the great confluence and accesse of excessive numbers of idle, indigent, dissolute and dangerous persons, And the pestering of many of them in small and strait roomes . . . have bene one of the chiefest occasions of the great Plague . . . no new Tenant or Inmate . . . [shall] reside in any such house . . . None of the foresaid Roomes, Houses, or places . . . [shall] be hereafter pestered with multitudes of dwellers.[36]

What is most striking about this passage is the double use of "pester" to describe the cramped space of urban life.[37] As in the comment from John Stow cited in the Introduction, that London is "too much pestered with people," the semantic distance between "pester" and "pestilence" seems minimal.[38] As in the dialogue between London and Westminster, here the "small and strait" space of the home, usually considered separate from the chaos of urban life, becomes an extension of the street, filled with the swarming multitudes. Both decrees draw their affective power from their claustrophobia, their sense that London has swollen too full to be healthy.

This connection between plague and population resonates in Dekker's frequent use of the purging metaphor to explain the presence of the plague. In *The Dead Tearme*, London explains to Westminster: "Nothing increaseth in vs as a delight in any pleasure, but to haue that pleasure taken away for a time . . . So is it to haue a Plague, for thereby the Superfluous numbers of people, which otherwise (if they increased) would deuore one another, are swept away" (sig. F1). In *Newes from Graues-end,* in the section titled "The necessitie of a Plague," he rhymes his way to a similar conclusion:

> We would conclude (still vrging pittie)
> A Plague's the Purge to clense a Citte:
> Who amongst millions can deny
> (In rough prose, or smooth Poesie)
> Of Euils, tis the lighter broode,
> A dearth of people, then of foode!
> And who knowes not, our Land ran o're
> With people, and was onely poore
> In hauing too too many liuing,
> . . .
> The medicine for a ryotous Land
> Is such a plague. (Sig. F4–F4v)

Dekker's point about plague versus famine is accurate as well as brutal, but the medical language of purging implies other levels of meaning, too. What is purged from the metaphorical urban body is urban bodies; the increase of those bodies through population growth suggests an urban body again growing out of order. All these associations suggest that the urban crowd is both symptom and antonym of the plague: the tangible referent, in whose bodies can be seen the random, inexorable energy of both the city and its disease.

A different sort of merging of city and plague can be observed in another of London's doubles, the explosion of literature about the city that intensified in the early seventeenth century, matching the city's population explosion. Dekker's urban pamphlets participate in this literary boom, and his writing is remarkably self-conscious about the interconnections between urban description, literary production, and the plague. *The Seuen Deadly Sinnes of London* opens with this imprecation against the readers of pamphlets:

> You are able (if you haue the tokens of deadly Ignorance, and Boldnes at one time vpon you) to breede more infection on in Pauls Church-yard, then all the bodies that were buried there in the Plague-time, if they had beene left still aboue ground. (Sig. *2)

The double face of the Churchyard, a place of crowded death during plague time, a place of bustling commerce otherwise—a place of the circulation of plague, and the circulation of books—resolves into one image, with the insatiable and fickle reading audience termed more deadly than plague.[39] But what is Dekker's own book but a plague token, part of the explosion of mercenary literature that fed on the corpses of 1603? Perhaps Dekker himself allows as much in his prefatory letter to *The Wonderful Year,* in which he says, in reference to the plague, "with which sickness, (to tell truth) this booke is, (though not sorely) yet somewhat infected" (sig. B2). At the end of *The Wonderful Year* Dekker turns from recounting the horrors of the plague in grim detail to recounting a series of morbidly comical tales about the plague, "cut out in sundry fashions." In vectoring these twice-told tales, Dekker shifts his work from first-hand reporting to the circulatory realm of the jestbook, emphasizing again the commercial nature of the project.

Dekker's complicity in plague production is also marked in one of his next pamphlets, *The Meeting of Gallants at an Ordinarie* (1604), which imagines a gathering of urbane Londoners shortly after the ebbing of the plague. One gallant, Signior Gingelspur, explains his tattered appearance:

> tis a Limbe of the fashion, and as commendable to goe ragged after a plague, as to haue an Antient full of holes and Tatters after a Battaile: And I haue seene fiue hundred of the same rancke in aparell, for most of your choyce and curious Gallants came vp in cloathes, because they thought it very dangerous to deale with Sattin this plague-time.[40]

With its diminishing, Dekker suggests, plague becomes merely an issue of fashion for the upper classes, its horrific message forgotten amid the return of metropolitan preoccupations. Satirical accounts such as these have often been taken as evidence of Dekker's militant politics; Healy, following Julia Gasper and Margot Heinemann, locates Dekker's work "within a radical English plague-writing tradition and firmly amidst the capital's political arguments about the management of its 'plagues', including its burgeoning underclass of the poor."[41] While this is certainly one level on which the pamphlet operates, it is important to recognize that Dekker includes himself in the attack. Gingelspur soon continues:

> I know an honest Host about London, that hath barreld vp newes for Gallants, like Pickled Oysters, marry your Ordinarie will cost you two shillings, but the Tales that he in Brine wilt be worth sixpence of the money: for you know tis great charges to keepe Tales long, and therefore he must be somewhat considered for the laying out of his Language. (Sig. B3v)

This set of cured tales is, in fact, what *The Meeting* becomes; as in *The Wonderful Year*, the pamphlet turns to recounting a series of humorous plague stories, in which the plague grotesquely provides the comic payoff for a variety of conventional narratives. In effect, Dekker casts himself as this "honest Host," who has prudently preserved the horrors of the plague for subsequent profit. If Dekker wants to criticize those who would disregard the spiritual warning of the plague, he does not close his eyes to his own appropriations. The author of *Lachrymae Londinenses*, written during the 1625 plague, in fact attacks exactly the sort of literature that Dekker frequently produced:

> If you expect in these ensuing Lines any scarce credible or feigned matters of wonderment, made in some Tauerne or on some Ale-bench, to tickle your Eares and helpe you to sing Care-away, you will be deceived: for there are enow, if not too many such Spuriall Pamphlets, which the Press hath of late already spewed out, (Broods of Barbican, Smithfield, and the Bridge, and Trundled, trolled and marshalled vp and downe and along the Streets; and haply the Contries also). (Sig. B2–B2v)

In this description, "Spuriall Pamphlets" about the plague—"Broods" born of unclean generation, or perhaps the purging of the presses— infest and infect the urban landscape: "Trundled, trolled, and marshalled vp and downe and along the Streetes." The increase and circulation of literature, like the increase and circulation of bodies, develops a symbiotic relation to the increase and circulation of plague.

Dekker's literary practice was deeply involved with the socially transforming power of the plague. His prose career was energized by the 1603 plague, perhaps in large part because the arrival of plague left him without theatrical employment for long periods in the ensuing decades.[42] The opposition noted above between the theater of plague and the narrative of plague recurs in the context of literary production;

for Dekker as for other writers, the persistence of plague created a constant tradeoff between the writing of pamphlets (circulatory, written for an unseen public audience) and the writing of plays (static, written for a particular place and time). After *The Wonderful Year*, which he published in the winter of 1603 as the plague ebbed, Dekker went on to write numerous pamphlets on the plague. Indeed, Dekker seems unable to stop talking about the plague, even when the plague is not really what he's talking about.

In *The Seuen Deadly Sinnes of London*, the sins that Dekker imagines bringing the plague into the city are not the traditional theological troop, but rather quotidian and venial aspects of London life: bankruptcy, lying, candle-light, sloth, apishness, shaving, and cruelty.[43] These sins express themselves in behaviors anatomized and ridiculed in scores of contemporary urban satires and complaints: living on credit, corrupt business practices, following fashion, and going to plays and taverns. Each sin bleeds into the next, and each breeds more sins, which in turn breed more, mocking the city's own circulatory and commercial patterns even as the book participates in them. The final sin, Cruelty, Dekker demonstrates in part by railing against forced marriages, impatient creditors and overbearing masters: in other words, the basic plot of every city comedy, including Dekker's own (sig. F2v–G3). A similar pattern appears in *The Ravens Almanacke*, published in 1609. In a mock-prognosticatory tone, Dekker writes of twelve "great and greiuous plagues" that will visit in the next year, beginning with "Saint Paulus plague":

> one of the heauiest, & that is, when a man hath neuer a penny in his purse, credit with this neighbors, nor a hold to hide his head in: alack, how many poore people will lye languishing of this disease? how many that haue bowling Alleys, nay, how many that walke in the middle Ile of Paules in reasonable good cloathes, will bee strucke with this plague?[44]

Other major visitations will include the plagues of drunkenness, cuckolds, spendthrift heirs, and scolding wives. Minor plagues will include the exhaustion of hired horses; a plague of beggary for "common fidlers"; a plague of catchpoles, "who this yeare shall dye so thick, that in all the 24. wardes in London . . . will there bee found one honest man liuing of that clapping vocation"; a "Hempen plague" for coney-catchers; and for players, "Saint Julians plague . . . that is, you shall weare gay cloathes, carrie lofty lookes, but . . . be with emptie purses at least twice a weeke" (Sig. C1–C1v).

Here is not so much plague devouring the city as the city devouring the plague, commodifying it, stripping it of its specificity, relocating it within the rhetorical and commercial patterns of the metropolis. The jests may seem a bit thin when we note that 4,300 people died of the plague in the year Dekker published this pamphlet. But rather than a mockery of the plague, Dekker's plastic appropriation of its rhetoric shows the inseparability of the plague and the city. For Dekker, plague becomes the master-metaphor, applicable to all aspects of urban life. As the plague became increasingly understood in social rather than theological terms, as an urban pathology engendered by urban complexity and disorder (particularly among the poor),[45] so was the city increasingly understood in terms of the plague. The rhetoric of the city and the rhetoric of the plague merge, due to their overlapping themes: circulation, uncontrollability, and inexplicable growth. With this merging, the idea of the city, the city as understood through its literature or its bodies, cannot be separated from the idea of the plague.

This inextricability of the city and the plague underlies Dekker's use of cannibalism to describe the plague in *The Wonderful Year*. Dekker speaks of "this *Anthropophagized* plague," adding in a side note that "Anthropophagi are Scitians that feed on mens flesh" (sig. C3). The use of the past participle "anthropophagized" is odd, creating some ambiguity as to agency and what is cannibalizing what. On a symbolic level, the geographical description at once asserts the alienness of the plague and its familiarity. The same trope appears in Davies' account:

> The London Lanes (themselues thereby to saue)
> Did vomit out their vndigested dead,
> Who by cart loads, are carried to the Graue,
> For, all those Lanes with folke were ouerfed. (Sig. K2)

The image of an invader conquering the city is replaced by one of the city feeding upon its citizens, consuming itself. Like the plague itself, the trope of urban cannibalism mixes levels of symbolic meaning, blending conceptual and material bodies. In plague time, London eats London. Or, as Volumnia, "the life of Rome," explains in *Coriolanus:* "I sup upon myself / And so shall starve with feeding" (5.5.1, 4.2.50–51).

* * *

There is a productive infelicity in associating the cold austerity of *Coriolanus* with Dekker's seriocomic rambles through the urban labyrinth. While Dekker draws the citizens that populate his work with a carnivalesque grotesqueness that is at once disarming and mockingly celebratory, the citizens of *Coriolanus* are always described with distaste. The tribune Brutus, representative of the people, speaks in the same tones as the nobility:

> the kitchen malkin pins
> Her richest lockram 'bout her reechy neck,
> Clamb'ring the walls to eye him; stalls, bulks, windows
> Are smother'd up, leads fill'd, and ridges hors'd
> With variable complexions, all agreeing
> In earnestness to see him. (2.1.208–13)

As many commentators have noted, *Coriolanus* is full of the horror of the urban body, in both its particular and collective forms.[46] In part the horror comes out of the difficulty of distinguishing between the two, on either an abstract level—what is the city but the people?—or a personal one: "As if a man were author of himself" (5.3.36). Coriolanus's hapless assertion to Volumnia is spoken in a familial context, but coming as it does at the moment of his threatened destruction of Rome, it carries the implication of urban self-fashioning as well.

Coriolanus is famously a play about the one and the many, and this basic division has driven the two schools of criticism of the play: psychological and psychoanalytic investigations into what authors Coriolanus's actions and words, and political interpretations of the social implications of the world the play presents. This critical split duplicates the binary grammar of plague literature; because of the social aspect of the disease, to write of the plague is inevitably to create divisions between private and public and between the individual and the society. Plague, however, creates such categories only in order to transgress them; the oppositions cannot be held separate and always collapse into each other. As Elana Gomel has commented (in a different though related context), the "body is no longer a unique vessel privileged to carry a uniquely refined subjectivity but rather a common corporeality of the sick community."[47] The events of *Coriolanus* similarly demonstrate that a separation between the body of the citizen and the body of the city is ultimately unsustainable. My perspective on this collapsing dichotomy (both literary and critical) is to approach the play in terms of "urban identity," by which I mean both how the city shapes the identities of its members and how the members understand their relationship to the city's own identity. As I suggested in the introductory chapter, in such a context the tribune Sicinius's comment, "What is the city but the people?" can be read less as a rhetorical assertion of the latent political power of the commoners than as a real question: what *is* the city? What does the city mean? I want to understand the play less as a *political* parable than as an *urban* parable, an example of the urban literature that flooded London in the early seventeenth century. And what this urban parable interrogates, I argue, is not only the generalized metaphor of a diseased body politic but also the specific and histori-cally inflected image of a city under plague.[48]

For Artaud, this image is a picture of a society on the verge of ecstatic collapse. Using imagery that goes back to Thucydides' description of the plague in Athens in 430 B.C.E. (with the crucial dif-ference that what Thucydides sees as devastation Artaud sees as a heroic fulfillment), Artaud imagines the advent of plague releasing individuals from moral strictures by dissolving the city. In an unex-pected intervention into the narrative structure of *Coriolanus* he writes, "The last of the living are in a frenzy: the obedient and virtu-ous son kills his father . . . The warrior hero sets fire to the city he once risked his life to save" (24). Speaking against this tradition in *Discipline and Punish*, Michel Foucault lists the regulations that went into effect in Vincennes in the seventeenth century after a severe out-break of plague, detailing the extent to which individuals were segre-gated, quarantined, and examined. Perhaps thinking specifically of Artaud's portrayal, he notes how "a whole literary fiction of the fes-tival grew up around the plague," but suggests:

> There was also a political dream of the plague, which was exactly its reverse: not the collective festival, but strict divisions; not laws trans gressed, but the penetration of regulation into even the smallest details of everyday life.[49]

Foucault's fantasy of total urban control is as revealing of his critical philosophy as Artaud's fantasy of organic dissolution is of his.[50] What makes the opposition pertinent is its similarity to the situation in *Coriolanus:* the opposing fantasies of a city threatened by the unfet-tered and self-indulgent activities of the populace, and a city threat-ened by the disciplinary powers of the state, controlling all aspects of human behavior. More allusive connections between *Coriolanus* and the plagued city discussed in the first half of this chapter might also be found; Dekker's description, quoted above, of how without plague "the Superfluous numbers of people . . . would deuore one another" is echoed in Coriolanus's evaluation of the Roman government: "the noble Senate, who / (Under the gods) keep you in awe, which else / Would feed on one another" (1.1.186–88).[51] If this conjunction seems to equate the authority of the city with the actions of the plague, it follows a logic extensively mapped in *Coriolanus.*

For something so central to urban life, and for something so frequently associated with theater, plague has an oddly liminal presence in the dramatic literature of early modern England. Perhaps because of official or informal censorship, perhaps because of the antagonistic relationship that existed between the theater and the plague,[52] or perhaps because of the sheer terror that representing plague-marked bodies in the crowded, contagious space of the theater would cause—there is very little plague theater in early modern London. Plague is almost never presented as a material context for the theater—Ben Jonson's *The Alchemist* is an important exception to this general rule[53]—but rather expresses itself through less immediately apparent routes.[54] An example of such a route is the hidden plague of *Coriolanus.*

In 1608, around the time that *Coriolanus* was written, the Colony of Virginia invited the City to begin forcibly shipping vagrants to the New World in order "to ease the city and the suburbs of a swarm of unnecessary inmates" who were "the very original of all plagues almost that happen in this kingdom."[55] This episode closely parallels an anecdote from Plutarch's "Life of Coriolanus" that Shakespeare does not include in his play. Plutarch relates that just as the plebeians of Rome were rioting over food prices, the city of Velitres offered its allegiance in the hopes that Rome would send it new inhabitants, as it had been decimated by plague. The leaders of Rome, especially Coriolanus, saw this as a marvelous opportunity at once to lessen the famine and to purge Rome of "many mutinous and seditious persones, being the superfluous ill humours that grevously fedde this disease."[56] "This disease" refers to sedition, but as in Dekker's purging metaphors the parallel is obvious: the excessive multiplicity of the crowd is itself the disease. The connection might be reinforced through Brutus's reference to "dissentious numbers pest'ring streets" (4.6.7), a description that once again plays on the double implications of "pester": to the plague city is sent the plague.

The presence of plague in *Coriolanus* is discursive rather than local. There is no actual plague in the cities of this play. Shakespeare elides the story of Velitres, perhaps because of its close resemblance to London's active deportation of vagrants. Traces of this story remain in the play, as when Coriolanus speaks of venting "our musty superfluity" (1.1.224–25), a desire recalled by Sicinius when he calls out, "Where is this viper / That would depopulate the city and / Be every man himself?" (3.1.261–63). But such traces can only be identified by going outside the realm of the play. Velitres becomes the hidden city, the anonymous location, the suppressed fact of the play, and in its absence plague is rhetorical rather than material. Plague is the symbolic subtext of the play, an infectious rhetoric typified only by its extreme adaptability to circumstance. In *The Wonderful Year* Dekker describes the plague as a "Cameleon-like sicknes" that appears "in such strange, and such changeable shapes" (sig. D3). The same pattern applies to the excessive discourse of the plague in *Coriolanus*. Plague fashions itself to all aspects of the play, a descriptive trope of enormous flexibility and power. Yet, as Dekker's convoluted plague grammar suggests (plague "as a plague," an "Anthropophagized plague"), the rhetorical effect of plague as a label is semantically paradoxical.[57]

Although most of the main characters speak through plague at times, the trope is most prominent in the speech of Coriolanus himself. References to plague crowd Coriolanus's speech, ranging from quick curses—"a plague—tribunes for them!" (1.6.43)—to complex descriptions of his relationship to the crowd. These passages, usually occurring at crucial moments in the play, limn Coriolanus's attempts to avoid the contagiousness of that relationship. The trajectory of these complex imprecations, designed to emphasize his separation from the crowd, serves instead to demonstrate the inextricability of Coriolanus and the common population.

Battling before the gates of Corioles, Coriolanus stops to excoriate the Romans who have fallen back from the fight:

> All the contagion of the south light on you,
> You shames of Rome! you herd of—Biles and plagues
> Plaster you o'er, that you may be abhorr'd
> Farther than seen, and one infect another
> Against the wind a mile! (1.4.30–34)

This remarkably dense image gives a clear sense of the complexities of plague and the crowd. Plague operates here as a descriptor, labeling something that Coriolanus cannot identify: the anacoluthon in the second line indicates the unnamability of the crowd as much as it indicates Coriolanus's rage. The plague becomes a way of understanding the crowd, of denoting and circumscribing its random and uncontrollable energies. The purpose of the plague here is not to sicken or destroy, but to stigmatize, to manifest on the bodies of the soldiers the shame they should feel. The disfiguring marks of plague mark the individual without identifying him, separate him from the anonymous denotation of "citizen" without naming him. In early modern London those found with plague tokens on their bodies were subjected to a host of disciplinary measures, as the plague orders demonstrate: "That to euery infected houses there be appointed two Watchmen, one for the day and the other for the night: and that these Watchmen haue a speciall care that no person goe in or out of such infected houses, whereof they haue the charge, vpon paine of seuere punishment."[58] The most prominent, and cruelest, practice was boarding up houses with the plague victims inside, left to die in total isolation from community, the door of the house marked with a cross that identified nothing but the illness.[59] In this regard, the curse can be understood with the intent to destroy the collectivity of the crowd, to render it particulate, atomized, unconnected. In this way the plague token becomes the mark of Cain, the first exile, the builder of cities.

The dash in line 31, however, is an emendation of the Folio text, which leaves the break unpunctuated; reading against Coriolanus's interrupted sentence, we can see that Coriolanus also names the crowd a "herd of biles and plagues." The label becomes inherent: by calling plague upon the crowd Coriolanus identifies the crowd with the plague. Told by the patricians to save both himself and the city by tempering his language, Coriolanus responds:

> As for my country I have shed my blood,
> Not fearing outward force, so shall my lungs
> Coin words till their decay against those measles
> Which we disdain should tetter us, yet sought
> The very way to catch them. (3.1.75–79)

Again, the language is dense and difficult to parse. Coriolanus here compares the crowd to plague spots, "measles," and claims that he at once abhors them and places himself in the way of infection. The dynamic of the previous passage has been reversed; here it is the crowd that threatens to infect Coriolanus, and by doing so, to disfigure him. Similarly, the comparison drawn by Coriolanus is to defense: as he has defended his city against the attack of outward force, now will he defend himself against the inward contagions of the city. The label of "measles," or plague tokens, is complex as well. Describing the crowd as tokens is significant. Plague has two parts, the unseen and imperceptible disease and the visible marks of its presence. A plague token is a sign of something else, a marker rather than a referent. The plague itself is invisible; it can only be seen through the manifestation of its sores. It was commonly believed to be spread by bad air, especially that from unburied bodies—a connection Coriolanus draws out when he speaks of the crowd's love as something he prizes "as the dead carcasses of unburied men / That do corrupt my air" (3.3.120–23). Throughout the play the crowd is also referred to in terms that refer to the insubstantiality (if also pungency) of air, suggesting a further linkage. As plague is unknowable except through the manifestation of its tokens, so the city seems unknowable except through its manifestation in the anonymous bodies of the crowd. With this label of "measles" Coriolanus reinforces Sicinius's suggestion that the city is but the people, and that both are the plague. What infects Coriolanus is not the crowd but Rome itself.

Yet to speak of this relationship in terms of the infection of the individual by the city is to maintain a distinction that the play pervasively undermines. Coriolanus is not disfigured by the plague; rather, he is figured by it. Although Coriolanus uses plague imagery to separate himself from the crowd while affirming their separation from the city, he is marked by the discourse himself. As Dekker and other writers describe the plague simultaneously as a conquering invader and as a corruption internal and inherent to the city, this double image repeats itself in the play. It is Coriolanus who is the plague, "this viper / That would depopulate the city" (3.1.261–62), the ill-omened planet that struck Corioles with pestilence (2.2.114). Thinking Coriolanus dead inside Corioles, Lartius eulogizes him: "A carbuncle entire, as big as though art, / Were not so rich a jewel" (1.4.55–56). The red glow of the carbuncle returns in the last act in Coriolanus's "eye / Red as 'twould burn Rome" (5.1.63–64), but more significant is that "carbuncle" one of the dozens of early modern words for a plague token.[60] "Carbuncle" at once symbolizes pure and jewel-like invulnerability and rottenness and infection. Coriolanus speaks the plague, and it speaks him. This is drawn out by the further parallel between the stigma of plague spots and Coriolanus's own stigmata, the scars and wounds he refuses to reveal. Like plague tokens, Coriolanus's cicatrices—formed in Rome's continual, invasive outward growth—connote the destruction of cities.

In Coriolanus's agonistic relationship with Rome we can see the urban subject trapped inside the interlocking structures of urban subjectivity and urban subjection.[61] As his name indicates, Coriolanus can only establish identity by destroying cities. When he arrives in Antium, he tells Aufidius that "only that name remains" (4.5.73). The attack on Rome is as much an attempt to reidentify himself as it is to find vengeance. " 'Coriolanus' he would not answer to," reports Cominius after his unsuccessful plea for Rome's survival:

> He was a kind of nothing, titleless,
> Till he had forg'd himself a name o'th'fire
> Of burning Rome. (5.1.11–15)

What name? Perhaps Coriolanus wishes not to be called Roman but Romanus—or even Romulus, in reference to the imaginary origins of the city. Here is the same desire manifested in Dekker's dismay at the quick regrowth of London after the 1603 plague: the idea that in order to achieve purity the city must be entirely destroyed, unbuilded to its beginnings. What defeats this purpose, at least in part, is Volumnia's dismissive naming strategy before the city gates: "To his surname Coriolanus longs more pride / Than pity to our prayers" (5.3.169–73). Here Volumnia reverses the meaning of his "Coriolanus" from conqueror of Corioles to subject of Corioles, a tactic underscored a few lines later when she says, "This fellow had a Volscian to his mother" (5.3.177). Attempting to fashion urban identity to his identity, and thus truly become the author of himself, Coriolanus instead finds himself caught in the symbolic framework of "citizen."[62]

Despite the importance that the characters attach to their specific cities, perhaps there is ultimately no difference between them beyond their titles. Challenged at Aufidius's door by a servant asking "where dwell'st thou?," Coriolanus replies, "Under the canopy . . . / I' th' city of kites and crows" (4.5.37–38, 42). Leaving Rome, Coriolanus had announced to the crowd, "Despising, / For you, the city, thus I turn my back; / There is a world elsewhere" (3.3.133–35); now, in his wandering, extravagant existence, he imagines the world elsewhere as an inescapable city—a nameless city whose nomadic, devouring inhabitants recall the "base and ravenous multitude" that survives Jonson's *Poetaster*. "Urban identity" contains another possible meaning than those I discussed above, especially in this early modern context: not uniqueness but sameness, lack of distinction.[63] The last scene of *Coriolanus* begins in Antium, Aufidius's city, but part way through the scene the city loses its location, at the moment Aufidius denies Coriolanus his name:

> Dost thou think
> I'll grace thee with that robbery, thy stol'n name
> Coriolanus, in Corioles? (5.6.88–90)

At once Antium and Corioles, symbolically this city is also Rome, as the assembled crowd, identical with their fickle Roman twin, turns from praising Coriolanus to excoriating him as the viper who depopulates the city: "Tear him to pieces! Do it presently! He killed my son! He killed my cousin Marcus! He killed my father!" (5.6.120–22).[64] These images of depopulation also imply Velitres, the hidden city of the plague and the play. And of course it is London as well; to dwell "under the canopy" is to dwell in the theater, the distracted and loosened Globe, the place of the crowd. There is ultimately only one city in the play, the chameleon city, like the chameleon plague that marks and defines it. Plague allows the city to be labeled, but in this labeling it obliterates its identity, leaving instead an excessively plastic trope signifying nothing and everything. Sicinius's question assumes a darker tone in this context, and threatens to dissolve not only the power of the Roman elite but also all the structures of urban significance that this book has been exploring. If the city is only the people, the anonymous crowds that throng through it with their random energy, then what is the city but "a kind of nothing," identifiable only by its ceaseless change and monstrous, uncontrollable growth? Scolding London for its sins and warning of the imminent return of plague, Dekker by way of example writes that Jerusalem "is now a dezert . . . it is rather now (for the abominations committed in it) no place at all."[65] All time is plague time in London, because London is always London. The threat of this anonymous city lies at the heart of the play. For *Coriolanus,* as for London, the city is the plague, the city of kites and crows, the city only of crowds.

Notes

Introduction

1. *The Riverside Shakespeare.* All citations of Shakespeare in this study are to this edition, unless otherwise noted.
2. My definitions of metaphor and metonymy, as a paradigmatic relationship based on similarity and a syntagmatic relationship based on contiguity, are based on the work of Roman Jakobson ("Two Aspects of Language and Two Types of Aphasic Disturbances").
3. Since the deconstructive logic of the supplement plays an important role in this study, a brief review of the term is probably in order. In Jacques Derrida's formulation, the double significance of the word "supplément" in French (meaning both "addition" and "substitute") is the hinge of a contradictory dynamic of both addition and replacement: "The supplement adds itself, it is a surplus, a plenitude enriching another plenitude, the *fullest measure* of presence. It cumulates and accumulates presence . . . . But the supplement supplements. It adds only to replace. It intervenes or insinuates itself *in-the-place-of;* if it fills, it is as if one fills a void" (*Of Grammatology,* 144–45). Throughout this study I argue that the relationship between the crowd and the idea (or ideal) of London follows the logic of the supplement.
4. Crowd theory gets its titular beginning in the work of Gustave Le Bon (*The Crowd: A Study of the Popular Mind*), whose approach to the psychology of the crowd was adopted and developed by Sigmund Freud ("Group Psychology and the Analysis of the Ego"). Other key figures include Neil Smelser (*Theory of Collective Behavior*) and Elias Canetti (*Crowds and Power*). See also J. S. McClelland, *The Crowd and the Mob: From Plato to Canetti.*
5. See George Rudé, *The Crowd in History:* "our main attention will be given to political demonstrations and to what sociologists have termed the 'aggressive mob' or the 'hostile outburst'—to such activities as strikes, riots, rebellions, insurrections, and revolutions" (4).
6. See E. J. Hobsbawm, *Primitive Rebels;* Rudé, *The Crowd in History;* E. P. Thompson, "The Moral Economy of the English Crowd in the Eighteenth Century." In making this extremely general claim I conflate

some disagreements within the field; Rudé, for example, was much opposed to the idea that the crowd was either "the people" or "the rabble" (*The Crowd in History*, 8–10).

7. Annabel Patterson, *Shakespeare and the Popular Voice*; Mikhail Bakhtin, *Rabelais and His World*.

8. Derek Keene, "Material London in Time and Space," 58.

9. *Oxford English Dictionary*, 2nd ed. sv. "Mob."

10. See Tim Harris, "Perceptions of the Crowd in Later Stuart London."

11. Roger Finlay, *Population and Metropolis*, 51. Cf. Vanessa Harding, "The Population of London, 1550–1700," which challenges the accuracy of some of Finlay's findings but does not offer other figures for this particular time period.

12. See Steve Rappaport, *Worlds Within Worlds*, 64–67.

13. See Paul Slack, "Perceptions of the Metropolis in Seventeenth-Century England," especially his discussion of Nicholas Barbon's late seventeenth-century defense of building and population growth, 175–78: "Barbon and his allies had won the battle over regulation; and although they had not wholly silenced opposing voices, they had also permanently altered the terms in which arguments about London were conducted" (178).

14. See, in particular, Karen Newman's recent work on satire and the urban space of London, in "Walking Capitals: Donne's First Satyre."

15. Henri Lefebvre, *The Production of Space*; Michel de Certeau, "Walking in the City," *The Practice of Everyday Life*.

16. Patricia Fumerton and Simon Hunt, eds., *Renaissance Culture and the Everyday*, 3.

17. Antonin Artaud, *The Theater and Its Double*, 7.

18. Lynch explains, "By this we mean the ease with which its parts can be recognized and can be organized into a coherent pattern. Just as this printed page, if it is legible, can be visually grasped as a relational pattern of recognizable symbols, so a legible city would be one whose districts or landmarks or pathways are easily identifiable" (*The Image of the City*, 2–3).

19. Lawrence Manley, *Literature and Culture in Early Modern London*, 125.

20. See especially the chapter "London and the Languages of Tudor Complaint," *Literature and Culture*, 63–122.

21. For an excellent summary of this historiographic debate, see Michael Berlin, "Reordering Rituals: Ceremony and the Parish, 1520–1640," 49–50.

22. See Rappaport, *Worlds within Worlds*, and Valerie Pearl, *London and the Outbreak of the Puritan Revolution* and "Change and Stability in Seventeenth-Century London."

23. See, for example, Slack, "Perceptions of the Metropolis"; cf. Peter Lake, "From Troynovant to Heliogabulus's Rome and Back." Margaret Pelling's essay "Skirting the City" is a significant exception to the general point I make here.

24. Jean Howard, "Women, Foreigners, and the Regulation of Urban Space in *Westward Ho*"; Garrett Sullivan, "The Beleagured City: Guild Culture and Urban Space in Heywood's *1 Edward IV* and Shakespeare's *2 Henry VI*," *The Drama of Landscape*; Andrew Gordon, "Performing London: the Map and the City in Ceremony"; Dillon, *Theatre, Court, and City*, 15.

25. An important exception to this general comment (although working toward somewhat different ends from this book) is Patricia Fumerton's recent essay, "London's Vagrant Economy: Making Space for 'Low' Subjectivity."

26. De Certeau, *Practice of Everyday Life*, 95. De Certeau's referent here is the postmodern city, not the early modern, but my discussion of the rhetoric of the building proclamations suggests its applicability to early modern London. As I discuss in chapter 1, de Certeau's imagining of a time when urban transparency was established that is now breaking down is a highly suspect historical narrative.

27. Emphasis in original.

28. Stow, *Survey of London*, I.165.

1   IMAGINARY NUMBERS: CITY, CROWD, THEATER

1. *Tudor Royal Proclamations*, II.466–67.

2. The original document reads "access of people" at this point (STC 8123.3); Larkin and Hughes's glossing of this as "excess" captures one half of the meaning of this phrase, its connection to overwhelming numbers, but elides the implication that London is too easy of access, too open to penetration and engrossment.

3. *Stuart Royal Proclamations*, I.171; see also I.193–95, I.345–47, I.398–400, I.428–31, I.485–88, and I.597–98.

4. *Les Reportes del Cases in Camera Stellata, 1593 to 1609*, 329.

5. Vanessa Harding, "City, Capital, and Metropolis: the Changing Shape of Seventeenth-Century London," 127.

6. On this point, also see John Schofield's "The Topography and Buildings of London, ca. 1600" and Lena Cowen Orlin's reading of Nicholas Treswell's property surveys in "Boundary Disputes in Early Modern London."

7. Stow, *Survey of London*, I.194; I.163; II.52; I.237. Kingsford notes of this last location, "The Cold Harbour became notorious as the dwelling-place of needy persons, and a sanctuary for debtors and vagabonds" (II.322). For dramatic citations, see *Epicoene* 2.3 and *Westward Ho* 4.2 (both noted in II.322).

8. See Patrick Collinson, "John Stow and Nostalgic Antiquarianism," 35.

9. For other references to building and subdividing, see I.126, I.163, I.165, I.211, I.242, II.4, II.21, II.28, II.52, II.66, II.72, II.73, II.74.

10. A slightly fuller explanation of Lefebvre's concepts of "representational space," "representations of space," and "spatial practice" would perhaps

be useful. Representational space is not just physical space but the experience of it as well, "space as directly *lived* through its associated images and symbols," the space "which the imagination seeks to change and appropriate" (Lefebvre, *Production of Space,* 39). Representations of space are theoretical, conceptual, and ideological: the spaces of private property, or urban planning, or social hierarchy, all of which attempt to *explain* rather than simply describe the world. Spatial practice is both a socioeconomic space and the space of daily routine, both what we do and the larger contexts that enable us to do it (and limit us from doing otherwise). I find Lefebvre's terminology somewhat idiosyncratic (and unstable within his discourse), and generally avoid it in this book; at some points I refer to representational space as "physical space," representations of space as "mental space," and spatial practice as "social space," although they would probably be more precisely described as "physical/mental," "mental/social," and "social/physical" spaces, respectively.

11. The building proclamations have often been understood in fairly cynical terms, as being used less to control the built environment of the city than to collect financial penalties from some of those who flouted the regulations. Although they were certainly used in this manner, especially under James and Charles, I believe that this sort of perspective underestimates the significance of the social and cultural issues at play in the proclamations—as well as overlooking the fact that actually enforcing the regulations would have been impossible. See Thomas G. Barnes's "The Prerogative and Environmental Control of London Building in the Early Seventeenth Century: The Lost Opportunity" for what remains the most substantial historical analysis of the legal use of the building proclamations. Although he notes the prevalence of financial penalties, Barnes takes the intent of the proclamations seriously; the "lost opportunity," in his reading, was due to their reliance on royal prerogative (i.e., proclamations) instead of Parliamentary statute: "At no time in the history of the Tudor and Stuart government was there a scintilla of authority in law for the position that buildings adhering to the realty could be demolished by virtue of a proclamation" (1358). Barnes also notes that there is "no evidence that any real attempt was made to enforce [the 1580 proclamation] until 1590" (1343); while this decade-long lapse might suggest an initial lack of compelling interest in controlling population growth, it also undermines the idea that the building proclamations were originally conceived of as a revenue source.

12. Keene, "Material London in Time and Space," 58.

13. Berlin, "Reordering Rituals: Ceremony and the Parish, 1520–1640," 51.

14. Archer, *The Pursuit of Stability,* 92. Archer treats parish life evenhandedly and at length in pages 76–99.

15. See "Reordering Rituals," 51–52.

16. Archer, "The Nostalgia of John Stow," 27, 28.

17. *Fovre Statvtes, Specially Selected and Commanded by his Maiestie . . .*, sig. P2–P2v. The statutes treat poor relief, the punishment of vagabonds, plague orders, and the prohibitions on new buildings; their joint publication suggests not only that James took these issues seriously but that he saw the regulation of building in London as closely related to these other documents of population control.

18. For the most extensive historical account of the social problem of vagrancy, see A. L. Beier, *Masterless Men.* Also see B. Roger Manning, *Village Revolts,* 157–86, and Linda Woodbridge, *Vagrancy, Homelessness, and English Renaissance Literature.* For an interesting approach to the congruent issue of the criminal underworld, see Bryan Reynolds, *Becoming Criminal.*

19. Reprinted in *Tudor Economic Documents,* 3:438. This document is not listed in the *Short Title Catalogue.*

20. For a contemporary example, see *Macbeth,* "as cannons overcharg'd with double cracks, so they/Doubly redoubled strokes upon the foe" (1.2.37–38).

21. That the number of discharged sailors was of particular concern is suggested by several royal proclamations (*Tudor Proclamations,* III.44, III.82, III.134, III.196). Impressment was a favorite tactic for removing masterless men from the city (Manning, *Village Revolts,* 194), but they had the unfortunate habit of coming back (often maimed) after being discharged. Between 1585 and 1602 over ten thousand men were pressed for soldiers in London and Middlesex (Manning, *Village Revolts,* 193); between 1580 and 1620 the percentage of London vagrants who were discharged soldiers rose from 1.5 percent to 12 percent (Beier, *Masterless Men,* 93).

22. *King James VI and I: Political Writings,* 225–26.

23. For further discussion of the idea of superfluity in the context of organic metaphors of the body politic, see James Holstun, "Tragic Superfluity in *Coriolanus.*"

24. Bakhtin, *Rabelais and His World,* 310.

25. In this analysis, and at many points in the book, I am indebted to Peter Stallybrass and Allon White's development of Bakhtinian paradigms in the context of urban space, especially their argument that "the human body, psychic forms, geographical space and the social formation are all constructed within interrelating and dependent hierarchies of high and low" (*The Politics and Poetics of Transgression,* 2).

26. I label these cities "imaginary" in part to connect with my chapter title, but also to acknowledge the connection between this opposition and a larger opposition between urban utopia and dystopia that pervaded understandings of early modern London, and perhaps are inherent to urban thought. See Slack, "Perceptions of the Metropolis," who writes that these two visions of the city, "in contemporary rhetoric as in reality . . . were bound together in a necessary and productive counterpoint" (163). As I suggest in the introduction, however, to

see these visions primarily in rhetorical terms risks minimizing the social realities to which they gesture.

27. De Certeau, *The Practice of Everyday Life*, 93.

28. For the difference between tactical and strategic practices see ibid., xviii–xx.

29. Gordon, "Performing London," 69–70. Although dealing primarily with mapping, Gordon's essay also pursues the relationship between de Certeau and early modern London's urban significance in a manner similar to my analysis, albeit in different directions and with somewhat different conclusions.

30. Mullaney, *Place of the Stage*, 10.

31. Lefebvre, *The Production of Space*, 229–36, 285–91.

32. Sullivan, *The Drama of Landscape*, 201. The important contribution that Lefebvre can make to early modern cultural studies is beginning to be recognized. As Peter Arnade, Martha C. Howell, and Walter Simons say in their introduction to a special volume of the *Journal of Interdisciplinary History* (32:4 [Spring, 2000]) on urban space in medieval and early modern Europe, "although the articles that constitute this volume were not written as direct responses to Lefebvre, it is his work, more than any other single tradition of scholarship, that throws into relief the issues they take up and illuminate" (517). See their subsequent discussion (517–38) for a superb summary of Lefebvre's theories and influence.

33. See Bakhtin, *Rabelais and His World*, 7.

34. Manley, "Sites and Rites," 39–40.

35. Archer, "Nostalgia of John Stow," especially 27–29.

36. Collinson, "John Stow and Nostalgic Antiquarianism," 28–29.

37. Archer, "Nostalgia of John Stow," 23.

38. See Lefebvre, *Production of Space*, 285–91.

39. For a analysis of Augustinian urban paradigms in early modern London, see Paster, *The Idea of London*. For a discussion of the function of the ideal city in Plato's *Republic*, see Michel Foucault, *The Use of Pleasure* (New York: Vintage Books, 1990), 70–72.

40. Cf. Rebeca Helfer's discussion of Spenser's *The Ruines of Time* in "The Art of Recollection."

41. Cf. *Richard II* 2.1.5–68.

42. *Fovre Statvtes*, sig. P3v.

43. Stow, *Survey of London*, II.205, II.206.

44. *A Breefe Discourse*, sig. A5v.

45. The doubleness of "articulation" was brought to my attention by the work of Marjorie Garber (see especially "Out of Joint") and by conversations with Carla Mazzio; although my application of the term is at some distance from that of either of them, I am indebted to them both.

46. See Sullivan, *The Drama of Landscape*, 213–14.

47. For an extensive and persuasive rebuttal to this now-traditional opposition of city and suburbs, see Joseph P. Ward, *Metropolitan Communities.*
48. Paul Griffiths, "Politics Made Visible," 177.
49. For discussions of the idea of the many-headed multitude, particularly in terms of representations, see Christopher Hill, *Change and Continuity in Seventeenth-Century England;* C. A. Patrides, " 'The Beast with Many Heads': Renaissance Views on the Multitude"; and Frederick Tupper, "The Shakespearean Mob." The most extensive analysis of this social attitude in political terms is found in Linebaugh and Rediker, *The Many-Headed Hydra.*
50. *The Plays of John Marston.*
51. See Manning, *Village Revolts,* 55–81, 221–29.
52. *Tudor Proclamations,* III.82. As Manning has argued, the imposition of martial law often exacerbated social tensions; it was not uncommon for large-scale arrests to lead to further riots, along with attempts to free arrested rioters from prison (202).
53. Quoted in Archer, *Pursuit of Stability,* 1.
54. Manning, *Village Revolts,* 200–02. See also K. J. Lindley, "Riot Prevention and Control in Early Stuart London"; Rappaport, *Worlds Within Worlds;* and Barbara Freedman, "Elizabethan Protest, Plague, and Plays."
55. Archer, *Pursuit of Stability,* 7.
56. Tim Harris, "Perceptions of the Crowd in Later Stuart London," 254.
57. *Tudor Proclamations,* II.232.
58. Christopher Hill, *The World Turned Upside Down,* 40.
59. Gilles Deleuze and Felix Guattari, *A Thousand Plateaus,* 33.
60. *Tudor Proclamations,* III.233. Elizabeth's fear of these libels was such that she offered the enormous reward of one hundred pounds to those who could provide the name "of any of the authors, writers, or dispersers of any of the said libels" (III.234).
61. The apparent context of this prologue is not, of course, solely an urban one, but I think Rumor's address to the urban theater audience as "my household" encourages this reading.
62. Fumerton, "London's Vagrant Economy," 208. Fumerton's study aims "to make space for a new notion of 'low' subjectivity" and suggests that "An originary trace of such an unbounded subject can be detected . . . in a newly emergent 'vagrant' economy that was centred on London" (207). Fumerton's interest in the mobile spaces of the city dovetails nicely with this study, although she ultimately points her discussion toward a theoretical argument about subjectivity that falls outside my concerns. See also Woodbridge, *Vagrancy,* 239–65. On this subject, see also John Twyning, *London Dispossessed;* as Twyning claims, "the vast majority of those who made London were in some way dispossessed from their livelihood and/or their family, but always

from the society and culture which had provided them with their identity. But the milieu in which they were to find new lives and identities was far from stable and their arrival created the very dynamic conditions of that instability" (1–2).

63. See Manley, *Literature and Culture,* 164–67, 487–89.
64. Stephen Gosson, *Plays Confuted in 5 Actions,* sig. B3.
65. Mullaney's *The Place of the Stage* remains exemplary in this regard. Also see Louis Montrose, *The Purpose of Playing.*
66. Heinemann, *Puritanism and Theatre,* 31–36.
67. Reprinted in E. K. Chambers, *Elizabethan Stage,* 4:316–17.
68. Reprinted in Chambers, *Elizabethan Stage,* 4:319–20.
69. Henry Crosse, *Vertues Common-Wealth,* sig. Q1. Another analysis of Crosse's pamphlet and other antitheatrical materials can be found in David Glimp's *Increase and Multiply,* which examines issues of population and governance in early modern England as they relate to literary practice and production. See especially chapter 3, "Staging Government," which intersects this study at a number of points.
70. Thomas Platter, in *The Journals of Two Travelers in Elizabethan and Early Stuart England,* 37; Robert Anton, *The Philosophers Satyrs,* sig. I3v.
71. *The Non-Dramatic Works of Thomas Dekker,* 2:53.
72. John Marston, *What You Will,* sig. E2.
73. Crosse, *Vertues Common-Wealth,* sig. Q1v.
74. Reprinted in Chambers, *Elizabethan Stage,* 4:340–41.
75. See Alfred Harbage, *Shakespeare's Audience,* 91.
76. Sir John Davies, "In Cosmum," *The Poems of Sir John Davies,* 136.
77. See Manning, *Village Revolts,* 202–03.
78. Crosse, *Vertues Common-Wealth,* sig. Q1; Freedman, op. cit.
79. Cf. Jeffrey Masten, "*More* or Less: Editing the Collaborative."
80. Anthony Munday et al., *Sir Thomas More,* 18–19.
81. Berlin, "Civic Ceremony in Early Modern London," 19.
82. Quoted in *Sir Thomas More,* 17. I do not mean to suggest that it was *only* the fact of rioting London crowds that disturbed Tilney; for an extended discussion of the issues involved, see Richard Dutton, *Mastering the Revels,* 80–87.
83. *Coriolanus* is truly an exception, in that the mob is not merely rehearsing or duplicating the actions of an elite leader. See Patterson, *Shakespeare and the Popular Voice,* 129–31.
84. Given that the play was performed by the Children of Pauls, an additional joke undoubtedly lurks in the expression "the children of Cheapside."
85. *The Alchemist and Other Plays,* 327–433.
86. Although I first read it long after this chapter was titled, I am indebted to Philip Pullman's *The Golden Compass* for this observation.

2 London's Mirror: Civic Ritual and the Crowd

1. Thomas Dekker, *Brittannia's Honor,* sig. A4.
2. See David M. Bergeron, *English Civic Pageantry 1558–1642,* 70–88. Bergeron's study is the foundation of all modern analysis of civic pageantry, and I have relied on it for informational purposes throughout this chapter.
3. Michel de Certeau, *The Practice of Everyday Life,* 93, 92.
4. Gilbert Dugdale, *The Time Triumphant,* sig. B2v. See Bergeron, "Gilbert Dugdale and Royal Entry of James 1 (1604)," and Andrew Gordon's comments on Dugdale (and on civic pageantry in general) in "Performing London."
5. Cf. Leah Marcus, *The Politics of Mirth,* 64.
6. Bergeron, *English Civic Pageantry,* 76.
7. Thomas Middleton's *The Triumphs of Truth,* the most expensive show, cost £1,300; the cheapest Jacobean show was Anthony Munday's *Sidero-Thriambos* (1618), which cost only £524. See *Collections III,* 85–88, 93–98.
8. Bergeron, *English Civic Pageantry,* 89. Also see Lawrence Manley, *Literature and Culture in Early Modern London,* 212–21.
9. Thomas Heywood, *Londini speculum: or, Londons mirror,* sig. C3v. For Heywood's civic pageants, see also *Thomas Heywood's Pageants: A Critical Edition.*
10. Anthony Munday, *Himatia-Poleos,* sig. B1–B1v. For Munday's civic pageants, see also *Pageants and Entertainments of Anthony Munday: A Critical Edition.*
11. *Collections III,* xxxii–xxxiii. For a somewhat different discussion of the relationship between some of the pageant texts and their performance, see David M. Bergeron, "Stuart Civic Pageants and Textual Performance."
12. See Leah Marcus, "City Metal and Country Mettle: The Occasion of Ben Jonson's *Golden Age Restored*"; Manley, *Literature and Culture;* Gail Kern Paster, "The Idea of London in Masque and Pageant"; Glynne Wickham, *Early English Stages,* 2:1.
13. Dekker, *Brittannia's Honor,* sig. B3v; Thomas Middleton, *The Triumphs of Truth,* sig. B4v.
14. Heywood, *London Ius Honorarium,* sig. B4.
15. This is not to suggest that London was governed by an oligarchy wholly indifferent to civic rule, nor to suggest that all of the power of civic government was in the direct hands of the mayor and aldermen; see Steve Rappaport, *Worlds Within Worlds,* 176–83, for a useful (if rather one-sided) corrective to this common point of view.
16. See Paul Seaver, "The Artisanal World," for an extensive analysis of the dynamics of wealth and office in the context of Dekker's *The Shoemaker's Holiday.*

17. And so, as Andrew Gordon puts it, "Where the monarchic city had been variously figured as the seat of kings and the *Camera Regia*, the London of the mayoral pageant is a place of political representation. The representation of the social body is structured according to the fiction of elective autonomy displayed in the formal habits of the representatives of civic authority, a fiction dependent upon repeated performance" ("Performing London," 81).
18. See Theodore Leinwand, "London Triumphing," 141.
19. Dekker, *Troia-Nova Triumphans,* sig. A3–A3v.
20. See Manley, *Literature and Culture,* 221–41, for an extended analysis of the processional route.
21. Charles Pythian-Adams, "Ceremony and the Citizen: The Communal Year at Coventry 1450–1550," 57–85.
22. Steven Mullaney, *The Place of the Stage,* 13.
23. "Fifty years before its appearance in 1598, Stow's *Survey of London* would have been superfluous. . . . Reading the city, as Stow does in his *Survey,* was something every citizen could be expected to do" (Mullaney, *The Place of the Stage,* 14). The idea of every citizen being able to read the city as Stow did seems frankly fantastical to me.
24. "Threatened" may seem too strong a word to describe the impact of suburban growth on the civic elite—especially given the revisionist historical work of Joseph Ward, who argues, "Despite the consensus among scholars that companies were impotent outside the City's walls and borders, many of London's guilds and—perhaps more important— their members exerted influence in the suburbs and liberties" (*Metropolitan Communities,* 28). On the other hand, the city guilds clearly had *less* influence in the suburbs than in London; in this regard, the overall effect of suburban population growth was to dilute the civic authority of the guilds. As I indicated in chapter 1, I have no desire to separate the city and suburbs into a rigid symbolic binary. Nevertheless, the significance of rapid and haphazard suburban growth to a ceremony designed to celebrate a coherent idea of London is considerable. On this point, see William Hardin, "Spectacular Constructions."
25. See Manley, "Of Sites and Rites," 53–54.
26. Walter Benjamin, *The Origin of German Tragic Drama,* 354.
27. See Gordon Kipling, "Triumphal Drama," 37–56.
28. Middleton, *The Trivmphs of Integrity,* sig. A3.
29. Munday, *Metropolis Coronata,* sig. B4v.
30. See Manley, *Literature and Culture,* 215.
31. Manley is conscientious about drawing attention to the political realities of the period: "The rise of the mayoral inauguration and its show to pre-eminence in London's civic year reflected the increasing domination of the City by a few elite companies, the cultic elevation of the Lord Mayor, and the widening gap between the leading City merchants and the expanding body of middling shopkeepers, artisans,

journeymen and apprentices who constituted the great majority of the citizen class" (262). Yet his emphasis is always squarely on a communal interpretation: "The shows . . . provided the lower echelons of Londoners with a genuinely innovative and compelling model of civic and economic achievement" (263).

32. For Turner's ritual model, see especially *The Ritual Process: Structure and Anti-Structure,* "Liminality and the Performative Genres," and *From Ritual to Theatre: The Human Seriousness of Play.*

33. Clifford Geertz, "Blurred Genres," 172.

34. See J. L. Austin, *How to Do Things with Words.*

35. Turner, *From Ritual to Theatre,* 112.

36. Pierre Bourdieu, *Language and Symbolic Power,* 113.

37. *Calendar of State Papers,* 58–63. Hereafter cited as Busino.

38. Bergeron discusses the research potential of the Venetian accounts in "Venetian State Papers and English Civic Pageantry," without offering much interpretation; Manley cites Busino's account in *Literature and Culture* without quoting it. The only actual analysis of part of this description I am aware of is R. M. Smuts, "Public Ceremony and Royal Charisma."

39. Munday, *Camp-bell,* sig. B2v. Also see Smutts, "Royal Charisma," 74–75, for a discussion of crowd noise at public rituals.

40. Heywood, *Londini Status Pacatus,* sig. C1v.

41. Reprinted in Frederick Fairholt, *Lord Mayor's Pageants,* 2:263.

42. Reprinted in Frederick Fairholt, *Lord Mayor's Pageants,* 1:163.

43. Middleton, *The Tryumphs of Honor and Industry,* sig. B4v.

44. Munday, *Sidero-Thriambos,* sig. C1v.

45. Middleton, *The Triumphs of Honor and Vertue,* sig. B2v.

46. John Webster, *Monuments of Honor,* sig. C2v.

47. Because of their complexity and sophistication, these two shows have attracted the majority of critical interest; see especially Leinwand, "London Triumphing." For a reading that emphasizes the constraints put on the mayor by the morality framework of the pageants, see Sergei Lobanov-Rostovsky, "*The Triumphes of Golde:* Economic Authority in the Jacobean Lord Mayor's Show."

48. After referring to "all spite that murmurs at the Choice / If at least such there be," Virtue makes explicit reference to the details of the coming confrontation, telling the mayor not to "feare the Stings of Envy, nor the Threates / Of her invenomd Arrowes, which at the Seates / Of those Who Best Rule, evermore are shot" (sig. B4).

49. Bristol, *Carnival and Theater,* 61.

50. Middleton, *The Triumphs of Truth,* sig. B3.

51. The contemporary double meaning of "beldams," widows and witches, compounds the ambiguity of the description.

52. For a discussion of the problem of refusing office, see Pearl, *London and the Outbreak of the Puritan Revolution,* 65, and Richard Wunderli, "Evasion of the Office of Alderman in London, 1523–1672."

As Wunderli says, "office evasion exposes us to the weak economic base of London that could not support the extraordinary expenses of population growth and Crown loans" (3).

53. "Tryumphes, are the most choice and daintiest fruit that spring from Peace and Abundance; Love begets them; and Much Cost brings them forth. . . . They are now and then the Rich and Glorious Fires of Bounty, State and Magnificence . . . Ryot having no hand in laying out the Expences, and yet no hand in plucking backe what is held decent to be bestowed. A *Sumptuous Thriftinesse* in these *Civil Ceremonies* managing all. For it were not laudable, in a City (so rarely governed and tempered) superfluously to exceed; As contrariwise it is much honour to her (when the Day of spending comes) not to be sparing in any thing" (sig. A3).

54. Munday, *Chruso-thriambos: The Triumphes of Golde*, sig. A4–A4v. It is possible that Middleton is explicitly recalling and criticizing this pageant, as he openly despised the shows that Munday produced.

55. As John Stow noted with some amusement, the red sword was that of St. Paul and had nothing to do with Walworth (*Survey of London*, I.221).

56. Munday, *Chrysanaleia: The Golden Fishing*, sig. C3.

57. Munday, *The Trivmphes of Re-Vnited Britania*, sig. B1v.

58. See *Collections III*, 2–3.

59. *The Life and Death of Jack Straw*, sigs. C4r–v, D4v–E2v.

60. Munday, *The Golden Fishing*, sig. A4–A4v.

61. For a discussion of the Jack Straw trope, see Brents Stirling, *The Populace in Shakespeare*, 131–50.

62. Richard Wilson, " 'A Mingled Yarn': Shakespeare and the Cloth Workers," 174.

63. See Michael Berlin, "Civic Ceremony in Early Modern London": "When in 1569 the lord mayor was asked by the Privy Council for an explanation of the city's failure to go ahead with the midsummer watch that year, the mayor's reply blamed the 'callinge and confluence of moche people to the cytie out of the countreye' " (19). See also chapter 1.

64. Manning, *Village Revolts*, 201–02.

65. *Stuart Royal Proclamations*, 1:361.

66. *The Dramatic Works of Thomas Heywood*, 6 vols. (New York: Russell & Russell, 1964).

67. My thanks to Garrett Sullivan for drawing my attention to this passage in a paper given at the 1998 RSA conference and for influencing my reading of the scene. See his chapter "The Beleagured City" in *The Drama of Landscape* for an extended discussion of the play.

68. *London 1500–1700: The Making of the Metropolis*, 45.

69. Hardin, "Spectacular Constructions," 112.

70. Ward discusses the New Corporation of the Suburbs of London extensively; see *Metropolitan Communities*, 19–45. The New Corporation

was "designed to regulate the activities of all traders and artisans that works in areas outside the lord mayor's jurisdiction up to three miles from the City, regardless of whether they already were members of City livery companies. . . . Those who wished to work in suburban London had to pay an entrance fee to the New Corporation that would then go to the Crown's use" (20). Perhaps unsurprisingly, the collection of fees quickly became the primary activity of the New Corporation.

71. As Ward comments, "The City governors' reaction to the Corporation was consistent with their predecessors' claim in 1610 that the City companies could have regulated the suburban economy had their powers been increased. As a result, they considered the Corporation 'very prejudicial' to the City privileges" (21).

72. See Hardin, "Spectacular Constructions," 130–32, for an extended discussion of this trope.

73. Heywood, *Londini Artium & Scientiarum Scaturigo,* sig. B4.

74. Heywood, *Londini Emporia, or Londons Mercatura,* sig. B3v–B4.

75. See especially Gail Kern Paster, "The Idea of London," 60.

76. See Walter J. Ong, "From Allegory to Diagram in the Renaissance Mind," 423–40.

77. Heywood, *Londini Sinus Salutis,* sig. C1.

78. William Fennor (ascribed), *Cornu-copiae,* sig. H1.

79. Robert Herrick, *Hesperides,* sig. Q4v–Q5.

80. *Pasquils Iestes Mixed with Mother Bunches Merriments,* sig. B1v–B2.

81. Dekker, *The Ravens Almanacke,* sig. D3.

3 "Shakespeare's London": The Scene of London in the Second Tetralogy and *Henry VIII*

1. On the function of anachronism in Shakespeare's history plays, see Phyllis Rackin, *Stages of History,* 86–145.

2. Like all generalizations, there are many important exceptions to this statement; for instance, Robert Weimann's *Shakespeare and the Popular Tradition* and *Author's Pen and Actor's Voice,* Garrett Sullivan's *The Drama of Landscape,* and Rackin's *Stages of History* are exemplary in their attention to theatrical space.

3. Of course, excellent critical work on Shakespeare's use of London has been done through these strategies; Leah Marcus's chapter on London in *Puzzling Shakespeare* is a good example.

4. *Oxford English Dictionary,* 2nd ed., s.v. "setting."

5. Or perhaps the Curtain; see Melissa D. Aaron, "The Globe and *Henry V* as business document," for a fascinating investigation as to which theater the play was intended for.

6. For more on the relationship between spatial and political hierarchies, especially in the context of court masques, see Stephen Orgel, *The Illusion of Power,* 37–43.

7. Greenblatt, *Shakespearean Negotiations,* 65. For a critical yet sympathetic reappraisal of the relationship between royal power and the theater, see Louis Montrose, *The Purpose of Playing.*

8. Christopher Pye, explicitly psychologizing Greenblatt's model, argues that in such moments "the subject is a function of the sovereign" (*The Regal Phantasm,* 4). This move pushes the analogy even further from a real location such as the playhouse, and furthermore replaces the implied collectivity of a theater audience with the private psychodrama of the individual.

9. This critical neglect is beginning to change; to take but one example, the *New History of Early English Drama* labels its first two sections "Early English Drama and Physical Space" and "Early English Drama and Social Space." My only criticism is to note that this format (coupled with comments in the editors' introduction) implies the independence of these two spaces.

10. Henri Lefebvre, *The Production of Space,* 11–12. The Foucaldian conception of space that underlies Greenblatt's critical approach is one of Lefebvre's targets in *The Production of Space;* with regard to Foucault's discussion of the space of knowledge in *The Archeology of Knowledge,* he comments, "Foucault never explains what space it is that he is referring to, nor how it bridges the gap between the theoretical (epistemological) realm and the practical one, between mental and social, between the space of the philosophers and the space of people who deal with material things" (4).

11. Edward Soja, *Thirdspace,* 8–12 and 53–82 passim. Soja considers this trialectical movement the master trope of Lefebvre's spatial paradigm, whether the terms involved are physical-social-mental space, natural-absolute-abstract space, or any of Lefebvre's other interrelated models.

12. In Bourdieu's model, *habitus* refers to an ingrained set of social dispositions (rules, concepts, perceptions, traditions, prejudices) that interacts with a particular *field* ("a space of possibles") to produce the space of social practice (*The Field of Cultural Production,* 64).

13. See Lawrence Manley, *Literature and Culture in Early Modern London,* 212–93. Also see Sydney Anglo, *Spectacle, Pageantry, and Early Tudor Policy,* for a foundational analysis of earlier royal entries.

14. Thomas Dekker, *The Magnificent Entertainment Giuen to King Iames,* sig. F2–F2v.

15. Lefebvre, *Production of Space,* 236.

16. Quoted in John Nichols, *The Progresses and Public Processions of Queen Elizabeth,* 3:220.

17. Victor Turner, *From Ritual to Theater,* 54, and throughout Turner's writings.

18. Lefebvre, *Production of Space,* 229–34, 285–91.

19. Turner, *From Ritual to Theater,* 47–51.

20. See, for example, *Discipline and Punish,* 197–98.

21. Stow, *Survey of London,* I.165.

22. David Kastan, "Proud Majesty Made a Subject," 459–75.
23. In practice Kastan does the same: "when the theatrical space is the city itself rather than the playhouse, the immediate danger of unregulated representation increases. Elizabeth, like the Lord Mayors, had used the city streets to stage pageants of authority, but the streets were not to serve as public access theaters" (468). I agree with Kastan's general point, but I think his analysis is exactly backwards; *pace* the antitheatricalists, it was not the theaters that made London a danger, but rather the reverse; the development of the theaters was intimately connected to the uncontrollable and dangerous growth of the city.
24. Cf. Greenblatt's discussion of Thomas More in *Renaissance Self-Fashioning*, 13–15.
25. In E. K. Chambers, *William Shakespeare: A Study of Facts and Problems*, 2:327.
26. Cf. *The Forms of Power and the Power of Forms in the Renaissance*, 3–4.
27. Dekker, *The Magnificent Entertainment*, sig. B3.
28. For an analysis of *camera regis* in the Lord Mayor's show, see Gail Kern Paster, "The Idea of London in Masque and Pageant," 52–56.
29. As Andrew Gordon puts it, "Dekker's text reads the city's temporary ceremonial topography in precise terms, transposing a network of spatial relations that describe degrees of proximity to the monarch onto the urban spaces of London" ("Performing London," 78).
30. Elias Canetti, *Crowds and Power*, 29–30.
31. Richard Schechner, *Performance Theory*, 106–47. Schechner argues that the basic polarity in performance is between entertainment and efficacy, not theater and ritual; the latter terms depend on contexts and functions that will not necessarily coincide with the performance's position on the entertainment–efficacy axis (120).
32. Rackin, *Stages of History*, 124, 133.
33. A theatrical control which depends, paradoxically, on his simultaneous relinquishing of political control. See Pye, *Regal Phantasm*, 84–88, for an excellent analysis of the theatrics of this scene.
34. For a superb reading of the complex textual and spatial issues catalyzed by Rumor's induction, see Harry Berger, Jr., *Making Trifles of Terrors*, 132–47.
35. Jonathan Goldberg, *Sodometries: Renaissance Texts, Modern Sexualities*, 145–47.
36. As Anthony B. Dawson has commented, "One thing that is forgotten in Henry's vision of national community is hierarchy, even as his phrase 'be he ne'er so vile' vividly recalls it" ("The Arithmetic of Memory," 56).
37. Goldberg, *James I and the Politics of Literature*, 163.
38. Annabel Patterson, *Shakespeare and the Popular Voice*, 81.
39. Pye speaks of "the histories, which began with Henry [V]'s death and conclude with his glory" (*Regal Phantasm*, 1); less brazen, Goldberg finesses the problem of endings by describing Henry V as

"the monarch who comes at the end of Shakespeare's second tetralogy and who must have seemed to Shakespeare the last English king he would show onstage" (*Politics of Literature,* 161). This type of elision is a common fate for *Henry VIII;* performed at least a year after Prospero first drowned his book, it offers an unwanted supplement to the classical unity of both the history plays and the Shakespearean canon as a whole.

40. Whether *Henry VIII* is "the last play" is, of course, open to question; both *The Two Noble Kinsmen,* which Shakespeare may have cowritten with John Fletcher, and the lost *Cardenio* are likely contemporaries of *Henry VIII.* All three plays are typically thought to involve collaboration. The crowd scenes in *Henry VIII* that bear the focus of my analysis of the play are typically attributed to Fletcher rather than Shakespeare; this attribution, and the fact of collaboration, matters little to the critical perspective I am employing (which emphasizes performative rather than creative links with the earlier history plays), but it is interesting that the scenes that I argue dismantle the courtly archetype of the city found in the Henriad, are generally considered "un-Shakespearean."

41. To label any Shakespeare play "politically quiescent" is, of course, to overlook the range and complexity of his negative capability, especially in matters of politics. Patricia Parker has argued that rather than endorse Tudor legitimacy, *Henry VIII* subtly undermines it by repeatedly drawing attention to the potential falsity of narrative, historical or otherwise (*Shakespeare From the Margins,* 53). While I accept the insight, I still think that the dynamic of the play tends strongly toward political and genealogical stability, especially in the case of Henry.

42. See Hugh M. Richmond, "The Resurrection of an Expired Form."

43. Despite the tactical expediency of charges of treason raised against Buckingham or Wolsey, for example, Henry's royal authority is unchallenged in the play.

44. In making this observation, I do not mean to suggest that the play is simple, or simply celebratory in its approach to Tudor history. On the contrary, a number of recent articles and book chapters have demonstrated the complexity of its historical perspective and practice—and the multiple ironies of the play's alternate title, *All is True.* As Barbara Kreps has commented, "In addition to itself *being* a depiction of the past, the play is also very often *about* the past: recounting, examining, interpreting it" ("When All is True: Law, History, and Problems of Knowledge in *Henry VIII,*" 167). See also, in particular, Zenón Luis-Martínez, " 'Maimed Narrations': Shakespeare's *Henry VIII* and the Task of the Historian"; Annabel Patterson, " 'All is True': Negotiating the Past in *Henry VIII*"; Anston Bosman, "Seeing Tears: Truth and Sense in *All is True*"; and Dennis Kezar, "Law/Form/History: Shakespeare's Verdict in *All is True.*" For the differences between Elizabethan and Jacobean history plays, see Ivo

Kamps's groundbreaking assessment of Stuart historical drama in the context of emerging philosophies of history in *Historiography and Ideology in Stuart Drama.*

45. Cited in the Arden *Henry VIII* (London: Methuen and Co., 1915), 6n28.

46. *Riverside Shakespeare,* 1007n.

47. This displacement introduces an important element of gender difference to the meaning of royal spectacle in *Henry VIII*; despite her ritual annointment, Anne's eroticized female body is not invested with the terrible majesty (and masculinity) of a monarch.

48. The presence of the Bishops might remind us of the Bishops that Gloucester uses as props in the Baynard's Castle scene (*Richard III* 3.7.95), but if *Henry VIII* intends a similar irony it is completely tacit.

49. As Simon Palfrey points out, "the comparison of the popular acclaim to 'many tunes' of a 'Tempest' at 'Sea' might suggest Shakespeare's frequent resort to just such weather to evoke the clamorous demotic voice" (*Late Shakespeare,* 201). To extend the point (and to anticipate the argument of chapter 4 somewhat), the exclamation of the Boatswain at the start of *The Tempest*—"What cares these roarers for the name of king?" (1.1.16–17)—can be seen as an allusion to that play's noisy theatrical audience and as a relevant intertext for the contemporaneous crowd scenes in *Henry VIII.*

50. Mikhail Bakhtin, *Rabelais and His World,* 310.

51. For a fascinating reading of issues of fecundity and unclean generation in the play in the context of the theater (albeit one that moves in different directions from this analysis), see David Glimp, *Increase and Multiply,* 101–14.

52. Leonard Tennenhouse, "Strategies of State and Political Plays," 124.

53. It is also worth noting that James's championing of rural pastimes occurred in the context of a political struggle with the mercantile elite of London. To James's mind, Puritan London was the enemy of traditional sports and games. See Marcus, *The Politics of Mirth,* especially the chapter on *The Vision of Delight* and *Christmas his Masque* (64–105).

54. *The King's Majesties Declaration to His Subjects, Concerning lawfull Sports to be used,* sig. B4v.

55. Such specificity characterizes Rabelais's use of carnival in Bakhtin's argument, who focuses on "the specific character of all Rabelaisian images, which combine a broad universalism and utopianism with extraordinarily concrete, obvious, and vivid traits, strictly localized and technically precise" (*Rabelais and His World,* 185).

56. Speech to Parliament, March 31, 1607. Reprinted in *King James VI and I: Political Writings,* 165.

57. Admittedly, this growth is occurring because of a failure in traditional hospitality by the landed nobility—that is, the fault is the country's, not the city's. Still, the terms in which James expresses this failure

suggests the power of the growing city as a symbol for various malfunctions in the body politic.

58. Cf. Peter Stallybrass and Allon White, *The Politics and Poetics of Transgression*, 6–26.

59. Bakhtin, *Rabelais and His World*, 7.

60. Canetti, *Crowds and Power*, 16.

61. The Porter's mispronunciation of "Parish" for "Paris" may have been a commonplace of the time, or it may be another level of wordplay, suggesting the religious component of the ceremony and referring to the parish, the community of the city. It is, however, impossible to read this as an example of genuine community, since the Porter obviously finds the populace's presence at this christening inappropriate.

62. See Andrew Gurr, *The Shakespearean Stage*, 120, 152.

63. This, of course, is historically accurate (at least by Holinshed's account), but the closeness of the allusion, especially considering that *Henry VIII* was probably staged at Blackfriars during the winter months, is significant. See Glynne Wickham's "The Dramatic Structure of Shakespeare's *King Henry the Eighth*." Cf. Ben Jonson's similarly self-conscious use of Blackfriars in *The Alchemist*; see R. L. Smallwood, " 'Here, in the Friars': Immediacy and Theatricality in *The Alchemist*."

64. In this context, it may be possible to read Henry's final words as ironic: he declares a holiday, not realizing that his subjects have already reached the same conclusion on their own.

65. Michel Foucault's comment on "the pleb" seems appropriate to this imagining of London: "There is always something which in some way escapes the relations of power; something in the social body . . . which is not all the more or less docile or reactive raw material, but which is the centrifugal movement, the inverse energy, that which escapes" (Meaghan Morris and Paul Patton, eds., *Michel Foucault: Power, Truth, Strategy*, 52).

4 Distracted Multitude: The Theater and the Many-Headed Monster

1. *Plato's Republic*, 235.

2. Deleuze and Guattari, *A Thousand Plateaus*, 16, 21. In treating the arborescent and the rhizomatic as an opposition I do some violence to Deleuze and Guattari's model; as they assert, "the root-tree and the canal-rhizome are not two opposed models: the first operates as a transcendent model and tracing, even if it engenders its own escapes; the second operates as an immanent process that overturns the model and outlines a map, even if it constitutes its own hierarchies" (20). It is also worth noting that Deleuze and Guattari explicitly associate images of many-headedness with the arbor (16); in this regard, I would suggest that the *figure* of the many-headed monster

itself is arborescent, but it attempts to capture, imperfectly, something rhizomatic.

3. Thomas Elyot, *The Book Named the Governor*, 6; Fulke Greville, *The Remains: Being Poems of Monarchy and Religion*, 183; Walter Raleigh, *Selections from His Historie of the World*, 36.

4. Christopher Hill, *Change and Continuity in Seventeenth-Century England*, 182–83.

5. Thomas Browne, *Religio Medici*, 76.

6. George Chapman, *Andromeda Liberata. Or the Nuptials of Perseus and Andromeda* (1614, STC 4964), sig. B2v–B3.

7. For a detailed discussion of the scandals surrounding Howard and Carr, see David Lindley, *The Trials of Frances Howard*.

8. Chapman, *A Free and Offenceles Iustification*, sig. *3v.

9. Among the important critical discussions of antitheatrical discourse in early modern England are Jonas Barish, *The Antitheatrical Prejudice*, Jean Howard, *The Stage and Social Struggle in Early Modern England*, and Louis Montrose, *The Purpose of Playing*. Also see the introduction of Michael Neill's *Issues of Death*, 22–29, and Bryan Reynolds's article, "The devil's house, 'or worse': Transversal power and antitheatrical discourse in early modern England."

10. I. G., *A Refutation of the Apology for Actors*, sig. E3; Stephen Gosson, *The Schoole of Abuse*, sig. A4.

11. Gosson, *Plays Confuted in 5 Actions*, sig. A4v, C2v–C3.

12. William Rankins, *A Mirrour of Monsters*, sig. C2; see Jeremiah 7.33, for example.

13. Gosson, *Schoole of Abuse*, sig. B6–B6v. On the "posterne" entry to the city, see Jeffrey Masten, "Is the Fundament a Grave?" 130.

14. I. H., *This Worlds Folly*, sig. B3. See Michael Neill, *Issues of Death*, 24–25 for a further discussion of this passage within the context of the plague.

15. Thomas Heywood, *An Apology for Actors*, sig. F3.

16. Anthony Munday (ascribed), *A 2nd and 3rd Blast of Retrait from Plaies and Theaters*, sig. F1–F1v.

17. "People at the theater are not *where* they should be . . . ; consequently, they are not *who* they should be, but are released into a realm of Protean shapeshifting with enormous destabilizing consequences for the social order" (Howard, *Stage and Social Struggle*, 27).

18. Gosson, *Plays Confuted*, sig. B1r–v.; Munday, *2nd and 3rd*, sig. D2v.

19. John Northbrooke, *A Treatise Wherein Dicing, Daucing, Vaine Plaies or Enterludes . . . are Reprooued*, sig. I2v.

20. John Rainoldes, *Th'Overthrow of Stage Plays*, sig. A2; Philip Stubbes, *The Anatomie of Abuses*, sig. N1v; Rankins, *Mirrour of Monsters*, sig. B2v.

21. Gosson, *Plays Confuted*, sig. D1. See Denis Kezar, "*Julius Caesar* and the Properties of Shakespeare's Globe," for an extended reading of this quotation.

22. Stubbes, *Anatomie,* sig. N1v–N2. On this passage, and on antithe-
    atricality in general, cf. Reynolds, "The devil's house, 'or worse.' "
23. *The Complete Works in Verse and Prose of Samuel Daniel,* 100.
24. "Thresholds to Memory": " 'Distracted' must not of course be read
    in Walter Benjamin's sense of 'distraction' (*Zerstreuung*)—as marking
    the modern mode of reception in a mass culture of reproducible
    entertainment; yet the ambivalence hinted at seems unmistakable and
    is inseparable from a larger process of social change affecting and,
    possibly, blurring the boundary between popular traditions in the
    theater and Early Modern consumer culture in a rapidly expanding
    marketplace" (12).
25. Though Weimann is reluctant to take this step, merely noting the
    problem of how the audience and the multitude are referred to in dif-
    ferent ways ("Thresholds to Memory," 14); my position, as I go on
    to demonstrate, is that the problem is only apparent.
26. *Oxford English Dictionary,* 2nd ed., s.v. "distracted."
27. *The Complete Works of John Webster,* 3.219. The meaning of the word
    "innovation" has been an editorial crux in *Hamlet* for generations.
28. *The Works of Thomas Middleton,* vol. 2.
29. Stow, *Survey of London,* II:197.
30. *The Plays and Poems of Philip Massinger.*
31. Richard Helgerson, *Forms of Nationhood;* see also Richard Wilson,
    " 'Is this a Holiday?': Shakespeare's Roman Carnival," for an especially
    extreme version of this argument in the context of *Julius Caesar.*
32. On this point and the larger issue of collective and atomized audiences,
    cf. Dawson and Yachnin, *Culture of Playgoing,* especially chapter 4.
33. *The Plays of John Marston.*
34. See Neill, *Issues of Death,* 44–50.
35. Cf. Dawson: "Just as there is a correlation between what happens
    metatheatrically within a play and what goes on within the playhouse,
    so what happens inside the theater—controlling visuality while
    acknowledging its devious abilities to escape management—can
    be seen as correlative to the position of the theater in the culture as a
    whole" (*Culture of Playgoing,* 102).
36. On the general subject of the War of the Theaters, see James
    Bednardz, *Shakespeare and the Poets' War.* Rosalyn Knutson, in
    Playing Companies and Commerce in Shakespeare's Time, has argued
    that the ascription of *Histriomastix* to Marston is mistaken; she would
    date it to perhaps a decade before the War of the Theaters, an event
    she thinks has been grossly exaggerated and misconstrued in our
    understanding of the relations between companies. While agreeing
    with the general thrust of Knutson's book, I find the evidence pre-
    sented against *Histriomastix* unpersuasive; apart from finding the play
    insufficiently trendy in its subjects, she supports her strongest point,
    about the unconventional cast size, by making assumptions about
    doubling practices that seem unnecessary to the play.

37. See Janette Dillon, *City, Court, and Theatre,* 79–95. I am indebted to Dillon's analysis in my subsequent readings of Jonson.
38. See Gail Kern Paster, *The Idea of the City in the Age of Shakespeare.*
39. *The Complete Plays of Ben Jonson,* vol. 1.
40. As Karen Newman comments on Donne's "Satyre I," "the homogeneous 'men of sort, of parts, and qualities' (105) they meet as they walk out . . . are by no means alike; much of the poem's action turns on the humorist's valuation of the various persons they meet" (208).
41. Martin Butler, "Jonson's London and its Theatres," 15.
42. *Cataline* also acknowledges the crowded city to a degree, through both occasional rhetoric and the device of a chorus, although the formal strictures of that play make it difficult to read its acknowledgment as a form of engagement.
43. Herbert Blau, *The Audience,* 216.
44. See Bruce Boehrer, *The Fury of Men's Gullets: Ben Jonson and the Digestive Canal.*
45. For Jonson's desire to play this public role, see Katherine Eisaman Maus, *Ben Jonson and the Roman Frame of Mind,* especially chapter 5 "Jonson and the Roman Social Ethos."
46. See Alan Sinfield, "*Poetaster,* the Author, and the Perils of Cultural Production," for a fuller discussion of these issues.
47. See Deleuze and Guattari, *A Thousand Plateaus,* passim.

5 "Rome, etc.": *Sejanus, Julius Caesar,* and the Prodigious City

1. *The Complete Plays of Ben Jonson,* vol. 2.
2. Recent and influential titles include: Coppelia Kahn, *Roman Shakespeare: Warriors, Wounds, and Women;* Clifford Ronan, *"Antike Roman": Power Symbology and the Roman Play in Early Modern England, 1585–1635;* Charles Wells, *The Wide Arch: Roman Values in Shakespeare;* Geoffrey Miles, *Shakespeare and the Constant Romans;* Charles Martindale, *Shakespeare and the Uses of Antiquity,* Vivian Thomas, *Shakespeare's Roman Worlds;* Gail Kern Paster, *The Idea of the City in the Age of Shakespeare;* Robert Miola, *Shakespeare's Rome;* Paul A. Cantor, *Shakespeare's Rome: Republic and Empire;* Julie Sanders, *Ben Jonson's Theatrical Republic;* Katherine Eisaman Maus, *Ben Jonson and the Roman Frame of Mind;* Jonathan Goldberg, *James I and the Politics of Literature: Jonson, Shakespeare, Donne, and Their Contemporaries.*
3. As Ronan tallies it, "forty-three extant vernacular plays date from the England of 1585–1635" (*"Antike Roman,"* 2).
4. Blair Worden's comment on Jonson is equally apt for Shakespeare: "His imagination anglicized Rome and romanized England" ("Politics in *Cataline:* Jonson and his Sources," 153). Of course, ancient Rome also stood as an alien, un-English location; for an interesting reading

from this perspective, see Christine E. Hutchins, " 'Who is here so rude that would not be a Roman?': England as Anti-Type of Rome in Elizabethan Print and *Julius Caesar.*"

5. As Richard Burt has commented, "Roman history was a discourse that one could not afford to ignore in the Renaissance. One had to make use of it. . . . The meaning of Roman history had to be articulated in and for the Renaissance present" (" 'A Dangerous Rome': Shakespeare's *Julius Caesar* and the Discursive Determinism of Cultural Politics," 111–12).

6. Miles, *Shakespeare and the Constant Romans,* 15.

7. My thinking on these points has been greatly influenced by the work of Rebeca Helfer; see her "The Art of Recollection: Ruin and Cultural Memory in Edmund Spenser's Poetry."

8. The dynamic I schematize here, of course, is in no way intended to encompass the enormous and complex subject of ancient Rome's significance in early modern England.

9. Paster, *The Idea of the City,* 5.

10. As Marjorie Garber notes, the archetypal Roman phrase, "Et tu, Brute?" is in fact an Elizabethan creation, first appearing in *The True Tragedie of Richard Duke of York* (1595). See *Shakespeare's Ghost Writers,* 54. My discussion of *Julius Caesar* in this chapter is significantly indebted to Garber's analysis of the play. As Ronan comments, "An Early Modern Roman play like *Caesar* exists in multiple chronotopes and tenses: especially the simple past of recent real-life Europe, and the 'progressive future' of the series of theatrical and political representations of assassinations from the year 1599 until practically the crack of doom" (*"Antike Roman,"* 24). Cf. Robert Miola's observation: "At the center of this vision stands the city of Rome. This 'city,' of course, Shakespeare defines variously: Rome is an extension of Collatine's household in *Lucrece,* a wilderness settlement in *Titus Andronicus,* a political arena in *Julius Caesar,* an Empire in *Antony and Cleopatra,* a sharply drawn *urbs* in *Coriolanus,* and a vaguely localized anomaly, part ancient, part modern, in *Cymbeline*" (*Shakespeare's Rome,* 16–17).

11. Nevertheless, *Julius Caesar* had many dramatic precedents; see Frank Kermode's introductory comments to the play in *The Riverside Shakespeare,* 1102.

12. Cf. John Drakakis, " 'Fashion it Thus': *Julius Caesar* and the Politics of Theatrical Representation": "In a culture in which those who would oppose theatrical representation continued to insist upon the power that inheres in the theatrical image itself, *Julius Caesar* is not so much a celebration of theatre as an unmasking of the politics of representation per se" (289).

13. William Rankins, *A Mirrour of Monsters,* sig. C2v.

14. Gosson, *Plays Confuted,* sig. C2.

15. Gosson, *Schoole of Abuse,* sig. C5.

16. "For in those daies everie part of the Romane empire was in health and sound; the riches of other townes made the common barnes to be large & big; citizens did abound in wealth and pleasure, so that it was verie hard in such aboundance of al things, for religion to continue pure, and manners uncorrupt. Then everie where Autors of filtie pleasure were cherished; for in al places men were fat" (Munday, *2nd and 3rd Blast,* sig. C3v–C4).

17. I. G., *Refutation,* sig. B2v.

18. Unlike the other examples, the *Refutation* postdates *Julius Caesar* and *Sejanus,* but it found earlier theatrical representation (and perhaps dramatic source) in Thomas Lodge's *The Wounds of Civil War,* in which the conqueror Scilla tells the city, "Your streetes, where earst the fathers of your state / In robes of purple walked vp and downe, / Are strewd with mangled members, streaming blood" (*The Complete Works of Thomas Lodge,* 3:9).

19. *Henry V* is typically dated to between March 27 and September 28, 1599, largely because of the reference to Essex later in the above quoted speech; *Julius Caesar* was seen by Thomas Platter on September 21, 1599. See *The Riverside Shakespeare,* 53.

20. *Shakespearean Iconoclasm,* 132. The connection between this passage in *Henry V* and the actual staging of Caesar's entry in *Julius Caesar* has been noted by a number of critics; see especially Barbara J. Bono, "The Birth of Tragedy: Tragic Action in *Julius Caesar.*"

21. See Robert Lacey, *Robert, Earl of Essex: An Elizabethan Icarus,* 230–32. For an interesting analysis of *Julius Caesar* in the local context of the Essex faction, see Wayne A. Rebhorn, "The Crisis of the Aristocracy in *Julius Caesar.*"

22. *OED,* s.v. "offal."

23. Frederick Tupper, "The Shakespearean Mob"; Annabel Patterson, *Shakespeare and the Popular Voice.* For a recent and pessimistic reappraisal of Patterson's position, see Jerald W. Spotswood, " 'We are Undone Already': Disarming the Multitude in *Julius Caesar* and *Coriolanus.*"

24. David Kranz, "Shakespeare's New Idea of Rome," 374–75.

25. For a comparison to Shakespeare's treatment of English plebeians, see Alexander Leggatt, *Shakespeare's Political Drama,* 158.

26. Cf. Paster, *Idea of the City,* 61.

27. Richard Wilson has interpreted the initial antagonism the play shows to its audience as "a declaration of company policy towards the theatre audience," a policy that he interprets as speaking to the company's alleged desire to "legitimate the Shakespearean stage and dissociate it from the subversiveness of artisanal culture" by turning it into a haven for bourgeois and aristocratic playgoers (" 'Is this a Holiday?': Shakespeare's Roman Carnival," 33). Cf. my comments in chapter 4 on theatrical attacks on crowded audiences; although such a desire (or anxiety) may well form a part of the theater's ambivalence

      toward its audience, I believe that it proposes too narrow a reading of an attitude rooted less in class distinction than sheer multiplicity.

28. Drakakis, " 'Fashion it thus': *Julius Caesar* and the Politics of Theatrical Representation," 284.

29. For a fascinating and somewhat parallel reading of the appropriability of ceremony and ritual in the play, see Naomi Conn Liebler, *Shakespeare's Festive Tragedy,* especially 90–92.

30. Of course, as Burt has pointed out, theatricality is not foolproof politics: "The conspirators' production is a dismal failure even before they manage to stage it" ("*Julius Caesar* and the Discursive Determinism of Cultural Politics," 115).

31. For significant links between the theater and the marketplace, see especially Jean-Christophe Agnew, *Worlds Apart* and Douglas Bruster, *Drama and the Market in the Age of Shakespeare.*

32. For an excellent reading, with somewhat different focuses, of *Julius Caesar* as an antitheatrical play, see Denis Kezar, "*Julius Caesar* and the Properties of Shakespeare's Globe." Kezar's focus here is on the idea of the stage as "a law court perverted" (18), an irresponsible theatrical space in which "the alterative gaze and indeterminate interpretation of the spectator" (20) violently appropriates the object of representation.

33. See Garber, "Out of Joint": "Dismemberment is the Hard Connective Tissue of Drama" (45).

34. See, for example, Brents Stirling, "Or Else it Were a Savage Spectacle," in *Unity in Shakespearean Tragedy;* Anne Barton (Righter), *Shakespeare and the Idea of Play,* Jonathan Goldberg, *James I and the Politics of Literature.*

35. I here paraphrase Stephen Gosson, as quoted in chapter 4: "The rudest of the people are sometime ravished with every giewgawe, sometime so heavie, that they runne together by heapes, they know not whither; and lay about with theire clobbes, they see not why." (Gosson, *Plays Confuted,* sig. D1).

36. Although the first scene of Act Four is ostensibly set in the city, it is presented in a private space that already looks away from the play; as I note below, the word "Rome" never appears in this scene.

37. See Sanders, *Ben Jonson's Theatrical Republics,* 28–29.

38. Of course, however the Germanicans are presented it seems likely that there is a fair degree of political sympathy between their views and Jonson's own; see, for example, Robert C. Evans, "*Sejanus:* Ethics and Politics in the Early Reign of James" and Sanders, *Ben Jonson's Theatrical Republics,* especially chapter 2.

39. Sweeney, *Jonson and the Psychology of the Public Theater,* 47–48, 50.

40. *The Complete Plays of Ben Jonson,* 2:233.

41. See Sweeney, *Jonson and the Psychology of the Public Theater,* for an extensive analysis of these attempts.

42. Ian Donaldson has suggested that "The Quarto . . . is a book eloquently and emphatically dissociating itself form the experience of the theatre where the play was evidently first performed with spectacular lack of success" (" 'Misconstruing everything': *Julius Caesar* and *Sejanus*," 100). This, I think, is only half the picture: rather, the quarto dissociates itself from the performance by drawing repeated attention (explicitly in the prefatory apparatus, implicitly in the text) to that performance.

43. Cf. Paul Yachnin's *Stage-Wrights*, which claims that the play effects a complex "legitimating self-representation" (118).

44. In contrast, Yachnin argues that "the play enhances the value of public, political selfhood by recording its tragic ineffectuality within the world of the play. . . . Jonson's tragic representation of the incapacity of public selves and public values registers the political powerlessness of the theater, but the play also offers itself as a morally good and effectual voice of protest within the Jacobean political arena" (*Stage-Wrights*, 111). While this reading makes sense out of the tensions the play inscribes, it does so at the price of the play's strange aggressive opacity; as Donaldson has commented, "this heavily-guarded fortress of a play is notoriously difficult of access, but arrows fly from its loopholes" (" 'Misconstruing Everything,' " 100). While Yachnin's play might be one we would expect from Jonson—with its rational perspective and civic aims—it does not seem to be the one we have been given.

45. Sanders has argued that "it is . . . inaccurate to state that the populace is marginalized in *Sejanus*, ostracized as it were to a point of nonappearance beyond or behind the palace walls; for the off-stage power of populace action is immense within the context of the play. Stage absence (as Tiberius's letter proves) carries a potency of its own within the operations of this playtext. Absence enables ambiguity and unpredictability and within these modes lies access to power" (*Ben Jonson's Theatrical Republics*, 30). While there are important connections to be made between the absence of Tiberius and the absence of the populace, to claim that the latter's nonappearance gives it "access to power" seems difficult to support, given how the crowd is used and the context of their sole set of actions in the play.

46. This awkwardness can perhaps be partly explained by Jonson's sources changing; faced with a substantial gap in Tacitus's account, Jonson turns to Dio's *Roman History* for the narrative of Sejanus's fall and thus incorporates the omens recounted in the latter text. On the other hand, Dio's treatment of the supernatural is substantially less theatrical than Jonson's, and Jonson was certainly under no compulsion to include them.

47. *Hamlet*, 1.5.97, 2.2.301

48. *Poetaster*: "Apological Dialogue," line 32.

49. See William E. Slights, *Ben Jonson and the Art of Secrecy*, 42–44.
50. *The Complete Plays of Ben Jonson*, 2:234.
51. Dio Cassius, *Dio's Roman History*, 7:217.
52. "They stamp on that face of greed and while yet he lives pluck out his eyes; others seize and carry off his severed arms. One cuts off his foot, another wrenches a shoulder from the torn sinews; one lays bare the ribs of the cleft spine, another his liver, his heart, his still panting lungs. There is not space enough to satisfy their anger nor room to wreak their hate" (Claudian, *Claudian*, 1:89, lines 410–17). As Slights notes, quoting the same passage, "Jonson kept Claudian's text completely intact" (*Ben Jonson and the Art of Secrecy*, 46).
53. As this statement implies, I consider *Antony and Cleopatra* as something other than an urban play.

6   "A Kind of Nothing": Plague Time in Early Modern London

1. Samuel Price, *Londons Remembrancer*, sig. C4v–D1.
2. The most influential account of plague in early modern England remains Paul Slack's *The Impact of Plague in Tudor and Stuart England*. See also Leeds Barroll, *Politics, Plague, and Shakespeare's Theater*; Charles F. Mullett, *The Bubonic Plague and England*; and F. P. Wilson, *The Plague in Shakespeare's London*. More recent important assessments include Raymond Anselment, *The Realms of Apollo*, Margaret Healy, *Fictions of Disease in Early Modern England*, and Richelle Munkhoff, "Searchers of the Dead: Authority, Marginality, and the Interpretation of Plague in England." The last two authors focus extensively on Thomas Dekker's work. For the more general topic of death in the early modern period, see Bruce Gordon and Peter Marshall, eds., *The Place of the Dead*, and Vanessa Harding, *The Dead and the Living in Paris and London, 1500–1670*.
3. Thomas Dekker, *The Wonderful Year*, sig. C3v. For a thorough analysis of Dekker's pamphlet literature in the context of urban dystopia, see John Twyning, *London Dispossessed*.
4. Antonin Artaud, *The Theater and Its Double*, 31.
5. John Davies, *Humours Heau'n on Earth; With . . . The Triumph of Death: Or, The Picture of the Plague, According to the Life; as it was in Anno Domini. 1603*, sig. L2–L2v. Cited hereafter as *The Triumph of Death*.
6. As Jonathan Gil Harris comments, "It is important not to underestimate the impact that epidemic diseases—most of all, perhaps, the notorious plague epidemic of 1603—had on the metaphorical as well as the literal language of Londoners" (55).
7. Slack, *Impact of Plague*, 145–48; *Analytical Index to the Series of Records Known as the Remembrancia*, 329–40.
8. *Orders Conceiued . . . in the Time of the Infection*, folio 3.

9. *Lachrymae Londinenses, or Londons Lamentations,* sig. B1–B1v.

10. *The Seuen Deadly Sinnes of London . . . Bringing the Plague with them,* sig. *2v. For an analysis of this pamphlet in social terms, see Twyning, *London Dispossessed,* 184–88.

11. This is not to say that there is no significant plague writing before 1603; Thomas Nashe's *Christ's Tears over Jerusalem,* to take the most obvious example, is a clear precursor to Dekker's pamphlets, and there are a variety of significant medical treatises and first-hand reports. See Healy, 54–87, for an excellent analysis of the literary heritage of plague writing. Still, the volume of plague-related materials that are published in the early seventeenth century create a different category for understanding the urban significations of plague. Healy notes that "between 1486 and 1604, 23 books exclusively concerned with the plague were published" (54); at least twice that many are extant from the next 30 years alone.

12. Dekker, *The Dead Tearme,* sig. G1.

13. James Godskall, *The Arke of Noah, for the Londoners that Remaine in the Cittie to Enter in,* sig. A2v.

14. Susan Sontag, *Illness as Metaphor,* 58. Sontag avowedly seeks to move away from metaphoric understandings of disease, but her rhetoric is both contradictory and culpable. See D. A. Miller, "Sontag's Urbanity."

15. Steven Mullaney uses this passage (identified as Nashe) to indicate the theatrical threat of the suburbs to the city (*The Place of the Stage,* 50).

16. See Terence Ranger and Paul Slack, eds., *Epidemics and Ideas,* 3.

17. *Shakespearean Negotiations,* 3.

18. Cf. Jacques Derrida, "La Parole Soufflée": "It is metaphor that Artaud wants to destroy" (*Writing and Difference,* 84). For a reading of *Coriolanus* through the lens of Derrida's analysis of Artaud, see Clark Lunberry, "In the Name of Coriolanus: The Prompter (Prompted)."

19. See Slack, *Impact of Plague,* 22–35.

20. Henoch Clapham, *An Epistle Discoursing Vpon the Present Pestilence,* sig. A3.

21. *Henoch Clapham His Demaundes and Answers Touching the Pestilence,* sig. A4. Admittedly, Clapham may have been equivocating on this point; according to this pamphlet he had been thrown into prison for promoting the idea that the plague was not infectious.

22. Dekker, *Newes from Graues-ende,* sig. C4v.

23. For an excellent account of the social issues of fleeing the plague, see Anselment, *The Realms of Apollo,* 98–100.

24. Sharon Achinstein, whose superb analysis of restrictions on the sale of ballads during plague time anticipates this portion of my discussion in some regards, points out that the plague was thought to reside in objects such as ballads and broadsheets; the circulation of this literature was as deadly as the circulation of bodies ("Plagues and Publication," 27–49).

25. Michel de Certeau, *The Practice of Everyday Life,* 93.
26. A similar pattern can be seen on the title page from *Lachrymae Londinenses:* "With, / A Map of the Cities Miserie: / Wherein may be seen, / A Iournall of the deplorable estate of the Citie, from / the beginning of the Visitation vnto this present."
27. Wilson, *Plague in Shakespeare's London,* 210–11. It was immigration, not new births, that caused London's population to rebound so quickly, of course.
28. See Slack, *Impact of Plague,* 185–86.
29. See Steve Rappaport, *Worlds Within Worlds,* 107.
30. Dekker, *The Whole Magnifycent Entertainment,* sig. B4.
31. *A Rod for Runaways,* sig. A2v. As the reference to "Physicke-Herbes," suggests, Dekker is presenting this, in seriocomic fashion, as a good thing.
32. William Muggins, *Londons Mourning Garment,* sig. D3v.
33. See *2 Samuel* 24:1–25, *1 Chronicles* 21:1–27.
34. *Orders Conceiued . . . in the Time of the Infection,* folio 3.
35. Healy, *Fictions of Disease,* 88.
36. *Stuart Royal Proclamations,* 1:47–48.
37. The same tone is struck in a 1609 Star chamber case, prosecuting under the building regulations, which warns of an "infinite number of people being pestered together breeding and norishing Infection" (*Fovre Statvtes,* sig. Q1).
38. The *OED* suggests that "pester" derives from a different root than "pest" (as in plague), but by the sixteenth century the two terms had influenced each other—doubtless due to the emphasis on overcrowding that the first term developed (*Oxford English Dictionary,* 2nd ed., s.v. "pester").
39. "In 1582, for example, no less than twenty-three parishes were using St. Paul's Churchyard, and it had become so crowded that scarcely any graves could be made without corpses being exposed" (Wilson, *Plague in Shakespeare's London,* 43). For a recent and extensive accounting of the churchyard's multiple activities, see Harding, *The Dead and the Living,* 86–93.
40. Dekker, *The Meeting of Gallants at an Ordinarie,* sig. B1v. The STC suggests Middleton as the more likely author of this pamphlet, but I agree with F. P. Wilson that the style and content clearly point to Dekker. See *The Plague Pamphlets of Thomas Dekker,* xvi–xx.
41. Healy, *Fictions of the Body,* 14. See also Julia Gasper, *The Dragon and the Dove,* and Margot Heinemann, *Puritanism and Theatre.*
42. See Barroll, *Politics, Plague, and Shakespeare's Theater.*
43. Dekker, *The Seuen Deadly Sinnes of London,* sig. *2 and passim.
44. Dekker, *The Ravens Almanacke,* sig. B4.
45. See Slack, *Impact of Plague,* 26–31.
46. In particular see Zvi Jagendorf, "*Coriolanus:* Body Politic and Private Parts": "everywhere we encounter legs, arms, tongues, scabs, scratches,

wounds, mouths, teeth, voices, bellies, and toes together with such actions as eating, vomiting, starving, beating, scratching, wrestling, piercing, and undressing" (458).

47. Elana Gomel, "The Plague of Utopias: Pestilence and the Apocalyptic Body," 415. The proximate subject of Gomel's observation is the death of Aschenbach from cholera in *Death in Venice,* but her analysis is intended to link together a wide variety of pestilential discourses.

48. Of course, there is a larger discourse of disease at work in the play (even for Shakespeare, *Coriolanus* seems particularly disease-ridden), but the historical specificity of the plague discourse warrants special attention.

49. *Discipline and Punish,* 197–98. The label of "dream" is appropriate (although Foucault evidently considers the dream fulfilled), especially in the context of seventeenth-century London; though efforts to control the plague in London had become increasingly coterminous with efforts to control the bodies of its citizens, correspondence between the city and the Privy Council continually recounts the failure of these measures to be enforced.

50. For an interesting analysis of Foucault's observations in the context of *Richard II* (albeit one that may credit the Elizabethan state with a greater degree of control over plague than they demonstrated), see Nick Cox, " 'Subjected Thus': Plague and Panopticism in *Richard II.*"

51. Similarly, Volumnia's description of her son in battle—"Like to a harvest-man task'd to mow / Or all or lose his hire" (1.3.36–37)— seems a possible source for Davies' description of the toil of Death: "There might ye see Death (as with toile opprest / Panting for breath, all in a mortall sweat) / Vpon each bulke or bench, himselfe to rest, / (At point to faint) his Haruest was so great!" (*Triumph of Death,* sig. K2v).

52. See Barroll, *Politics, Plague, and Shakespeare's Theater,* but cf. Barbara Freedman, "Elizabethan Protest, Plague, and Plays."

53. See Cheryl Lynn Ross, "The Plague of *The Alchemist.*" For a more recent and excellent analysis, see Mathew Martin's chapter on *The Alchemist* in *Between Theater and Philosophy.*

54. Keir Elam, examining *Timon of Athens* and several other plays, has suggested that "bubonic contagion comes to constitute for Shakesperian drama a paradigm for language itself, especially in performance" (" 'I'll plague thee for that word,' " 20). See also Eric S. Mallin's chapter "Word and Plague in the Second Quarto *Hamlet,*" in *Inscribing the Time: Shakespeare and the End of Elizabethan England.*

55. *The Annals of the Barber Surgeons of London,* 121–23. Their impetus was doubtless a proclamation made by James in 1603, demanding that "incorrigible or dangerous Rogues should . . . be banished or conveyed" to "places and parts beyond the Seas" (*Stuart Royal Proclamations,* 1:50); see also Healy, *Fictions of Disease,* 88–91.

56. *Plutarch's Lives of the Noble Grecians and Romans*, 2:156. The omission of the Velitres story is also discussed by James Holstun in "Tragic Superfluity in *Coriolanus.*"

57. For a broader analysis of the paradoxes of the play's rhetoric, see Yvonne Bruce, "The Pathology of Rhetoric in *Coriolanus.*"

58. *Orders Conceiued . . . in the Time of the Infection*, folio 1.

59. "That euery house visited be marked with a red Crosse of a foote long, in the middle of the Doore, euident to be seene, and with these vsuall printed wordes: that is to say, Lord haue mercy vpon vs to be set close ouer the same Crosse, there to continue vntill lawfull opening of the same house" (ibid., folio 2).

60. This specific usage is not noted in the *OED*, curiously, but it is everywhere in Dekker and other early modern plague writers; see, for example, Thomas Lodge's *A Treatise of the Plague:* "The Carbuncle is a malignant pustule proceeding from bloud very hote and gross in substance, which causeth the adustion thereof, an vlcer with an Eschare or crust in the skin, swelling and red, raising thorow the inflammation thereof" (sig. I4).

61. Lunberry comments, "For Coriolanus there *is* no world elsewhere . . . Rome is the sole location within which his identity can be understood *as* identity, his presence understood as presence" ("In the Name of *Coriolanus,*" 239). While this may be true, it is important to stress his identity's lack of stability within Rome as without.

62. See Peter Stallybrass, "Shakespeare, the Individual, and the Text": "A person was *civis,* a member of the *civitas* . . .; one was not an individual" (594). My discussion of "identity" is deeply indebted to Stallybrass's examination of the word "individual."

63. According to the *OED*, the idea of identity as "the condition or fact that a person or thing is itself and not something else" develops only in the late seventeenth century, particularly in the context of John Locke's writings (*Oxford English Dictionary,* 2nd ed., s.v. "identity").

64. As Bruce has noted, "The play's final scene . . . is, after all, in many ways a repetition of the first scene of the play" ("The Pathology of Rhetoric," 110).

65. Dekker, *The Seuen Deadly Sinnes,* sig. A1v.

BIBLIOGRAPHY

A Breefe Discourse, Declaring and Approuing the Necessarie and Inuiolable Maintenance of the Laudable Customes of London. London, 1584, STC 16747.

Aaron, Melissa D. "The Globe and *Henry V* as Business Document," *Studies in English Literature, 1500–1900* 40.2 (Spring 2000): 277–92.

Achinstein, Sharon. "Plagues and Publication: Ballads and the Representation of Disease in the English Renaissance." *Criticism* 34.1 (Winter 1992): 27–49.

Agnew, Jean-Christophe. *Worlds Apart: The Market and the Theater in Anglo-American Thought.* Cambridge: Cambridge University Press, 1986.

Analytical Index to the Series of Records Known as the Remembrancia. London: E. J. Francis, 1878.

Anglo, Sydney. *Spectacle, Pageantry, and Early Tudor Policy.* Oxford: Oxford University Press, 1969.

The Annals of the Barber Surgeons of London. London: Blades, East & Blades, 1890.

Anselment, Raymond. *The Realms of Apollo: Literature and Healing in Seventeenth-Century England.* Newark: University of Delaware Press, 1995.

Anton, Robert. *The Philosophers Satyrs.* London, 1616, STC 686.

Archer, Ian W. "The Nostalgia of John Stow." In David L. Smith, Richard Strier, and David Bevington, eds., *The Theatrical City: Culture, Theatre, and Politics in London, 1576–1649.* Cambridge: Cambridge University Press, 1995.

———. *The Pursuit of Stability: Social Relations in Elizabethan London.* Cambridge: Cambridge University Press, 1991.

Arnade, Peter, Martha C. Howell, and Walter Simons, eds. *Journal of Interdisciplinary History* 32.4 (Spring, 2000).

Artaud, *Antonin. The Theater and Its Double.* New York: Grove Weidenfeld, 1958.

Austin, J. L. *How to Do Things with Words.* 2nd ed. Cambridge, MA: Harvard University Press, 1975.

Bakhtin, Mikhail. *Rabelais and His World.* Trans. Helene Iswolsky. Bloomington: Indiana University Press, 1984.

Barish, Jonas. *The Antitheatrical Prejudice*. Berkeley: University of California Press, 1981.

Barnes, Thomas G. "The Prerogative and Environmental Control of London Building in the Early Seventeenth Century: The Lost Opportunity." *California Law Review* 58 (1970): 1332–63.

Barroll, Leeds. *Politics, Plague, and Shakespeare's Theater: The Stuart Years*. Ithaca: Cornell University Press, 1991.

Barton (Righter), Anne. *Shakespeare and the Idea of Play*. London: Penguin, 1967.

Beaumont, Francis and John Fletcher. *Philaster: or, Love lies a-bleeding*. Ed. Andrew Gurr. London: Methuen, 1969.

Bednardz, James. *Shakespeare and the Poets' War*. New York: Columbia University Press, 2001.

Beier, A. L. *Masterless Men: The Vagrancy Problem in England 1560–1640*. New York: Methuen, 1985.

Beier, A. L. and Roger Finlay, eds. *London 1500–1700: The Making of the Metropolis*. New York: Longman Inc., 1986.

Benjamin, Walter. *The Origin of German Tragic Drama*. Trans. John Osborne. London: NLB, 1977.

Berger, Jr., Harry. *Making Trifles of Terrors: Redistributing Complicities in Shakespeare*. Stanford: Stanford University Press, 1997.

Bergeron, David M. *English Civic Pageantry 1558–1642*. Columbia, SC: University of South Carolina Press, 1971.

———. "Gilbert Dugdale and Royal Entry of James 1 (1604)." *The Journal of Medieval and Renaissance Studies* 13.1 (Spring 1983): 111–25.

———. "Stuart Civic Pageants and Textual Performance." *Renaissance Quarterly* 51.1 (Spring 1998): 163–83.

———. "Venetian State Papers and English Civic Pageantry." *Renaissance Quarterly* 23.1 (Spring 1970): 37–56.

———, ed. *Pageantry in the Shakespearean Theater*. Athens: University of Georgia Press, 1985.

Berlin, Michael. "Civic Ceremony in Early Modern London." *Urban History Yearbook* (1986): 1–24.

———. "Reordering Rituals: Ceremony and the Parish, 1520–1640." In Paul Griffiths and Mark S. R. Jenner, eds., *Londinopolis: Essays in the Cultural and Social History of Early Modern London*. Manchester: Manchester University Press, 2000.

Blau, Herbert. *The Audience*. Baltimore: Johns Hopkins University Press, 1990.

Boehrer, Bruce. *The Fury of Men's Gullets: Ben Jonson and the Digestive Canal*. Philadelphia: University of Pennsylvania Press, 1997.

Bono, Barbara J. "The Birth of Tragedy: Tragic Action in *Julius Caesar*." *English Literary Renaissance* 24.2 (Spring 1994): 449–70.

Bosman, Anston. "Seeing Tears: Truth and Sense in *All is True*." *Shakespeare Quarterly* 50.4 (Winter 1999): 459–76.

Bourdieu, Pierre. *The Field of Cultural Production: Essays on Art and Literature*. New York: Columbia University Press, 1993.

————. *Language and Symbolic Power.* Trans. Gino Raymond and Matthew Adamson. Cambridge, MA: Harvard University Press, 1991.

Browne, Thomas. *Religio Medici.* Ed. Jean-Jacques Denonain. Cambridge: Cambridge University Press, 1955.

Bruce, Yvonne. "The Pathology of Rhetoric in *Coriolanus.*" *The Upstart Crow* 20 (2000): 93–115.

Bruster, Douglas. *Drama and the Market in the Age of Shakespeare.* Cambridge: Cambridge University Press, 1992.

Burt, Richard. " 'A Dangerous Rome': Shakespeare's *Julius Caesar* and the Discursive Determinism of Cultural Politics." In Marie-Rose Logan and Peter L. Rudnysky, eds., *Contending Kingdoms: Historical, Psychological, and Feminist Approaches to the Literature of Sixteenth-Century England and France.* Detroit: Wayne State University Press, 1991.

Butler, Martin. "Jonson's London and Its Theaters." In Richard Harp and Stanley Stuart, eds., *The Cambridge Companion to Ben Johnson.* Cambridge: Cambridge University Press, 2000.

Calendar of State Papers and Manuscripts Existing in the Archives and Collections of Venice, and in Other Libraries of Northern Italy. London, 1900.

Canetti, Elias. *Crowds and Power.* Trans. Carol Stewart. New York: The Viking Press, 1962.

Cantor, Paul A. *Shakespeare's Rome: Republic and Empire.* Ithaca: Cornell University Press, 1976.

Chambers, E. K. *The Elizabethan Stage.* 4 vols. Oxford: Oxford University Press, 1923.

————. *William Shakespeare: A Study of Facts and Problems.* 2 vols. Oxford: Clarendon Press, 1930.

Chapman, George. *Andromeda Liberata. Or the Nuptials of Perseus and Andromeda.* London, 1614, STC 4964.

————. *A Free and Offenceles Iustification, of a Lately Publisht and Most Maliciously Misinterpreted Poeme: Entituled Andromeda Liberata.* London, 1614, STC 4977.

Chapman, George, Ben Jonson, and John Marston. *Eastward Ho,* ed. R. W. Van Fossen. Manchester: Manchester University Press, 1979.

Clapham, Henoch. *An Epistle Discoursing Vpon the Present Pestilence. . . .* London, 1603, STC 5340.

————. *Henoch Clapham His Demaundes and Answers Touching the Pestilence.* London, 1604, STC 5343.

Claudian, *Claudian.* 2 vols. Loeb Classical Library. Trans. Maurice Platnauer. London: William Heinemann, 1922.

Collinson, Patrick. "John Stow and Nostalgic Antiquarianism." In J. F. Merritt, ed., *Imagining Early Modern London: Perceptions and Portrayals of the City from Stow to Strype.* Cambridge: Cambridge University Press, 2001.

Cox, John D. and David Scott Kastan, eds. *New History of Early English Drama.* New York: Columbia University Press, 1997.

Cox, Nick. " 'Subjected Thus': Plague and Panopticism in *Richard II*." *Early Modern Literary Studies* 6.2 (2000).

Crosse, Henry. *Vertues Common-Wealth, or The High-Way to Honour*. London, 1603, STC 6070.5.

Daniel, P. A. *Notes and Conjectural Emendations*. London, 1870.

Daniel, Samuel. *The Complete Works in Verse and Prose of Samuel Daniel*. Ed. Alexander Grossart. 4 vols. London: privately printed, 1885.

Davies, John. *Humours Heau'n on Earth; With . . . The Triumph of Death: Or, The Picture of the Plague, according to the Life; as it was in Anno Domini*. 1603. London, 1609, STC 6332.

———. *The Poems of Sir John Davies*. Ed. Robert Krueger. Oxford: Clarendon Press, 1975.

Dawson, Anthony B. "The Arithmetic of Memory: Shakespeare's Theatre and the National Past." *Shakespeare Survey* 52 (1999): 54–67.

Dawson, Anthony B. and Paul Yachnin. *The Culture of Playgoing in Shakespeare's England: A Collaborative Debate*. Cambridge: Cambridge University Press, 2001.

De Certeau, Michel. *The Practice of Everyday Life*. Trans. Steven Randall. Berkeley: University of California Press, 1984.

Dekker, Thomas. *Brittannia's Honor: Brightly Shining in Seuerall Magnificent Shewes or Pageants. . . .* London, 1628, STC 6493.

———. *The Dead Tearme. . . .* London, 1608, STC 6496.

——— (ascribed). *Lusts Dominion: or, The Lascivious Queen*. London, 1657, Wing L3504a.

———. *The Magnificent Entertainment Giuen to King Iames. . . .* London, 1604, STC 6510.

———. *The Meeting of Gallants at an Ordinarie. . . .* London, 1604, STC 17781.

———. *Newes from Graues-ende Sent to Nobody*. London, 1604, STC 12199.

———. *The Plague Pamphlets of Thomas Dekker*. Ed. F. P. Wilson. Oxford: Clarendon Press, 1925.

———. *The Ravens Almanacke*. London, 1609, STC 6519.2.

———. *A Rod for Runaways. . . .* London, 1625, STC 6520.

———. The *Seuen Deadly Sinnes of London. . . . Bringing the Plague With Them*. London, 1606, STC 6522.

———. *The Shoemaker's Holiday*. Ed. J. B. Steane. Cambridge: Cambridge University Press, 1965.

———. *Troia-Nova Triumphans. London Triumphing. . . .* London, 1612, STC 6530.

———. *The Whole Magnifycent Entertainment: Given to King James. . . .* London, 1604, STC 6513.

———. *The Wonderful Year. 1603. . . .* London, 1603, STC 6535.3.

Dekker, Thomas and Thomas Middleton. *The Roaring Girl*. Ed. Paul A. Mulholland. Manchester: Manchester University Press, 1987.

Deleuze, Gilles and Felix Guattari. *A Thousand Plateaus: Capitalism and Schizophrenia*. Trans. Brian Massumi. Minneapolis: University of Minnesota Press, 1987.

Derrida, Jacques. *Dissemination*. Trans. Barbara Johnson. Chicago: University of Chicago Press, 1981.

———. *Of Grammatology*. Trans. Gayatri Chakravorty Spivak. Baltimore: Johns Hopkins University Press, 1976.

———. *Writing and Difference*. Chicago: University of Chicago Press, 1977.

Dillon, Janette. *Theatre, Court, and City, 1595–1610: Drama and Social Space in London*. Cambridge: Cambridge University Press, 2000.

Dio Cassius, *Dio's Roman History*. Trans. Earnest Cary. 9 vols. Loeb Classical Library. London: William Heinemann, 1914.

Donaldson, Ian. " 'Misconstruing everything': *Julius Caesar* and *Sejanus*." In Grace Ioppolo, ed., *Shakespeare Performed: Essays in Honor of R. A. Foakes*. Newark: University of Delaware Press, 2000.

Drakakis, John. " 'Fashion it Thus': *Julius Caesar* and the Politics of Theatrical Representation." In Ivo Kamps, ed., *Materialist Shakespeare: A History*. London: Verso, 1995.

Dugdale, Gilbert. *The Time Triumphant Declaring in Briefe, the Ariual of Our Soueraigne Liedge Lord, King Iames.* . . . London, 1604, STC 7292.

Dutton, Richard. *Mastering the Revels: The Regulation and Censorship of English Renaissance Drama*. London: Macmillan, 1991.

Elam, Keir. " 'I'll plague thee for that word': Language, Performance, and Communicable Disease." *Shakespeare Survey* 50 (1997): 19–27.

Elyot, Thomas. *The Book Named the Governor*. Ed. S. E. Lehmberg. London: J. M. Dent & Sons Ltd., 1962.

Evans, Robert C. "*Sejanus*: Ethics and Politics in the Early Reign of James." In Julie Sanders with Kate Chedgzoy and Susan Wiseman, eds., *Refashioning Ben Jonson: Gender Politics, and the Jonsonian Canon*. London: Macmillian Press Ltd., 1998.

Fairholt, Frederick. *Lord Mayor's Pageants: Being Collections Towards a History of these Annual Celebrations*. 2 vols. London: The Percy Society, 1843.

Fennor, William (ascribed). *Cornu-copiae, Pasquils Night-cap.* . . . London, 1612, STC 10782.5.

Finlay, Roger. *Population and Metropolis: The Demography of London 1580–1650*. Cambridge: Cambridge University Press, 1981.

Foucault, Michel. *Discipline and Punish: The Birth of the Prison*. Trans. Alan Sheridan. New York: Vintage Books, 1979.

———. *The Use of Pleasure*. New York: Vintage Books, 1990, 70–72.

Fovre Statvtes, Specially Selected and Commanded by His Maiestie. . . . London, 1609, STC 9341.

Freedman, Barbara. "Elizabethan Protest, Plague, and Plays: Rereading the 'Documents of Control.' " *English Literary Renaissance* 26.1 (Winter 1996): 17–45.

Freud, Sigmund. "Group Psychology and the Analysis of the Ego." *The Complete Psychological Works of Sigmund Freud*. Trans. James Strachey. London: The Hogarth Press, 1955.

Fumerton, Patricia. "London's Vagrant Economy: Making Space for 'Low' Subjectivity." In Lena Cowen Orlin, ed., *Material London, ca. 1600*. Philadelphia: University of Pennsylvania Press, 2000.

Fumerton, Patricia and Simon Hunt, eds. *Renaissance Culture and the Everyday*. Philadelphia: University of Pennsylvania Press, 1999.

G., I. *A Refutation of the Apology for Actors*. London, 1615, STC 12214.

Garber, Marjorie. "Out of Joint." In David Hillman and Carla Mazzio, eds., *The Body in Parts: Fantasies of Corporeality in Early Modern Europe*. New York: Routledge, 1997.

———. *Shakespeare's Ghost Writers: Literature as Uncanny Causality*. New York: Methuen, 1987.

Gasper, Julia. *The Dragon and the Dove: The Plays of Thomas Dekker*. Oxford: Clarendon Press, 1990.

Geertz, Clifford. "Blurred Genres: The Refiguration of Social Thought." *American Scholar* (Spring 1980): 170–92.

Glimp, David. *Increase and Multiply: Governing Cultural Reproduction in Early Modern England*. Minneapolis: University of Minnesota Press, 2003.

Godskall, James. *The Arke of Noah, for the Londoners That Remaine in the Cittie to Enter in. . . .* London, 1604, STC 11935.

Goldberg, Jonathan. *James I and the Politics of Literature: Jonson, Shakespeare, Donne, and Their Contemporaries*. Baltimore: Johns Hopkins University Press, 1983.

———. *Sodometries: Renaissance Texts, Modern Sexualities*. Stanford: Stanford University Press, 1992.

Gomel, Elana. "The Plague of Utopias: Pestilence and the Apocalyptic Body." *Twentieth Century Literature* 46.4 (Winter 2000): 405–33.

Gordon, Andrew. "Performing London: The Map and the City in Ceremony." In Andrew Gordon and Bernhard Klein, eds., *Literature, Mapping, and the Politics of Space in Early Modern Britain*. Cambridge: Cambridge University Press, 2001.

Gordon, Andrew and Bernhard Klein, eds. *Literature, Mapping, and the Politics of Space in Early Modern Britain*. Cambridge: Cambridge University Press, 2001.

Gordon, Bruce and Peter Marshall, eds. *The Place of the Dead: Death and Rembrance in Late Medieval and Early Modern Europe*. Cambridge: Cambridge University Press, 2000.

Gosson, Stephen. *Plays Confuted in 5 Actions*. London, 1582, STC 12095.

———. *The Schoole of Abuse*. London, 1587, STC 12098.

Greenblatt, Stephen. "Murdering Peasants: Status, Genre, and the Representation of Rebellion." In Stephen Greenblatt, ed., *Representing the English Renaissance*. Berkeley: University of California Press, 1988.

———. *Renaissance Self-Fashioning: From More to Shakespeare*. Chicago: University of Chicago Press, 1980.

———. *Shakespearean Negotiations*. Berkeley: University of California Press, 1988.

———, ed. *The Forms of Power and the Power of Forms in the Renaissance*. Norman: Pilgrim Books, 1982.

Greville, Fulke. *The Remains: Being Poems of Monarchy and Religion*. Ed. G. A. Wilkes. Oxford: Oxford University Press, 1965.

Griffiths, Paul. "Politics Made Visible: Order, Residence, and Uniformity in Cheapside, 1600–45." In Paul Griffiths and Mark S. R. Jenner, eds., *Londinopolis: Essays in the Cultural and Social History of Early Modern London*. Manchester: Manchester University Press, 2000.

Griffiths, Paul and Mark S. R. Jenner, eds. *Londinopolis: Essays in the Cultural and Social History of Early Modern London*. Manchester: Manchester University Press, 2000.

Gurr, Andrew. *The Shakespearean Stage* 1574–1642. Cambridge: Cambridge University Press, 1992.

H., I. *This Worlds Folly: or, A Warning-Peece Discharged Upon the Wickednesse Thereof*. London, 1615, STC 12570.

Harbage, Alfred. *Shakespeare's Audience*. New York: Columbia University Press, 1941.

Hardin, William. "Spectacular Constructions: Ceremonial Representations of City and Society in Early Stuart London." Unpublished Ph.D. dissertation. University of North Carolina at Chapel Hill, 1995.

Harding, Vanessa. "City, Capital, and Metropolis: the Changing Shape of Seventeenth-Century London." In J. F. Merritt, ed., *Imagining Early Modern London: Perceptions and Portrayals of the City from Stow to Strype*. Cambridge: Cambridge University Press, 2001.

———. *The Dead and the Living in Paris and London, 1500–1670*. Cambridge: Cambridge University Press, 2002.

———. "The Population of London, 1550–1700: A Review of the Published Evidence." *London Journal* 15.2 (1990): 111–28.

Harris, Jonathan Gil. *Foreign Bodies and the Body Politic: Discourse of Social Pathology in Early Modern England*. Cambridge: Cambridge University Press, 1998.

Harris, Tim. "Perceptions of the Crowd in Later Stuart London." In J. F. Merritt, ed., *Imagining Early Modern London: Perceptions and Portrayals of the City from Stow to Strype*. Cambridge: Cambridge University Press, 2001.

Healy, Margaret. *Fictions of Disease in Early Modern England: Bodies, Plagues, and Politics*. New York: Palgrave, 2001.

Heinemann, Margot. *Puritanism and Theatre: Thomas Middleton and Opposition Drama under the Early Stuarts*. Cambridge: Cambridge University Press, 1980.

Helfer, Rebeca. "The Art of Recollection: Ruin and Cultural Memory in Edmund Spenser's Poetry." Unpublished Ph.D. dissertation. Columbia University, 2003.

Helgerson, Richard. *Forms of Nationhood: The Elizabethan Writing of England*. Chicago: University of Chicago Press, 1992.

Herrick, Robert. *Hesperides: Or, the Works both Human & Divine*. London, 1648, Wing H1596.

Heywood, Thomas. *An Apology for Actors*. London, 1612, STC 13309.

———. *The Dramatic Works of Thomas Heywood*. 6 vols. New York: Russell & Russell, 1964.

———. *Londini Artium & Scientiarum Scaturigo.* . . . London, 1632, STC 13347.

———. *Londini Emporia, or Londons Mercatura.* . . . London, 1633, STC 13348.

———. *Londini speculum: or, Londons mirror.* . . . London, 1637, STC 13349.

———. *Londini Status Pacatus: or, Londons Peaceable Estate.* . . . London, 1639, STC 13350.

———. *London Ius Honorarium.* . . . London, 1631, STC 13351.

———. *Thomas Heywood's Pageants: A Critical Edition*. Ed. David M. Bergeron. New York: Garland Publishing, Inc., 1986.

Hill, Christopher. *Change and Continuity in Seventeenth-Century England*. New Haven: Yale University Press, 1991.

———. *The World Turned Upside Down: Radical Ideas During the English Revolution*. London: Penguin Books, 1975.

Hobsbawm, E. J. *Primitive Rebels: Studies in Archaic Forms of Social Movement in the Nineteenth and Twentieth Centuries*. New York: W. W. Norton, 1968.

Holstun, James. "Tragic Superfluity in *Coriolanus*." *ELH* 50.3 (Fall 1983): 485–507.

Holy Bible. Authorized Version. Cleveland: World Publishing, n.d.

Howard, Jean. *The Stage and Social Struggle in Early Modern England*. New York: Routledge, 1994.

———. "Women, Foreigners, and the Regulation of Urban Space in *Westward Ho*." In Lena Cowen Orlin, ed., *Material London, ca. 1600*. Philadelphia: University of Pennsylvania Press, 2000.

Hughes, Paul L. and James F. Larkin, eds. *Stuart Royal Proclamations*. 2 vols. Oxford: Clarendon Press, 1973.

———, eds. *Tudor Royal Proclamations*. 3 vols. New Haven: Yale University Press, 1969.

Hutchins, Christine E. " 'Who is here so rude that would not be a Roman?': England as Anti-Type of Rome in Elizabethan Print and *Julius Caesar*." *The Ben Jonson Journal* 8 (2001): 207–27.

Jagendorf, Zvi. "*Coriolanus*: Body Politic and Private Parts." *Shakespeare Quarterly* 41.4 (Winter 1990): 455–69.

Jakobson, Roman. "Two Aspects of Language and Two Types of Aphasic Disturbances." In Krystyna Pomorska and Stephen Rudy, eds., *Language and Literature*. Cambridge, MA: Harvard University Press, 1987.

Jonson, Ben. *The Alchemist and Other Plays*. Ed. Gordon Campbell. Oxford: Oxford University Press, 1995.

———. *Cataline.* Ed. W. F. Bolton and Jane F. Gardner. Lincoln, NB: University of Nebraska Press, 1973.

———. *The Complete Plays of Ben Jonson.* 4 vols. Ed. G. A. Wilkes. Oxford: Clarendon Press, 1981.

———. *Poetaster.* Ed. Tom Cain. Manchester: Manchester University Press, 1995.

Kahn, Coppelia. *Roman Shakespeare: Warriors, Wounds, and Women.* New York: Routledge, 1997.

Kamps, Ivo. *Historiography and Ideology in Stuart Drama.* Cambridge: Cambridge University Press, 1996.

Kastan, David Scott. "Proud Majesty Made a Subject: Shakespeare and the Spectacle of Rule." *Shakespeare Quarterly* 37.3 (Autumn 1986): 459–75.

Keene, Derek. "Material London in Time and Space." In Lena Cowen Orlin, ed., *Material London, ca. 1600.* Philadelphia: University of Pennsylvania Press, 2000.

Kezar, Denis. "*Julius Caesar* and the Properties of Shakespeare's Globe." *English Literary Renaissance* 28.1 (Winter 1998): 18–46.

———. "Law/Form/History: Shakespeare's Verdict in *All is True.*" *Modern Language Quarterly* 63.1 (March 2002): 1–30.

The King's Majesties Declaration to His Subjects, Concerning lawfull Sports to be used . . . . London, 1618, STC 9238.9.

Kipling, Gordon. "Triumphal Drama: Form in English Civic Pageantry." *Renaissance Drama* 8 (1977): 37–56.

Knutson, Rosalyn. *Playing Companies and Commerce in Shakespeare's Time.* Cambridge: Cambridge University Press, 2001.

Kranz, David. "Shakespeare's New Idea of Rome." In P. A. Ramsey, ed., *Rome in the Renaissance: The City and the Myth.* Binghampton, NY: Center for Medieval and Early Renaissance Studies, 1982.

Kreps, Barbara. "When All is True: Law, History, and Problems of Knowledge in *Henry VIII.*" *Shakespeare Survey* 52 (1999): 166–82.

Lacey, Robert. *Robert, Earl of Essex: An Elizabethan Icarus.* London: Weidenfeld and Nicolson, 1971.

Lachrymae Londinenses, or Londons Lamentations . . . . London, 1626, STC 16753.

Lake, Peter. "From Troynovant to Heliogabulus's Rome and Back: 'Order' and Its Others in the London of John Stow." In J. F. Merritt, ed., *Imagining Early Modern London: Perceptions and Portrayals of the City from Stow to Strype.* Cambridge: Cambridge University Press, 2001.

Le Bon, Gustave. *The Crowd: A Study of the Popular Mind.* London: T. Fisher Unwin, 1896.

Lefebvre, Henri. *The Production of Space.* Trans. Donald Nicholson-Smith. Oxford: Blackwell Publishers, 1991.

Leggatt, Alexander. *Shakespeare's Political Drama: The History Plays and the Roman Plays.* London: Routledge, 1988.

Leinwand, Theodore. "London Triumphing: The Jacobean Lord Mayor's Show." *Clio* 11.2 (1982): 130–62.

Les Reportes del Cases in Camera Stellata, 1593 to 1609. London: Privately Printed, 1894.

Liebler, Naomi Conn. *Shakespeare's Festive Tragedy: The Ritual Foundations of Genre.* New York: Routledge, 1995.

The Life and Death of Jack Straw, A Notable Rebell in England, Reprinted in John S. Farmer, ed., *Tudor Fascimile Texts.* London, 1911.

Lindley, David. *The Trials of Frances Howard: Fact and Fiction at the Court of King James.* New York: Routledge, 1993.

Lindley, K. J. "Riot Prevention and Control in Early Stuart London." *Transactions of the Royal Historical Society* 33 (1983): 109–26.

Linebaugh, Peter and Marcus Rediker. *The Many-Headed Hydra: Sailors, Slaves, Commoners, and the Hidden History of the Revolutionary Atlantic.* Boston: Beacon Press, 2000.

Lobanov-Rostovsky, Sergei. "*The Triumphes of Golde*: Economic Authority in the Jacobean Lord Mayor's Show." *ELH* 60 (1993): 879–98.

Lodge, Thomas. *The Complete Works of Thomas Lodge.* 3 vols. London: Hunterian Club, 1883.

———. *A Treatise of the Plague* . . . . London, 1603, STC 16676.

Londons Looking-glass. London, 1621, STC 18327.

Luis-Martínez, Zenón. " 'Maimed Narrations': Shakespeare's *Henry VIII* and the Task of the Historian." *Explorations in Renaissance Culture* 27.2 (2001): 205–43.

Lunberry, Clark. "In the Name of Coriolanus: The Prompter (Prompted)." *Comparative Literature* 54.3 (Summer 2002): 229–41.

Lynch, Kevin. *The Image of the City.* Cambridge, MA: MIT Press, 1960.

Mahood, M. M. "Bit Parts in *Richard III*." In Hugh Macrae Richmond, ed., *Critical Essays on Shakespeare's* Richard III. New York: G. K. Hall & Co., 1999.

Mallin, Eric S. *Inscribing the Time: Shakespeare and the End of Elizabethan England.* Berkeley: University of California Press, 1995.

Manley, Lawrence. *Literature and Culture in Early Modern London.* Cambridge: Cambridge University Press, 1995.

———. "Sites and Rites." In David L. Smith, Richard Strier, and David Bevington, eds., *The Theatrical City: Culture, Theatre, and Politics in London, 1576–1649.* Cambridge: Cambridge University Press, 1995.

Manning, Roger B. *Village Revolts: Social Protest and Popular Disturbances in England, 1509–1640.* Oxford: Clarendon Press, 1988.

Marcus, Leah. "City Metal and Country Mettle: The Occasion of Ben Jonson's *Golden Age Restored*." In David M. Bergeron, ed., *Pageantry in the Shakespearean Theater.* Athens: University of Georgia Press, 1985.

———. *The Politics of Mirth: Jonson, Herrick, Milton, Marvell, and the Defense of Old Holiday Pastimes.* Chicago: University of Chicago Press, 1986.

———. *Puzzling Shakespeare: Local Reading and its Discontents.* Berkeley: University of California Press, 1988.

Marston, John. *The Malcontent and Other Plays.* Ed. Keith Sturgess. Oxford: Oxford University Press, 1997.

———. *The Plays of John Marston.* Ed. H. Harvey Wood. London: Oliver and Boyd, 1939.

———. *What You Will.* London, 1607, STC 17487.

Martin, Mathew. *Between Theater and Philosophy: Skepticism in the Major City Comedies of Ben Jonson and Thomas Middleton.* Newark: University of Delaware Press, 2001.

Martindale, Charles. *Shakespeare and the Uses of Antiquity.* New York: Routledge, 1990.

Massinger, Philip. *The Plays and Poems of Philip Massinger.* Eds. Philip Edwards and Colin Gibson. Oxford: Clarendon Press, 1976.

Masten, Jeffrey. "Is the Fundament a Grave?" In David Hillman and Carla Mazzio, eds., *The Body in Parts: Fantasies of Corporeality in Early Modern Europe.* New York: Routledge, 1997.

———. "*More* or Less: Editing the Collaborative." *Shakespeare Studies* 29 (2001): 109–32.

Maus, Katherine Eisaman. *Ben Jonson and the Roman Frame of Mind.* Princeton, NJ: Princeton University Press, 1984.

McClelland, J. S. *The Crowd and the Mob: From Plato to Canetti.* London: Unwin Hyman Inc., 1989.

Merritt, J. F., ed. *Imagining Early Modern London: Perceptions and Portrayals of the City from Stow to Strype, 1598–1720.* Cambridge: Cambridge University Press, 2001.

Middleton, Thomas. *The Sunne in Aries.* London, 1621, STC 17895.

———. *The Tryumphs of Honor and Industry.* London, 1617, STC 17899.

———. *The Triumphs of Honor and Vertue . . . .* London, 1622, STC 17900.

———. *The Trivmphs of Integrity . . . .* London, 1623, STC 17901.

———. *The Triumphs of Truth . . . .* London, 1613, STC 17903.

———. *The Works of Thomas Middleton.* Ed. A. H. Bullen. 8 vols. Boston: Houghton, Mifflin and Company, 1885.

Miles, Geoffrey. *Shakespeare and the Constant Romans.* Oxford: Clarendon Press, 1996.

Miller, D. A. "Sontag's Urbanity." In Henry Abelove, Michèle Aina Barale, and David M. Halperin, eds., *The Lesbian and Gay Studies Reader.* New York: Routledge, 1993.

Miola, Robert. *Shakespeare's Rome.* Cambridge: Cambridge University Press, 1983.

Montrose, Louis. *The Purpose of Playing: Shakespeare and the Cultural Politics of the Elizabethan Theatre.* Chicago: University of Chicago Press, 1996.

Morris, Meaghan and Paul Patton, eds. *Michel Foucault: Power, Truth, Strategy.* Sydney: Feral Publications, 1967.

Muggins, William. *Londons Mourning Garment, or Funerall Teares.* London, 1603, STC 18248.

Mullaney, Steven. *The Place of the Stage: License, Play and Power in Renaissance England.* Chicago: University of Chicago Press, 1988.

Mullett, Charles F. *The Bubonic Plague and England: An Essay in the History of Preventive Medicine*. Lexington: University of Kentucky Press, 1956.

Munday, Anthony (ascribed). *A 2nd and 3rd Blast of Retrait from Plaies and Theaters*. London, 1580, STC 21677.

———. *Camp-bell or the Ironmongers Faire Feild*. London, 1609, STC 18265.

———. *Chruso-thriambos: The Triumphes of Golde . . . .* London, 1611, STC 18267.

———. *Chrysanaleia: The Golden Fishing . . . .* London, 1616, STC 18266.

———. *Himatia-Poleos The Triumphs of Olde Draperie . . . .* London, 1614, STC 18274.

———. *Metropolis Coronata, the Trivmphes of Ancient Drapery . . . .* London, 1615, STC 18275.

———. *Pageants and Entertainments of Anthony Munday: A Critical Edition*. Ed. David M. Bergeron. New York: Garland Publishing, Inc., 1985.

———. *Sidero-Thriambos, Or Steele and Iron Triumphing . . . .* London, 1618, STC 18278.

———. *The Trivmphes of Re-Vnited Britania . . . .* London, 1605, STC 18279.

——— et al. *Sir Thomas More*. Ed. Vittorio Gabrieli and Giorgio Mechiori. Manchester: Manchester University Press, 1990.

Munkhoff, Richelle. "Searchers of the Dead: Authority, Marginality, and the Interpretation of Plague in England." *Gender and History* 11.1: 1–29.

Neill, Michael. *Issues of Death: Mortality and Identity in English Renaissance Tragedy*. Oxford: Clarendon Press, 1997.

Newman, Karen. "Walking Capitals: Donne's First Satyre." In Henry S. Turner, ed., *The Culture of Capital: Property, Cities, and Knowledge in Early Modern England*. New York: Routledge, 2002.

Nichols, John. *The Progresses and Public Processions of Queen Elizabeth*. 3 vols. London: John Nichols & Son, 1823.

Northbrooke, John. *A Treatise wherein Dicing, Daucing, Vaine Plaies or Enterludes with Other Idle Pastimes . . . Are Reprooued*. London, 1579, STC 18671.

Ong, Walter J. "From Allegory to Diagram in the Renaissance Mind: A Study in the Significance of the Allegorical Tableau." *The Journal of Aesthetics and Art Criticism* 17.4 (June 1959): 423–40.

Orders Conceiued . . . in the Time of the Infection . . . . London, 1608, STC 16723.

Orgel, Stephen. *The Illusion of Power: Political Theater in the English Renaissance*. Berkeley: University of California Press, 1975.

Orlin, Lena Cowen. "Boundary Disputes in Early Modern London." In Lena Cowen Orlin, ed., *Material London, ca. 1600*. Philadelphia: University of Pennsylvania Press, 2000.

Oxford English Dictionary, 2nd ed. Oxford: Clarendon Press, 1989.

Palfrey, Simon. *Late Shakespeare: A New World of Words.* Oxford: Clarendon Press, 1997.

Parker, Patricia. *Shakespeare from the Margins: Language, Culture, Context.* Chicago: University of Chicago Press, 1996.

Pasquils Iestes Mixed with Mother Bunches Merriments . . . . London, 1609, STC 19451.5.

Paster, Gail Kern. "The Idea of London in Masque and Pageant." In David M. Bergeron, ed., *Pageantry in the Shakespearean Theater.* Athens, GA: University of Georgia Press, 1985.

———. *The Idea of the City in the Age of Shakespeare.* Athens: University of Georgia Press, 1985.

Patrides, C. A. " 'The Beast with Many Heads': Renaissance Views on the Multitude." *Shakespeare Quarterly* 16.2 (Spring 1965): 241–46.

Patterson, Annabel. " 'All is True': Negotiating the Past in *Henry VIII.*" In R. B. Parker and S. P. Zitner, eds., *Elizabethan Theater: Essays in Honor of S. Schoenbaum.* Newark: University of Delaware Press, 1996.

———. *Shakespeare and the Popular Voice.* Oxford: Basil Blackwell Inc., 1989.

Pearl, Valerie. "Change and Stability in Seventeenth-Century London." *London Journal* 5 (1975): 3–34.

———. *London and the Outbreak of the Puritan Revolution: City Government and National Politics, 1625–1643.* Oxford: Oxford University Press, 1961.

Pelling, Margaret. "Skirting the City." In Paul Griffiths and Mark S. R. Jenner, eds., *Londinopolis: Essays in the Cultural and Social History of Early Modern London.* Manchester: Manchester University Press, 2000.

Plato. *Plato's Republic.* Trans. G. M. A. Grube. Indianapolis: Hackett Publishing Co., 1974.

Plutarch. *Plutarch's Lives of the Noble Grecians and Romans, Englished by Sir Thomas North, Anno 1579.* 4 vols. London: David Nutt, 1895.

Pollard, A. W., G. R. Redgrave, W. A. Jackson, F. S. Ferguson, and Katharine Pantzer. *The Short Title Catalogue of Books Printed in England . . . 1475–1640.* London: Bibliographic Society, 1976–1991.

Price, Samuel. *Londons Remembrancer.* London, 1626, STC 20332.

Pye, Christopher. *The Regal Phantasm: Shakespeare and the Politics of Spectacle.* New York: Routledge, 1990.

Pythian-Adams, Charles. "Ceremony and the Citizen: The Communal Year at Coventry 1450–1550," In Peter Clark and Paul Slack, eds., *Crisis and Order in English Towns 1500–1700: Essays in Urban History.* London: Routledge & Keegan Paul, 1972.

The Queenes Maiestie Perceiving the State of the Citie of London . . . . London, 1580, STC 8123.3.

Rackin, Phyllis. *Stages of History: Shakespeare's English Chronicles.* Ithaca: Cornell University Press, 1990.

Rainoldes, John. *Th'Overthrow of Stage Plays.* London, 1599, STC 20616.

Raleigh, Walter. *Selections from His Historie of the World, His Letters, etc.* Ed. G. E. Hadow. Oxford: Clarendon Press, 1917.

Ranger, Terence and Paul Slack, eds., *Epidemics and Ideas. Essays on the Historical Perception of Pestilence.* Cambridge: Cambridge University Press, 1992.

Rankins, William. *A Mirrour of Monsters . . . .* London, 1587, STC 20699.

Rappaport, Steve. *Worlds within Worlds: Structures of Life in Sixteenth-Century London.* Cambridge: Cambridge University Press, 1989.

Razzell, Peter, ed. *The Journals of Two Travelers in Elizabethan and Early Stuart England.* London: Caliban Books, 1995.

Rebhorn, Wayne A. "The Crisis of the Aristocracy in *Julius Caesar.*" *Renaissance Quarterly* 43.1 (Spring 1990): 75–111.

Reynolds, Bryan. *Becoming Criminal: Transversal Performance and Cultural Dissidence in Early Modern England.* Baltimore: Johns Hopkins University Press, 2002.

———. "The Devil's House, 'or Worse': Transversal Power and Antitheatrical Discourse in Early Modern England." *Theatre Journal* 49.2 (May 1997): 143–69.

Richmond, Hugh M. "The Resurrection of an Expired Form: *Henry VIII* as Sequel to *Richard III.*" In John W. Velz, ed., *Shakespeare's English Histories: A Quest for Form and Genre.* Binghampton, NY: Medieval & Renaissance Texts & Studies, 1996.

Robertson, Jean and D. J. Gordon, eds. *Collections III: A Calendar of Dramatic Records in the Books of the Livery Companies of London.* Oxford: Malone Society, 1954.

Ronan, Clifford. *"Antike Roman": Power Symbology and the Roman Play in Early Modern England, 1585–1635.* Athens: University of Georgia Press, 1995.

Ross, Cheryl Lynn. "The Plague of *The Alchemist.*" *Renaissance Quarterly* 41.3 (Autumn 1988): 439–58.

Rudé, George. *The Crowd in History: A Study of Popular Disturbances in France and England 1730–1848.* New York: John Wiley & Sons, Inc., 1964.

Sanders, Julie. *Ben Jonson's Theatrical Republics.* London: Macmillian Press, Ltd., 1998.

Schechner, Richard. *Performance Theory.* New York: Routledge, 1988.

Schofield, John. "The Topography and Buildings of London, ca. 1600." In Lena Cowen Orlin, ed., *Material London, ca. 1600.* Philadelphia: University of Pennsylvania Press, 2000.

Seaver, Paul. "The Artisanal World." In David L. Smith, Richard Strier, and David Bevington, eds., *The Theatrical City: Culture, Theatre, and Politics in London, 1576–1649.* Cambridge: Cambridge University Press, 1995.

Sennett, Richard. *Flesh and Stone: The Body and the City in Western Civilization.* New York: W. W. Norton & Co., 1994.

Shakespeare, William. *Henry VIII.* London: Methuen and Co., 1915.

———. *The Riverside Shakespeare.* 2nd ed. Boston: Houghton Mifflin Co., 1997.

Siemon, James R. *Shakespearean Iconoclasm.* Berkeley: University of California Press, 1985, 132.

Sinfield, Alan. "*Poetaster*, the Author, and the Perils of Cultural Production." In Lena Cowen Orlin, ed., *Material London, ca. 1600*. Philadelphia: University of Pennsylvania Press, 2000.

Skeat, W. W., ed. *Shakespeare's Plutarch*. London: Macmillan and Co., 1875.

Slack, Paul. *The Impact of Plague in Tudor and Stuart England*. London: Routledge & Kegan Paul, 1985.

———. "Perceptions of the Metropolis in Seventeenth-Century England." In Peter Burke, B. Harrison, and Paul Slack, eds., *Civil Histories*. Oxford: Oxford University Press, 2000.

Slights, William E. *Ben Jonson and the Art of Secrecy*. Toronto: University of Toronto Press, 1994.

Smallwood, R. L. " 'Here, in the Friars': Immediacy and Theatricality in *The Alchemist*." *The Review of English Studies* 32.126 (May 1981): 142–60.

Smelser, Neil. *Theory of Collective Behavior*. New York: Free Press of Glencoe.

Smith, David L., Richard Strier, and David Bevington, eds. *The Theatrical City: Culture, Theatre, and Politics in London, 1576–1649*. Cambridge: Cambridge University Press, 1995.

Smuts, R. M. "Public Ceremony and Royal Charisma: The English Royal Entry in London, 1485–1642." In A. L. Beier, David Cannadine, and James M. Rosenheim, eds., *The First Modern Society: Essays in English History in Honour of Lawrence Stone*. Cambridge: Cambridge University Press, 1989.

Soja, Edward. *Thirdspace: Journeys to Los Angeles and other Real-and-Imagined Places*. Oxford: Blackwell Publishers, 1996.

Sommerville, Johann Press, ed. *King James VI and I: Political Writings*. Cambridge: Cambridge University Press, 1994.

Spotswood, Jerald W. " 'We are undone already': Disarming the Multitude in *Julius Caesar* and *Coriolanus*." *Texas Studies in Literature and Language* 42.1 (Spring 2000): 61–78.

Stallybrass, Peter. "Shakespeare, the Individual, and the Text." In Lawrence Grossberg, Cary Nelson, and Paula Treichler, eds., *Cultural Studies*. New York: Routledge, 1992.

Stallybrass, Peter and Allon White. *The Politics and Poetics of Transgression*. Ithaca: Cornell University Press, 1986.

Stirling, Brents. *The Populace in Shakespeare*. New York: Columbia University Press, 1949.

———. *Unity in Shakespearean Tragedy: The Interplay of Theme and Character*. New York: Columbia University Press, 1956.

Stow, John. *A Survey of London*. Ed. C. L. Kingsford. 2 vols. Oxford: Clarendon Press, 1908.

Stubbes, Philip. *The Anatomie of Abuses*. London, 1584, STC 23377.5.

Sullivan, Garrett. *The Drama of Landscape: Land, Property, and Social Relations on the Early Modern Stage*. Stanford: Stanford University Press, 1998.

Susan Sontag, Susan. *Illness as Metaphor*. New York: Farrar, Straus and Giroux, 1978.

Sweeney, John. *Jonson and the Psychology of the Public Theater.* Princeton: Princeton University Press, 1985.

Tawney, R. H. and Eileen Power, eds. *Tudor Economic Documents.* 3 vols. London: Longmans, 1924.

Tennenhouse, Leonard. "Strategies of State and Political Plays: *A Midsummer Night's Dream, Henry IV, Henry V, Henry VIII.*" In Jonathan Dollimore and Alan Sinfield, eds., *Political Shakespeare: New Essays in Cultural Materialism.* Ithaca: Cornell University Press, 1985.

Thomas, Vivian. *Shakespeare's Roman Worlds.* New York: Routledge, 1989.

Thompson, E. P. "The Moral Economy of the English Crowd in the Eighteenth Century." *Past and Present* 50 (February 1971): 78–120.

Tupper, Frederick. "The Shakespearean Mob." *PMLA* 27 (1912): 486–523.

Turner, Victor. *From Ritual to Theater: The Human Seriousness of Play.* New York: Performing Arts Journal Publications, 1982.

———. "Liminality and the Performative Genres." In John J. MacAloon, ed., *Rite, Drama, Festival, Spectacle.* Philadelphia: Institute for the Study of Human Issues, 1984.

———. *The Ritual Process: Structure and Anti-Structure.* Ithaca: Cornell University Press, 1969.

Twyning, John. *London Dispossessed: Literature and Social Space in the Early Modern City.* New York: St. Martin's Press, 1998.

Ward, Joseph P. *Metropolitan Communities: Trade Guilds, Identity, and Change in Early Modern London.* Stanford: Stanford University Press, 1997.

Webster, John. *The Complete Works of John Webster.* Ed. F. L. Lucas. Boston: Houghton Mifflin Company, 1928.

———. *Monuments of Honor* . . . . London, 1624, STC 25175.

Weimann, Robert. *Author's Pen and Actor's Voice: Playing and Writing in Shakespeare's Theatre.* Cambridge: Cambridge University Press, 2000.

———. *Shakespeare and the Popular Tradition: Studies in the Social Dimension of Dramatic Form and Function.* Baltimore: Johns Hopkins University Press, 1978.

———. "Thresholds to Memory and Commodity in Shakespeare's Endings." *Representations* 53 (Winter 1996): 1–20.

Wells, Charles. *The Wide Arch: Roman Values in Shakespeare.* New York: St. Martin's Press, 1993.

Wickham, Glynne. "The Dramatic Structure of Shakespeare's *King Henry the Eighth*: An Essay in Rehabilitation." *Proceedings of the British Academy* 70 (1984): 149–66.

———. *Early English Stages: 1300 to 1660.* 3 vols. London: Routledge and Kegan Paul, 1963.

Wilson, F. P. *The Plague in Shakespeare's London.* Oxford: Oxford University Press, 1927.

Wilson, Richard. " 'Is this a Holiday?': Shakespeare's Roman Carnival." *ELH* 54.1 (Spring 1987): 31–44.

———. " 'A Mingled Yarn': Shakespeare and the Cloth Workers." *Literature and History* 12.2 (Autumn 1986): 168–79.

Woodbridge, Linda. *Vagrancy, Homelessness, and English Renaissance Literature*. Urbana: University of Illinois Press, 2001.

Worden, Blair. "Politics in *Cataline*: Jonson and his Sources." In Martin Butler, ed., *Re-Presenting Ben Jonson: Text, History, Performance*. New York: St. Martin's Press, 1999.

Wunderli, Richard. "Evasion of the Office of Alderman in London, 1523–1672." *London Journal* 15.1 (1990): 3–18.

Yachnin, Paul. *Stage-Wrights: Shakespeare, Jonson, Middleton, and the Making of Theatrical Value*. Philadelphia: University of Pennsylvania Press, 1997.

Index